may all your
dreams come true!

Love,

Julie

HEATHER VALENCIA
AND
ROLLY KENT

QUEEN OF

THE STORY OF A YAQUI DREAMING WOMAN

DREAMS

SIMON & SCHUSTER

NEW YORK   LONDON   TORONTO   SYDNEY   TOKYO   SINGAPORE

Simon & Schuster
Simon & Schuster Building
Rockefeller Center
1230 Avenue of the Americas
New York, New York 10020

Designed by Nina D'Amario/Levavi & Levavi
Manufactured in the United States of America

1   3   5   7   9   10   8   6   4   2

Library of Congress Cataloging-in-Publication Data
Valencia, Heather.
Queen of dreams : the story of a Yaqui dreaming woman /
[Heather Valencia and Rolly Kent].
p.   cm.
1. Valencia, Heather.   2. Religion—Biography.
3. Yaqui Indians—Rites and ceremonies.
4. Yaqui Indians—Social life and customs.
I. Kent, Rolly.   II. Title.
BL73.V35A3   1991
299'.784—dc20
[B]   91-2534
                                             CIP

ISBN 0-671-69447-2

Grateful acknowledgment is made to Timoteo Barker
for permission to reprint his poem "Eternity."

ACKNOWLEDGMENTS

I would like to express my gratitude to these people who so strongly supported me in the telling of this story: Frank Lister, Koshare; Blair Sabol, the sorceress; Al Lowman, the cardinal; Ralph Blum, the wizard; Greg Mosher, Grey Eagle; Catherine Oxenberg, the princess; Rolly Kent, my cherished collaborator; my editors, Bob Bender and Barbara Gess; and that Lightning Pilot.

—HV

Thanks to M and M.

—RK

To Anselmo Valencia Tori
and
all the Dreaming Women
who brought into being
such a magnificent part of
Grandmother's great dream.

CONTENTS

ETERNITY

A holding back
from grasping at
what is rightfully
due
& simply moving
into what is
coming toward you
opens up
a crack
just wide enough
for you
to crawl through
into your destiny.

—Timoteo Barker

PREFACE
An Appointment

THE MAGIC OF CLOUDS IS SECRET. THE CLOUDS WHEN I WAS A GIRL ON THE Mississippi were like flat-bottomed boats, they were floating islands, they were the subcontinents of a world much older than this one, passing over me in remnants, cloud-shards broken loose from the ancient place where they started. The magic was like a residue, a sediment in which lyrical artifacts suggested a larger story. I knew all that separated me from the whole story was time, not space—space was only an illusion. For how easily I could reach up my arms from where I lay and stir around the clouds and everything would change and rearrange. The sky was the place of journeys, just like the land or the rivers and oceans—space where the magic of cloud-life could happen. And the clouds were torn charts that contained directions and significations about the life and times of the girl I was, lying on her back on the bluffs of the river in summer. The clouds rolled over and through me. They told me everything, but they told it without any regard for order. I had no idea if I was seeing past, present or future. So even though I saw the magic, what to make of it was still the clouds' secret.

And then, at the age of eleven, a dream came into me and

suddenly, if rudimentally, I had a perspective by which to see a shape and a direction. From eleven until I was fourteen, I dreamed of a beautiful man. He was the man I would one day come to know as Anselmo Valencia Tori, the spiritual leader of the Yaqui Indian Nation of Sonora, Mexico, and Arizona. The force of our connection was so intense in the dream that once it began, I lived my life in the shape of its calling. The memory of the dream quickened my life in a world that was slow, flat and stifling. I had been hypnotized like the snake that believes God's diamond eye follows it everywhere. Like the snake, for a long time I chased after it, not knowing that what I wanted I already had.

There is an amount of power that comes to us when we cross over from childhood into maturity. The advent of the man in the dream marked that crossing for me; when I at last came to Anselmo Valencia I also crossed over a border to which the journey of many lifetimes had brought me. Before I came to Yaquiland to live with Anselmo and his people, I struggled with men about power and with myself about good and evil. My life at Yaqui actively demonstrated that I could be in both the dream place and the concrete reality we think of as the "real world." With Anselmo I learned that good and evil are kinetic, inseparable, forces, which together create the dynamics of the universe. My life with him showed me I was neither good nor evil, but a crucible for the mixing of those elements. Finally, as powerful a magician and contemporary leader as Anselmo was, as real a man as any ten men I have ever before or since met, he claimed very little for himself except his superb ability to deer sing. For me, he released the full potential of my dreaming gift. Together we dreamed and sang, and in that partnership I learned that to dance the world is a woman's high privilege. With Anselmo Valencia I heard the songs that come to us all from the beginning of time.

I went with my twelve-year-old son, Bobby, on April Fool's Day, 1980, to a little hill topped with a white cross near the Papago cemetery at the Mission San Xavier del Bac in Tucson. It was the Tuesday before the Easter weekend, and I had an appointment that afternoon to meet the spiritual chief of the Yaqui people.

I had sat for a long time by myself while Bobby scouted and ran around the desert. It was a beautiful, warm spring day. The desert was beginning to thicken lushly with all sorts of white and yellow and red wildflowers. The sun was in my face as I sat looking south. The heat and the hypnotic swish of cars on the interstate highway to Mexico, the mysterious mountains with their igneous, reptilian personalities, the big saguaros backlit to blackness with sunlight, the golden-silver aura of needles blazing . . . the world came so fully into my senses that it overwhelmed me. The buzz of flies, the smell of grass, creosote . . . in the full Arizona sun I mused over a dream I'd received in answer to a prayer. For months I'd been restless and unhappy in my marriage and didn't know what to do about it.

My aunt Charmaine had taught me how to pray in the full moon, and that's what I had done on the night of the full moon in October 1979. In the dream I had that same night, I became a hummingbird in the land of the long-armed cactus, the saguaro. Something drew me to a particular saguaro, a stately, ancient one with many outraised arms. In the dream, the air grew more dense as I flew toward this saguaro, pulled through hot and cold currents, through air heavy with the perfume of orange blossoms. I come closer to its green, needle-studded surface as if approaching an emerald and amethyst planet. Like me, the saguaro vibrates so furiously it glows with a nearly molten, ruby intensity. The closer I get, the faster the saguaro vibrates until we cannot resist each other and merge.

"Mom!" Bobby yelled, startling me from the reverie. He scrambled up the rocky hill behind me, and I turned around. "Mom! Come here, quick! There's a man smoking a cigarette and he's floating in thin air! Come right now, come right now!"

I followed Bobby back over the hill to a place near the big whitewashed wooden cross. "He was right here, Mom, right here. Look!" Bobby picked up a crumpled wrapper from a pack of Camels.

"What did he look like?"

"He was, like, Indian, with a black hat and dark glasses. He was just smoking, right here, sitting about three feet off the ground, Mom. In the middle of thin air." I sat down for a while where we found the cigarette wrapper to see if I could sense anything about the man, but I couldn't.

Before my appointment to see Anselmo Valencia that afternoon, I decided to drive around the Yaqui village. I promptly got lost. Bobby and I stopped at the end of the village facing the big mountains far to the west where I could see the telescopes on Kitt Peak Observatory and miles and miles of empty desert between. We drove on until the dirt road ended at a small pile of dirt and rocks with a cross on top. We parked inside a wire fence that went around two sides of a cemetery, and walked toward the graves at the westward end of a large field.

It was the most amazing cemetery I had ever seen. There were mounds of dusty, rose-colored dirt heaped up over the dead who were laid to rest in uneven rows. Some graves didn't even have crosses. There were graves covered with bright and fading plastic flowers. There were graves with small, crude handmade crosses and graves with well-kept whitewashed wooden ones. Some graves had little dishes of water. One grave had a piece of birthday cake and a can of Coors placed where the stomach of the departed one would have been. There were lots of tall glass candles with the faces of the saints. In the northwest corner were tiny graves with broken children's toys. A color snapshot of a two-year-old was all that identified one small grave.

I was overwhelmed with feeling. All my life the spirits of the dead have comforted me, but I had never seen a place of the dead like this one. I noticed a glow to one of the graves on the southeast boundary of the cemetery and walked over. Even if I hadn't seen the glow, I'd have known it was the grave of someone special. There was a small concrete shrine erected at the head of the grave, with a niche in it for the Virgin of Guadalupe and a white cross on top. At the base of the shrine there were calla lilies growing, and in their midst was a broken teapot which had been painted to look like an apple, bright red with emerald spout and handle. The apple had been decorated with a smile and Disney-style eyes with large black pupils and wide white ovals around them. As I looked at the teapot, something pressed within me, like small birds lifting their wings. A radiant light poured from the eyes of the teapot; I was so startled I gasped, for the light from the pot was illuminating the fabric of my pink dress, touching my heart. A wave of emotion swept over me and for a moment there was in me an understanding of the woman who was buried here. I knew she was kind and generous to many, many people. I felt she had summoned me there.

Bobby called and I went to join him, looking back over my shoulder at the grave. It was time to go meet Anselmo Valencia at the Yaqui tribal offices.

"Bobby, did you see anything unusual about any of the graves?"

"Yes," he said, "a teapot on one. Why?"

"I felt something there."

"Me, too."

I nodded. We got in the car. My heart was racing so fast my hand shook. I let Bobby put the key in the ignition. "Does the map show how to get to the tribal offices?"

Bobby looked over the map I'd drawn when Anselmo Valencia had dictated instructions to me over the phone. I had no idea where I was going, so I just followed a road. That's what I had always done.

1 ⌘ THE RIVER

I WAS BORN, LIKE HUCKLEBERRY FINN, TO FOLLOW THE RIVER. WHEN THE river didn't get me far enough, I turned my back to it and took the bigger river of the sky. I rode horses with an orphan's abandon, having seen that earth is the true mother, and when the horses tired, there was starlight, firelight, the enchanted light of the flowers . . . I was born to be the queen of dreams.

All my life, forces vaguely visible at the edges have made their way toward the center of things. The night of my birthday, the first person to see me, besides my mother, was her showgirl roommate and friend, Harriet. Harriet took care of her beautiful looks—she loved mirrors—and she took care of Mother because my father was away at war. Harriet had hurried over from Manhattan to the Jersey side of the river, still dressed in her stage costume, having received backstage the telegram announcing my birth. It was the day of the vernal equinox; a storm was blowing hail and snow into the ashen streets. The lights in the hospital went out and came on and went off again without warning. Harriet, whom my mother remembered as being dark as an Egyptian courtesan, sat next to the bed, alternately swiveling her head and her mirror as if to line up the two faces that they might coalesce into one steady image. As she preened her exotic looks, a small feather fell from her headpiece.

"Let's see," said Harriet, snapping her compact shut as she pressed together her bright red lips. "Let's see, let's see. A good name for a girl." She twirled the green feather as she mused. My mother, who was nearly spent, leaned toward her as if Harriet were a candle or an answer.

"How about 'Heather'? You get it, honey?" she asked my mother, twirling the feather in front of my mother's eyes, "you get it?" My mother beamed her approval. Harriet cooed that I was made all the more pretty by her name for me. Taking off her headdress, she swaddled me in it and picked me up. "Oh, sweet little thing," she said, "Oh, Heather."

The war ended. Aunt Harriet disappeared into the underworld with her Mafia boyfriend. My father came home from the Pacific theater and took my mother away. For most of my early life I was a strange kind of orphan—I knew who my parents were, saw them on occasion, but I did not miss them. Another war was beginning where the Second World War left off, a war for the Third World, the Fourth World, stack them up like layers of rainbow—at some point it isn't even a matter of number. Let's just say the fight was on for the world inside me, though I wouldn't know this for years to come.

From that feather bed across the river from Manhattan, and the dingy hospital where I was born, by degrees, and often at night, I made my way westward from one relative to another until I arrived at the country home of my father's parents, the Winnings, in Hannibal, Missouri. Along the way I heard stories of my parents, of my birth, the war. My folks were down on their luck and trying very hard; my parents were now in the Midwest, studying at college; they were preparing a new life that I, too, poor little thing, would soon be part of.

I never felt poor. I never felt unwanted, or resented. Quite the opposite: wherever I was sent, the household seemed to reorganize around my presence. In their spacious ranch house in the country, on the high bluffs that faced the eastern riverbank across the Mississippi, the parents of my father doted on me in every way. Of course they had expectations for me, which emerged over the course of my education and initiation into life in Hannibal. They were good Missourians, true emissaries of the show-me attitude in which reality is as reality does. They were not much for words, thoughts, subtleties. Life was a ladder—not Jacob's, but a short, stout stepladder that had its solid functionality. They had climbed up and shown me I was to do the same if I wanted to get what I wanted, because the first lesson of life, learned at Grandmother's and Grandfather's knees, was that you can get what you want, though not by wishes, which were not their kings, but by old-fashioned elbow grease.

During those first five years when nobody was my parents, I never knew I should want it to be otherwise. I was connected to aunts and uncles and cousins, even my grandparents' parents, through a tight yet elastic web of relatives who were my people. Not often, but occasionally, the strangers my grandparents called "your mother and father" would disturb my equilibrium.

I remember visiting my mother and father for a weekend somewhere in the country once. My mother was looking out the window toward the emerald fields below and beyond the house. The sun in her face and eyes made her sing just to me, "The corn is as high as an elephant's eye! Oh, what a beautiful morning!" She lifted the window open, and together we stuck out our heads and smelled the green corn. I love that green! I love my mother. And the corn is as high as my eye. It's all in the field in front of the house and I run out to feel it. The tender leaves flutter against me like thousands of green, green wings as I run through. I could never tire of the green; when I stop and listen I hear from the closeness of my breath the rustle of so many green and yellow corn snakes hatching from the swishing corn. Over my head where I sit, and over my arms and down my front and across my legs, the little snakes ripple and dance and ask me for a song: "Oh, what a beautiful corn, oh, what a beautiful hay!"

My mother is dusting me off, holding my hand as we walk out of the cornfield. She says, I worried about you, Heather, don't run off like that again, but I tell her about the lady of the corn and her green fingers that play songs until your skin can't stand it and you start to sing, didn't you hear her singing, Mom?

* * *

What I knew was that wherever I was I was the center of the people, the house, the grass, the corn, in those childhood days, before I moved back with my parents, before the magic and the darkness made themselves known; before boys and wild horses, before Kansas and Chief George Allen, before the word "Yaqui," and the Dark Lord, before the name Anselmo Valencia. I was the little blond queen of all I could see; from the shiny white porch to the well-kept beds of tulips and daffodils, the big and little boats in the brown river that flowed from a giant's white cloud in the broad blue sky.

By the time I was four I was reading to myself. By the time I was five I was like the mind of the land, the river, the sky—whatever I wanted or thought or dreamed, it came through, like weather, like sun or rain or dark or shine, it came in many forms, but when it appeared, it turned out to be what I'd wanted.

When I awoke one morning, my grandmother told me to be quiet. "Your mother and father have come home! They came in very late last night, so be quiet." And suddenly it was all different. From the beginning of those days when my parents moved in with me and my grandparents, I was afraid of my father. But I loved my mother. I was very proud of her when we'd walk down the street and she held my hand tight in her bright nail-polished hand. Men would whistle, and my mother would smile and say it was nice to be two beautiful girls, wasn't it? But a few months later, when my brother was born, I knew he was the real reason they'd come back to be a family. After the baby was born, my grandparents helped to get a mortgage on a house just for the family. One day I was queen of all I inhabited, the next I lived in a red brick duplex on Fifth Street. I pushed my baby brother down a flight of stairs and was kept indoors for the next two weeks. I sat at the top of the same stairs, minus the baby carriage, and watched the rain outside the narrow screen door below do the crying for me.

At the end of my imprisonment, the sun was out. So Nature expressed what was inside me, and it was long before I saw that outside and inside are different thoughts, different places. But that day, alone outside the house, I understood that sometimes being the center of things has its costs.

*   *   *

Early September, the first day of kindergarten at the Lutheran
school. We enter the room with its wooden floors reeking of
polish. My shoes squeak as if my heels have turned into mice. I
turn around to look for them, but the mice are gone. My grandfather, who has driven me because my father has just started
work for the phone company, stops to say "Hello, darlin' " to
one of the women. He's somebody everybody knows.

Across the room a black-and-white spotted horse hangs by
silver from the ceiling. It's my horse, the moment I see it it
becomes mine, and I walk up to the girl on the spotted horse and
tell her so. She coasts to a stop, her dark braids that were falling
behind her head as she pumped the horse come to rest, framing
her face like an Indian maiden's. She looks at me, jumps off, and
sits down nearby.

I plant myself on the red saddle and take the red reins and my
first day in Lutheran kindergarten the spotted pony and I swing
and gallop, gallop and swing. All day I ride the black-and-white
horse—I pull back and we swing forward, she takes off through
the playground, down the streets of the town, out onto the
prairie whose grasses are long and blond and full of the thick
rich sunlight. She gallops toward the sun, with each gallop we
ride across the world, across months and years, until we are
galloping so fast the horse's legs are fluid as fire and wind.

In my sleep I am riding dark horses, I ride them until they all
tire and then I ride the horses that are like the earth, dark red
and brown. And these, too, tire, so I must ride the horse that
will last, but I cannot find this horse. Whenever I am in the
dream, I'm flowing like the river. When I look up, the big black
sky is shaking some stars from its mane.

It is Thanksgiving. Nanny, my great-grandmother, has just
presented me with an enormous strand of pearls. Her daughter,
my grandmother, is furious. "Mother, you can't be serious!
Heather's a child, put them away for her until she's old enough
to understand what they are."

"Nonsense!" Nanny says. "I may never see the child again.
She gets them here and now. Come here, sweetheart," Nanny
bestows the pearls on my neck. In a minute Grandma has pulled
me aside and wags her finger in my face. "If you lose these,

young lady, I will do a bean, Heather, I'll do a bean!" I try to think of Grandma and the bean, but don't understand how to relate them together.

All during dinner I feel like I am wearing a circle of strange light. I look down at them; they look like the moon in the windowpane on a cold night. Or my eyes as they move toward the window and merge with another pair of eyes coming from the outside to look at me . . .

It's because I want a horse so much. All these horses in my wishes, I want to ride at least one. It's because of horses that I am kneeling by the elm tree, scraping away the frost with a big silver spoon. I know what I am doing—this spot belongs to the Moon.

When the hole is deep enough I take off the necklace and kiss it. I say some words to the Moon Mother, how much I love you, Moon, my lady. I am your daughter, Moon. Send a gold horse if you like these. I cover over the gift with earth.

The next day, Grandma is furious again because I cannot find the necklace. It's just as she said, she was afraid of this, she told her mother I was too young. "What have you done with them, Heather? Tell me right now." Grandma is saying each word as if it is making a big bubble in her mouth that might explode if she's not careful. "But honestly, Grandma, I don't know. I had it on last night, Grandma, maybe someone took it."

She's not buying it, she knows I've done something with them, she knows and she is going to get to the bottom of it. I am worried when she says this, because I see her looking throughout the world for anything with a bottom to get to—scouring everywhere before the Moon has a chance to take my offering. I have no idea how long the Moon takes.

Christmas. After all the other presents have been given, just one remains: a gold statue of a horse high on the mantle. It has a red ribbon on its neck, but no name tag. Grandma says it couldn't be for Heather—she's gotten over the pearls and is teasing, I hope—but when no one comes forward for it my great grandfather takes it down from the mantle. "Santa must have left it for . . . Heather!"

It's not a real horse, but the Moon Mother has heard my prayer. The next day I go out to the tree in the backyard and try to dig in the frozen ground. I want to know for sure if the Moon took my gift. But the ground is too hard, and I am forced to believe it—until spring, when the crocuses bloom. By then I've gotten used to believing; should I dig to see? I dig. The pearls are gone—the Moon Mother kept them!

From then on I made altars. I created them in secret places and offered the Moon jewels, pretty rocks, and fossils, which were plentiful on the bluffs of the Mississippi. I would place my gifts on a flat rock at the base of a tree or among wild rose vines. If a ladybug landed on me, it was good luck, but their cadavers were power objects and went on my altars. I loved the emerald and iridescent Japanese peach beetles, which augured wealth and ended up in my treasure box as well as on ledges out on the bluffs, on fallen logs, in little niches carved by water and wind.

I loved certain saints, as well as certain stars, in addition to the Virgin Mary and Venus with her vivid, shiny heart, which she held out to anyone who wished to touch it, low in the sky. I liked St. Michael the Archangel, slayer of demons, and carried his prayer card with me wherever I went. In our new house, with its banisters running up three flights of stairs, the dark each night, not my mother, walked upstairs with me. Why was my mother always frightened? "Don't worry," my mother said. I was a big girl now, and everything else was just imagination. If I confided I was scared of dark shapes coming toward me, she'd say, "Oh, Heather, don't be silly." Or, if she was tired, "Stop being so selfish and get upstairs." The sight of the crucifix made me faint—I hated the statue of God bleeding on the cross, so I wore St. Michael around my neck. St. Michael was a warrior, his sword raised high at the ready. I clutched him as I went upward toward my room.

My favorite Mary was a dark Indian standing on a crescent moon. She looked like one of the beautiful Indian women who visited my dreams and rode ponies with me. There were three, sometimes four, dark-skinned ladies who rode with me in my dreams. These dreams were so real, I felt the fluid rhythm of the ponies and the wind through my hair. Then, a little older, I'd get onto my bike and ride out into the streets and lanes that went into the country and around the town, and scout for horses. I'd find them out at pasture. I'd ditch my bike, roll under the barbed wire and go up to the horses. I'd seen Tom Mix feed horses in movies with a slice of apple in his hand. I did the same thing. As the horse took my offering I'd loop a string around his neck and lead him over to a tree stump or a fence so I could mount him. Then I'd ride the bareback, gleaming arc of everything I felt.

Whatever I dreamed was real like that. I was the horse and I'd ride the horse. I was the dream and no hand had to offer apples to entice me to follow. The dreams of flying made me ache for the freedom of the stars. Often I went to the stars. But in the stars was a place where, if I went beyond its bounds, I'd never get back to my mother, I'd never see her again. When I felt that fear I'd start to plummet, and fear led to fear. I'd get scared I'd hit earth and break apart. But I didn't die, and I didn't lose my mother. I'd just be in a confined world, and that was frustration enough. I always wanted the green lands of the dream, the waterfalls and hot springs, and caves brimming with orchids, volcanoes erupting rainbows.

People began to appear in my dreams, people who were familiar, like my mother and grandmother, but who weren't exactly them either. One of my dream grandmothers was an Indian woman who wore a robe of mountain-lion fur. She was my protector. She fed me a sweet black pudding made from little seeds. She also gave it to the dead, and I was honored to share the tribute.

My parents put my brother and me to bed early—he's sleeping in his bed on one side of my room. It is dusk, and I am looking out of my upstairs bedroom window. My brother has settled into rhythmic finger-sucking. My father has scared us both into absolute, not-one-peep silence. Through the closed door I can hear the muffled voices from the new black-and-white TV—it sounds like something caught in a big tin can. Now and then the laughter spills out, but then something snaps a lid on again.

Who is moving in the yard below, by the elm trees, in the bed of tiger lilies? I have seen fairies lots of times—they are shy, like tiny deer. I have seen them only at a distance before now, and in dreams. I press my face as far into the rusty screen as it will go so I can get a better angle by which to see. Who is making the faint music, who is making a song that comes to my window in a strange, quick language whose notes are formed by light? I can hear, all at once, a chorus attended by a thousand sand-grain-sized bells, I can see brilliant orange and pink lights in the bed of tiger lilies. The sound is so beautiful it is painful to hear from my room. I start to cry softly—I dare not arouse my father's fury—for my room is separated from the garden of the fairies' dream fire. Their song is so exquisite, the screen smells like iron, my lips fill with salt—

Something like a hummingbird darts by the window, then coasts in midair, face-to-face with me. Twilight on her heart-shaped face, her poppy-colored lips, eyes like a cat with clear green pupils. She's covered with a stardusting of freckles, her ears pink shells. She wears her copper hair in a bird's next, wild, wild thicket of hair that is like fire, and clouds full of thread-sized lightning bolts. What tiny bird of the exotic, elfin world roosts there? Some twiggy tendrils snake down her delicate neck. I can't tell if her gold-and-peridot dress is clothing or skin—the wings seem made of nothing but motion itself behind her miniature, girl-like arms. She has perfect breasts and a tiny waist just visible through some sort of webbed veil. Her toes and fingernails are painted red. There is pollen in her hair.

A shimmer gets through the screen into my eyes, and she directs my attention over the treetops toward the west. Twilight has become like fireworks in the electric blue sky. Everything is glowing—the elm tree, the street, the houses—all backlit by a mysterious brilliance. My heart has expanded so much that its joy is like a bubble transporting me with the fairies. I lean out to follow the Queen of the Tiger Lilies as she waves from her red dragonfly and rides into the tiger stripes of the boughs of trees against the sky.

My father comes into the room and closes the door. He lies in bed with me. The air is too thick; it makes me swelter. I can hardly breathe. When he touches me between my legs, I cry out; all the fairy dust vanishes. My father puts the pillow over my face. You have to get very still to breathe inside something like that. If you keep crying the thing that is deep down in the darkness will come and take your breath away forever. My father never needed the pillow again. I only cried the first time.

The Queen visited me in dreams. I went on looking for a horse to ride—even then I was practicing escape. If there were no horses to ride in pastures, the bike was a pony. Sometimes in spring I'd just sit on the fence rails, covered with small, fragrant rosebuds, and ride the wild roses to the center of my desire. In school, my teachers encouraged me to read—more books on horses, horses of the cowboys, of Indians and conquistadors and the knights of old. I painted murals all afternoon, with mesas I'd never seen in real life, and clouds like the dream songs. I'd look out a window and there was the dream fire the Queen had brought and left, like a shawl, a perfumed hankie, a carpet woven from the clouds where the silkworms nest. That easily I could induce a vivid dream. By the time I was ten I was riding big rawboned nags with the Elder brothers, my peer descendants of the famous outlaw gang, and Bobby Drennan let me ride his red mare, Shawnee.

From time to time, my mother hired Lydia Burton to babysit. People made fun of Lydia because even though she was rich, they said, she liked to pick through garbage cans like a crazy woman. When I was eleven, she embroidered a silk handkerchief for me. She put pink and yellow flowers in one corner, set against a scalloped field of pale gold silk. In February of that year, Lydia slipped on the ice by a neighbor's garbage can and broke her hip. Her sister put her in a convalescent home at the bottom of Hill Street.

Lydia Burton came crying to me in dreams one night. She was heartbroken, she said. She knew I was a dreamer and could see her. She told me it was her birthday and she wished I would come visit her.

The next afternoon, I went into the weathered brick building. I climbed the stairs with my hand over my nose to keep from gagging on the smell of Pine Sol and urine. I found her bed and took her hand. She opened her small bleary eyes and her fingers squeezed back when she saw who it was.

"Thank you," she said. "Thank you. I'm so glad you've come, Heather. So glad."

Lydia pressed my hand against her eyes. We both sat there, silent. She set my hand down and looked me straight in the eye. "I want you to dream me into summer, Heather. I don't want to see another birthday like this."

Toward the end of the month I dreamed Lydia Burton was running in a meadow wearing a dress exactly like the handkerchief she'd given me. A tall, handsome man in a brown pin-striped suit waited for her in the middle of a meadow. Lydia ran toward his arms . . .

Lydia Burton passed away in her sleep the same night I dreamed her into summer. That was the first time I helped someone die.

That July I went to Girl Scout camp. I was not a joiner, certainly not a Girl Scout, but camp was escape from my father, if only for three weeks. Scout activities dulled me into nervous restlessness. By the beginning of my second week at camp, I tried each night to bring to myself dreams that would alleviate the boredom. I expected to dream. But the dream that came, and continued over the next three years in serial form, was so powerful that it became more real than my ordinary life.

It was so humid, the night inside the cabin had turned to syrup. I lay in a lower bunk listening to the insect hum of the Missouri summer night. Suddenly I was in a crystal ship, landing somewhere above the palm trees, watching emissaries from the Dark Lord climb the path to the rock ledge where my ship has landed. They open the hatch; I understand what comes next, for everything in my life has been a prelude to this moment. I rise and accept the honors from the ministers—gifts of shells and bright feathers, and the gratitude of the ministers for my journey to this place which is so foreign compared to the island temple from which I've traveled through the sky.

We step out from the crystal interior of the ship. I look over my shoulder into the pilot's window—he is slumped into a deep sleep and will not wake up. Down the beach I look up a last time at the high perch where the ship is quickly being overgrown by the jungle. Already the pilot has become a tiny skeleton in the cockpit.

I have no remorse. Rather, I am in an elevated and excited state. I am taken with courtesy, yet I am clearly being guarded. The wariness of the party suggests I have come to a place at war. We enter a cave. We walk in darkness a long time. I realize the capital toward which we proceed is within a mountain, and that my journey in the ship of crystal has been across both space and time. I am not surprised when I understand these things. My excitement is for what is yet to be.

We reach daylight. The air is alive with bird song and the spectacular flights of big and little birds across a series of stunning bridal falls and pools of hot and cold water . . . From some temple-like dwellings with intricately carved stone façades a lithe, dark man in ceremonial clothes approaches me. As soon as I see him I remember everything—his bright headpiece of long green and blue feathers, punctuated with red plumes; the cape likewise of feathers; the staff with the eagle head; the jaguar loincloth; the leather bag of medicine on his chest—I say his name, and there are flowers everywhere, where his footprints came toward me it is all yellow and white petals.

I am dressed in green feathers. I have my arm in his. We are standing there before his people—everyone is so happy they can't shower us with enough flowers. We stand shoulder to shoulder and I remember one more thing: I've come so far to marry the Dark Lord beside me.

I had long ago become adept at dreaming myself into another world. I was also used to the disappointing sense that upon awakening I was less free in the real world than in the dream place. But it was always a question of places traded. In class, in bed, wherever I went into the dream, it was eleven-year-old Heather, twelve-year-old Heather. This dream, however, was a shock. The Heather of this dream was a fully grown woman, and she had no apparent awareness of me dreaming her from Girl Scout camp on the bluffs of the Mississippi. I not only awoke hungry for the arms of my king; I felt doubly alone because the queen I was didn't seem to remember me either. Where prior to this dream I'd been able to travel distances to other places, the world of those two royal beings was impenetrable to my will. It was the first time I ever dreamed a dream with its own life, its own time. Though I was desperate to get back to the life that was just beginning with the man in the dream, I was nonetheless excited that I had crossed over from one era of time to another. In ordinary dreams, I had conjured the knights of King Arthur or riverboat gamblers. But those dreams were more like plays with historical costumes and settings, like movies, child's play.

I lay down in the bushes and grass, near an ancient burial ground the camp director had made off-limits. We weren't supposed to go alone to the grave of "Indian Joe," she said. That was a special place owned by the university, and the camp could go there only with permission. It was very warm and peaceful. I lay down and watched the big clouds shape and unshape, until the sky and the dream turned into one thing and I was back with the dark man, my husband.

Some time after my arrival from the island temple beyond the sea, I am in my room. I have come to this place at a very difficult time in the history of the Dark Lord's people—a terrible war has been wasting the resources and energy of everyone. My value to the people, despite the fact that I am from outside their present-day world, is apparently critical: my husband is worried that I might be kidnapped by his enemies. It is also known that some of the enemies of the people are traitors within the community, so extra vigilance is necessary in protecting me. When the Dark Lord is away, I am taken into the confidences of many women.

I am used to being completely telepathic with the Dark Lord. In my homeland, all people were completely telepathic. It is an effort for me to converse in ordinary language. At first there is a great deal to learn and assimilate of an ordinary, functional nature. Later, I long for someone like myself in the dream. Even though I am always in touch with my husband, even when he is at the battle front, I am in many ways alone.

What drew me, the dreamer, back and back again to the Dark Lord was, at first, unbridled physical passion. The Dark Lord in the dream initiated me into forms of sexual expression I had no idea were possible. There in Girl Scout camp, in the dream place, I knew in my body the sheer exhilaration of lovemaking. The Dark Lord knew me so well, as I knew him, that my body at orgasm would keep expanding until it reached beyond me and I'd awaken, sure that everyone who saw me would know what I had been doing.

So sex was the flame that I'd have been content to be consumed by, and I flew back to it at every chance I had. Oddly, though, it never burned me up, and after the first flush of the dream, during the first week, if I was with the Dark Lord, the dream would go on and on past lovemaking. There was a great deal to do and I began to have a detailed life. But as soon as I would feel frustrated or constrained even in the slightest, the world I was in would suddenly cease and I would have to return to Missouri while the dream continued. It had its own integrity, its own rules, its own momentum and timing.

I was so taken up with the reality of the dream that I didn't do camp chores. I skipped meals and scheduled activities to go off on my own somewhere where I could lie down and get back to the Dark Lord. Because the dream was so powerful, it completely transformed me at camp from a polite citizen to a problem child. By the third week, my parents were asked to please come take me home, as I was a disruptive influence on other campers. The ride back to Hannibal was long on silence and cigarette smoke. I felt my mother's confusion, my father's anticipation.

At home my mother wanted to talk with me. She came into the room and sat on my bed. In a kindly way, she asked how I was feeling. Did I want to talk about what had happened that got me sent home? Protect me, I wanted to tell my mother. I assumed she must have known what my father was doing to me, her daughter. Then I realized she was so scared of him herself that he'd hypnotized her into not seeing it at all. Though I was a child being used, it was my mother who was the more fragile.

So I told her about the dreams, because I thought that would cheer her up. As I was telling her about the Dark Lord and the amazing jungle kingdom in which I was queen, I saw the skepticism which she blew into the air with every drag on her cigarette. But I wanted to believe in my mother, so I carried on about the man who was my husband, describing his wonderful hands, his fine intelligence, his tiger-bright fierceness. "Oh, Heather!" my mother burst out. "When are you going to stop this? There are no more Indian chiefs! It's just a dream, it's just a dream!"

I was so hurt that she didn't believe or understand me. I knew, then and there, that absolutely no one was going to save me from my father. The only way out was indeed what the dream indicated—I had to be a grown woman to have my own world.

My mother got up. She was so agitated she was wringing her hands the way you squeeze water from cashmere. At the door she folded her arms and faced me, but without looking into my eyes. "I'm just afraid your imagination is going to get you in big trouble, Heather. What are you going to do when we're not around to protect you? What are you going to do? Think about that, Heather."

But the dream had already given me a perspective I'd never before had. I saw, with disappointed clarity, that I was the protector of my mother. She could be the child, but strength was expected of me.

My husband is saying that he is a man, *not* God. Nevertheless, his people must believe he is God. Otherwise there will not be unity, and disorder and danger will attend the people.

Not all of his people accepted his deity, so he carried out many executions in a quite ruthless fashion. Before long, his people referred to him as the Lord of Death. I am brought into the council of women. My husband and I create six sons and daughters, each of whom is the manifestation of an aspect of divinity.

No escaping it—it was in the world of the dream that I was consciously living my destiny. When Zyla, which was my dream name, made love, I, too, cried out in the throes of lovemaking. At the births of her children, I knew the same measure of pain she knew. The dream was real because it was in my body. What was missing was the critical element of reciprocity of awareness. Without Zyla aware of me, even though I knew and felt everything she felt, I was exiled to the remote reality of Hannibal. Zyla slipped like grains of sand through my twelve-year-old fingers every time I awoke from her world. I had no idea how to get to the dream place, other than going to sleep to dream myself there. That was the only control I had.

I told the dreams only to my best friend, Della, and her mother. Mrs. Wells, I noticed, got very excited and asked if I wouldn't draw what I'd dreamed. As it turned out, hers was an easy request to meet. Suddenly I had something to pour myself into, and I drew and sketched dozens of scenes from the dream. Over the next several months, with Mrs. Wells as my tutor, I learned quite a bit about painting, and at the same time I gave Mrs. Wells some visual verifications of what she'd at first suspected when I narrated the dreams—a few days after the first drawings from the dream of the Dark Lord, she returned from the library with some heavy books that were full of plates and drawings of pre-Columbian art and artifacts. All three of us were astounded at the remarkable similarities between symbols and regalia I had drawn from the dreams and the pictures in the books of art from the ancient Americas and the illustrated Mayan legends of the feathered serpent, Quetzalcoatl. I'd never seen the art of these Indians, yet my images were theirs.

The dream of the Dark Lord was unpredictable, and it came when it chose to come, which was often, though not every night, between that summer and the fall of my fourteenth year. Over those many months, as the dream went on and on, I became accustomed to living in two places at once. It didn't seem to make any difference that there was a historical connection between my dreaming and the Mayan world before the white man came. That knowledge was useful only to the girl I was, the girl who, as the dream intensified, saw the more clearly that nothing in Hannibal was as interesting, as beautiful—or as ruthless. For the Dark Lord and his Queen came and went as they pleased, leaving me the orphan of my own sweet dream.

I wanted no connection to my bloodlines. I was happy to be anything but my father's. Still I'd glean fragments of my father's orphaned past and through offhand comments and anecdotes told by my grandmother Winning and my father's sisters, my aunts, I constructed a short history of my father's youth. My father had two mothers—I knew and loved Grandma Winning. But how come she wasn't the "real" one? My father's other mother was a small oval photograph at Aunt Sissy's house, nothing romantic about her: she was short, toothless, pregnant. She stood at a big pot, grinning, barefoot, and though the photo seemed less specific and more faded each time I saw it, she took root in my imagination.

Her name was Elizabeth Dark Water, the perfect name for this Cherokee woman who seemed part of the eternal black and white the photo portrait showed shimmering on my aunt's dresser. Elizabeth had married a Cornish miner in Pocahontas, Illinois. My father's blood father was a drunk who'd made with Elizabeth seven other half-breed brothers and sisters. Sixteen days after my father was born, Elizabeth Dark Water died.

My grandfather Winning's parents were Scots with big hearts. My great-grandparents lived near the small town where Elizabeth and her coal-miner husband lived, and they knew the man's habits of working double shifts and hard drinking. The family lived in a one-room shack which the father seldom visited, except to sleep off his binges. Then he'd go off to work or drink again. He gave little to his family except money for food. So my great-grandparents started bringing clothes and food to Elizabeth Dark Water, and when she died, they adopted little Eddie. In turn, when my great-grandfather died, on his deathbed he made my grandfather promise to take over as Eddie's adoptive father. My grandparents were newlyweds, eager to enjoy the Roaring Twenties in St. Louis. But despite Grandma's protests—for she wanted no children—my grandfather felt honor-bound to take Eddie, who subsequently passed from one culture to another, one generation to another. In their reluctant, often nonchalant care, he grew up spoiled, courted trouble and those who also liked trouble, as if he were practicing for when I'd appear.

It was as dark as winter got in Hannibal and my father was driving us somewhere. The streets were empty; the only light seemed to come from the dashboard. I was fourteen, but my father told me I looked ten years older than my age. "Fred Himmel wants to date you." Mr. Himmel was an old man, and extremely wealthy.

"No," I said, "Forget it. I'm not going out with an old man."

"I'll tell you what, he may be old, but he wants you, Heather, and he'll give you anything you want if you marry him, I guarantee it. It could make all of us rich."

"No! You can't just sell me to some old man! I don't want to talk about it."

"Think about your future. I'll sign the papers; it'll all be legal and the best part is you'd have all his money by the time you were in your twenties. He doesn't have more than ten years in him, tops."

"The only good thing about this stupid idea is that I'd get away from you," I said.

"Think you're smarter than I am? Hell, if I had my brain and your body, I could do anything I wanted. Don't you know women have all the power?"

I didn't know how to dream my father away, but change was coming. The door between winter and spring hinged on my birthday. A few weeks later, early in April, we were again in the car. I noticed a good-looking blond boy leaning against a phone booth. I smiled. He smiled. My father burst out, "I know that kid, I know his father, Bill Eliott. Lee—that's the kid's name. I saw the way he looked at you. Stay away from him. He's nothing but trouble."

"That's ridiculous," I said, thinking that no one was more trouble than my father was. "I don't know him at all."

"Yeah, well, just make sure you don't. He's a hoodlum just like his father."

But my interest in Lee was piqued by my father's reaction. Secretly it delighted me that Lee Eliott had aggravated my father. I was going to make it my business to know this Lee Eliott. I began at that moment in the car to conjure Lee. I wished upon his image. I knew the rest would come.

A few nights later I was coming out of my swim class at the Y. There was Lee, shooting pool by himself in the lobby. He was tall and suntanned, with an unruly shock of dishwater-blond hair that nearly obscured his blue eyes. I wanted Lee because to want this boy and no other was to begin exerting pressure for my freedom. I decided that day to make some part of Hannibal's reality as potent as my dreams. I came into the lobby and walked in front of him. I leaned against a pillar, folded my arms against my sweater, and smiled. Lee missed one shot, then another and another. Finally he looked up from the pool table and laughed. "I can't make a shot with you standing there looking like that. What's your name?"

"Heather."

"What are you doing now?"

"Breaking your concentration."

Lee shrugged, put down the pool cue and took my arm. Without a word we both walked smiling out of the Y and he escorted me home like we'd always known each other. A week later we lay under the lilacs on the grounds of the old Cruikshank mansion and kissed. Lee's gang was out there in the darkness, keeping watch for their friend. The air was full of springtime; the river was below us, beyond the bluffs where the mansion was. If Lee was a troublemaker, trouble was what I wanted more of. I knew the stories I heard about shoplifting and break-ins were true, but I didn't care. His family, who were working class and not on my grandparents' country club list, seemed undisturbed by any such rumors. They also seemed to like me. They made no pretenses about anything.

My Dark Lord visited me less frequently as Lee and I pursued being boy- and girlfriend. The Dark Lord, unquestionably, was my *true* love, though Lee Eliott was my true friend. I was in *this* world, in Hannibal, respectably repressed Hannibal, and at least Lee was a kindred spirit who understood the dark side of our town and longed, with me, for freer skies and minds. As my father's job increasingly took him away from home for days at a time, suddenly I was under the spell of hope.

All fall Lee and I met covertly, sometimes during school nights if my father was away, on weekends under the guise of acceptable social events, like football games or Catholic Youth Organization meetings. Around Thanksgiving my friend Selene slipped me the key to her house—she and her family were going for the winter to their second home in Florida. She didn't say anything—just grinned.

Through the dark halls of the empty house, I guided Lee toward Selene's bedroom. At first we lay in our clothes on top of

Selene's bed. But after we'd made love for the first time, it was so safe and cozy, we thought, in Selene's room, that Lee and I got under the covers. Every Saturday till midnight, the pumpkin hour, we would lie close together and discuss Hannibal, life, the future, dreams. I never told Lee about the Dark Lord. But I told him all about my father, and, as it turned out, he knew quite a lot about my dad. Both his father and his older friend Crystal went drinking at the same bar my father went to, the Alibi. Lee knew from them that my father was keeping women on the side, that he had substantial debts with bookies, and that he and a second man had a scam for bilking money from lonely women they would meet at country clubs and golf courses throughout the tri-state area.

It wasn't Lee's love that freed me from my father. My father was too much until he became a story—and it was the story that Lee provided. When Lee would lie beside me, my arm across his chest, my head on his shoulder or by his, I'd hear tales of my father and Hannibal's mighty and powerful citizens, revealing their dark and petty purposes, and slowly, over weeks, the sway of Hannibal undid itself.

Lee and I were so much alike. We were both good students. He was the editor of his school newspaper, I a writer for mine. He, too, had grand visions about what life could offer—beyond the rich mainstream expectations to which, it was assumed, a smart kid like Lee, a great athlete to boot, would surely rise like cream.

But Lee's secret life was among the kids from the hidden world of Hannibal. The children of the carnies, Gypsies, Cajuns, blacks, roughnecks, bootleggers had that allure that came from being on the slippery banks of the mainstream where a fuller, richer, freer life seemed to happen. Lee was the leader and the youngest member of a band of juvenile delinquents. We both liked going against the grain of what was acceptable, and because we kept getting away with it, we thought we'd always get away with it. We told Lee's gang not to bother keeping watch for us when we went into Selene's place. There was no need to waste their time.

There had been light snow one evening when Lee and I sneaked into Selene's house, in a silly mood, giggling. I led Lee into the master bedroom. We slipped beneath the bed coverings and were kissing. At the same moment we both heard loud footsteps on the hall floor; then someone was shining a flashlight on the bed.

"How'd you get in here?" a man's voice was saying. I stood up with the sheet around me and tried to see past the light.

"Leon? Is that you?" I knew it was Leon, the groundskeeper, but I needed some time to think. "Selene gave us a key to the house, Leon," I said as I walked toward him. "She said we could use it any time we wanted."

"I don't think Selene's mother would like that too much. I don't suppose your mother would like it either. What do you think she'd say if she knew you were with a boy? Where is he anyway?"

Lee stood up and said his name to Leon. Then I turned on the tears. I started sniffling how Selene had told us to come to the house whenever we wanted, and if Leon knew what an awful family life I had he'd understand. If my father found out he'd kill me for sure, I'd have to run away. My life, I told him, would be over. I was really crying by then, standing very close to Leon. "You're not going to tell my parents, are you, Leon? Please, we'll never do it again, I swear!"

Leon wasn't sure whether to be uncomfortable or stern. Through my fingers that stifled my sobs I saw him hesitate. I waited a beat, then moved a little closer. "Okay," Leon said. "But give me them keys. And this is the last time I want to see you two here! You're not so smart, you know. Feet leave tracks when it snows." He turned with his small triumph, and Selene's keys, and left. Lee flashed the thumbs-up sign for my performance. We dressed quickly but kissed a long time by the front door, then went out into the cold midnight.

It was my mother's wish that I become confirmed in the Catholic religion. I went to classes during the early part of the new year and to confession for the first time in many, many months. As it happened, the priest of our church was a golfing partner of my father's. When I confessed that my father had been sexually abusing me for the past seven years, instead of a prescription of Hail Marys and prayers for mercy, the priest shot back, "Young lady, I know what you're doing with the Eliott boy—no wonder your father is upset, can you blame him? Whatever he's doing to you, you're tempting him to it, just like you've done with that boy. I advise you to stay away from him and do what your father tells you."

From that time on I began to comprehend the extent of the gap between what I dreamed and what I lived in Hannibal. I had to choose the life I wanted. Still, it would take me many more years to have the experience that readied me, once and for all, to cut the ties between my kind of dreaming and Hannibal's.

After I first had sex with Lee, the dream of the Dark Lord ceased. His absence presented me with another kind of choice: since the biggest danger in my life was my father, and since the Dark Lord had vanished, I could lament and feel hopeless, or find my way by a different route back to the dream. For the dream signaled me, from its separate time and place where I was a grown woman living her destiny, that the straightest way to paradise was to grow up and not stay a child.

Crystal got sent to jail for fencing stolen goods. He was twenty-one and his sentence put an end not only to the "gifts" Lee bestowed whenever I wanted records, a necklace, a ring; it ended the gang itself. Snake had tipped off the police that if they went to Crystal's garage they'd find a little surprise. What they found was a small warehouse full of hi-fi equipment, kitchen appliances, 45 rpm records, cheap jewelry, and clothes. Snake betrayed everyone in the gang—except Lee.

Lee and I were sitting alone in his small, dark room toward the end of winter, 1962. Lee was staring out the window. Suddenly he leaned forward and looked at me.

"What's the matter?" I said. "Are you okay?"

"We have to stop."

"Stop?" I said, feeling my heart rise. "Are you saying you're tired of me?"

"Every time we're together, I feel like lightning is about to strike. What if you get pregnant? That's it for both of us, Heather, our futures will be dead."

I yelled at Lee. "Well, I feel like I've been struck by lightning! You just want to be free from me so you can follow that little blond who chases around after you." There were always girls following Lee, and it was true that he did not discourage their interest. "You're not going to find a better girlfriend than me, Lee, no matter how many girls you have!"

But to my surprise, Lee was not about to get into an argument by trying to defend himself. "Listen to me. It's different. Those girls are staying here in Hannibal, and they are going to be swallowed by Hannibal. You're someone special, and you're going to go places no one else in Hannibal can even dream of. Do you want to trade that for getting pregnant? Because if we keep seeing each other, there's no way we can stop having sex. I like it too much to be able to stop when we're together."

I looked away. Neither of us said anything for several minutes, and we didn't look at each other. My mind was racing—I wasn't happy about giving up so much pleasure with a boy, and the happiness of each other's company. But what Lee said was true. Quietly I told him that he was right, that he was the best friend I'd ever had, and I loved him. I did want my freedom. If that meant parting, we had to do it.

"Except," I said, "you have to take me to the prom. I want to leave dancing."

Lee and I were walking in Riverside Park Cemetery after the prom was over. It was spring again in Hannibal. The grass was silver where the moon hit it, black where the shadows of trees fell between the headstones. We leaned against the big mausoleum of one of the lumber barons in Hannibal's past.

"This is the part of the cemetery I like best," I said to Lee. The headstones were gleaming marble in the moonlight, almost as if they glowed from within. We stood quiet for a while, then strolled over to the bluffs.

"Well," Lee said, "this is it." We were looking south, down the big river that slid beneath the path of moonlight on the surface. Lee put his arm around my shoulders. We gazed downriver a long time. From all sides, around us, above and below, I could feel the presence of the dead. Riverside was the oldest, most unkempt cemetery in town, and I'd always liked it for that reason—something of the wildness of human life was still allowed here. From along the moonlit water, every now and then a disembodied voice would rise in a laugh or hoot that made an echo. As I listened for three, four rings of echoing, it would gradually grow so quiet, I seemed to hear the nineteenth century sighing, all overgrown with its weeds and gaudy angels, its faded wealth and iron, its little cupids tooting bugles.

It was Lee sighing. I couldn't help laughing at us dressed up so gaudily ourselves as if in tribute to the old century that had laid to rest its loved ones in such ostentation of grief. I took hold of both Lee's hands and said, "Look up," and leaned back so far I was half-horizontal. Lee turned me slowly and the sky started to wheel, the moon in the center, the stars like bright drops of water that spun off the moon.

The dead again! That starlight showering above us was broadcast so many centuries ago, long before there was a Midwest or even a river. The power that shone from those stars could easily now be dust; yet starlight is always fresh, always seen as if for the first time.

"Look at the stars, Lee. Go ahead. You won't feel so alone."

We both spun slowly and easily off of one another's arms. Then Lee pulled me back upright. We walked giddily back toward the car. The wet grass and weeds got the bottom of my white dress wet, and my feet were soaked with the dew. "Thank you," I said to Lee. "Thank you so much." He smiled.

"You know, I just can't tell you how grateful I am to *you*," Lee said, and paused. Then he smirked, "So I won't." We both laughed. As we walked away from the bluffs among the graves, I saw in a sudden vision that the adoring little girl who followed him everywhere was going to get pregnant. I saw them carrying a baby. But I didn't tell Lee. We kissed, he drove me home, and I never saw him again.

Even after the Dark Lord ceased to come to me through dreams, the stars would entrance me and draw me. Theirs was a power greater than mine. I didn't know what the power was, but I thought there were, somewhere, people like the stars who knew where to go to find the Dark Lord.

2⊟ BRIDE OF THE PHARAOH

THERE WAS WILD LAUGHTER IN THE STREET BELOW. I LOOKED OUT: "WHO'S that?" I thought. I must have asked my question aloud. My roommate came to the window. "Oh, it's Allen Hunter," she said. "Lucky girls."

Allen Hunter was being carried from the dorm by blond girls from wealthy Chicago suburbs. His entire left leg gleamed in a new full-leg plaster cast. As the girls pretended to drop him their shrieks flew up like scattered leaves; Allen lay serenely smiling, his arms folded across his chest like a young pharaoh. He wore a white T-shirt and plaid Bermuda shorts and one penny loafer with no sock. The sun was all on his face, his eyes were closed. The girls bounced him, they stroked his leg, they signed his cast—he remained still, unperturbed, unaroused.

Exactly below me, he floated as the girls clowned and teased. "Allen," my roommate mused. "Mmmm, what a catch!"

A month later he was escorting me, a freshman at the University of Kansas, to Homecoming '63. One year later we married. All-American Allen. Who were you that serene afternoon? That beautiful prince passed out of your body as if he were a passenger who embarked on a different course, and I, foolish I, fell from the window into the arms of All-American Al, Brother Al, frat president, Captain Al with the football wound and the limp in his leg, agribusiness Al, roots heavy with the frost of money.

Allen Hunter, below my window. I took that effigy for the real man. Along the way I conceived a son. Along the way I finally received the blessings of my grandmother, who approved my eminent good sense in marrying Al Hunter in whom she saw the future writ larger than a paycheck. And my mother, oh, my poor mother, trapped in her fear of my father! How happy she was for my escape to Kansas and the beautiful Oz of marriage to Al!

All the dried roses of my memory of Allen, all the star-blurred nights in his sports car, the roads that all led in a circle to desire and ended at a duplex on Manhattan Street in Lawrence, Kansas. He thought I was the goddess, the moon, the deer-girl and had to have me because he'd had every kind of girl he'd ever wanted. It was so easy, looking back: all I had to do was refuse him. From then on he couldn't resist.

Yes, and what did I see? I saw what I needed to see in order to seal shut forever the way back to Missouri and my father. I see you still, Al, down there beneath my window, young prince reposed in the eight arms of American beauty!

Such a little thing to want someone, and how it alters everything, sex! Behind your eyes the Virgin darted among ancient trees. I thought you would be my pharaoh; I didn't see Pluto in his black chariot.

Spring came and I finally said yes to Allen. We made love all night at a motel in Columbia. Driving out of the motel lot, we both laughed at the marquee of the Holiday Inn: "Hunter Enterprises—Made in Columbia!" Al's fraternity loved a good joke.

Everything was fun, everything was alive and dancing, as if the voluptuous seizure of springtime emanated from us. Al got a job at a big milling company in Kansas City. From a banking family in southern Kansas, and five years my senior, he knew the value of plans; all that was missing from Al's plans senior year was me. I don't know at what point around his graduation

I started getting apprehensive—the voice of my grandmother's Missouri mule-headedness jarred me: "Don't act nuts, Heather. Use good sense. Think of your future." I liked college, especially my art classes; I had received a scholarship to the University of Kansas and a career in the arts is what I assumed I'd pursue after graduation. I loved drawing, was very good at it, and had a natural talent for textile design. Nothing in the ordinary world except art came close to the power and reality of the dream. So I thought college would be a marriage of the practical and the dream realms; art school and I seemed designed for each other. Allen Hunter and I were not—I knew it all along, though I refused to admit it.

We were out at the Lawrence, Kansas, dump in July of 1964. The sky was almost white from the unrelenting afternoon heat. I had no Bob Dylan albums, I hadn't heard of Vietnam, I hadn't heard of Yaqui. Still, something larger than us was on the land, it prickled even when the heat went away at nighttime, and then you felt as if a layer of scratchy, yellow insulation had been lifted from your entire body. The country was about to strip the fibers of sleep from the good old fifties and I, too, felt a foreboding I could not assign a name.

"Come on," Al had said. "Let's go have some fun." Where are we going, I asked. "To the dump to shoot rats."

Rats were among the subjects that greatly interested me as a girl in grade school. I remember doing reports: "The Bee and the World of the Hive," "Snakes: Our Friends," and "Madame Spider." But rats had always intrigued me. I was always drawn to animals who had a strong group existence. I was curious about the habits of rats and downright fascinated by their various human personae, especially the Rat King and the Gypsies, the rat as King of Thieves and the animal familiar of Lord Ganesh, the master of the material realm. The fact that anyone had even written about animal familiars encouraged me. It meant that someone else also knew spirits existed in nonhuman forms.

Al took the rifle from its boot, withdrawing it smartly, quickly. He lifted the stock to his shoulder, fired. A red soup can shrieked backwards.

"Here, try it." He liked to show me how to do things, as if the man's world were penetrable by the oil of how-to. Hold it like this. Look at it like this. Try it like this. Watch me do it. Bang. Crack. Whizz. Pow. How.

When I was ten, my father had forced me to shoot a shotgun. He liked to take me out to target-shoot. I was a natural shot with a pistol and .22 caliber rifles, but I'd never shot a big weapon, and I had hated shotguns ever since during an earlier outing my father had accidentally hit my brother with birdshot. Aiming for some quarry in a field, he hadn't seen my brother and me and several pellets hit my brother's chest.

My father pointed to a downy woodpecker up in a tree, not more than twenty feet away. "Kill it," he ordered. I couldn't. I didn't even lift the shotgun. "If you kill it," my father said, "I won't come into your room tonight."

Without hesitation I raised the gun and fired. The bird blew up right before me. And my father lied, he came anyway, power gone wild. It was the last time I ever believed anything he promised. Instead I hid my power and didn't reveal it in any thing or way he might control.

I played with Allen's gun, but let him do the shooting. I didn't want him to know I was a better shot than he was. I have something to tell you, Al, I said. What, he said, squeezing and popping and cocking his gun. My father used to shoot rats in the spring. He used to wait for them to crawl into the hallway, on the radiator pipes. He sat in the hallway waiting for rats. I stood behind him looking from my room through a crack in the door. He sat there a long time, he was patient, he was Indian somewhere in the back of himself, Cherokee. I watched him, I watched his patience, with his back turned to me, in the dark hall, in his dark shirt, sitting on a box, with the rifle across his legs. I stood there as long as he sat. Maybe he knew I was behind him. He was raping me, Al. I was little, I was hoping I was so stealthy he'd never feel me enter his shadow with a knife in my hand, with the wish in my heart that he would shoot himself through the head, that the rat would shoot him, that the comet in God's eye would find him out and slice through the roof and seize him. I stood peeking out and almost smelled the sizzle of his flesh after God's wounding—

The rat slammed back against the wall, then sank between the wall and the pipe. My father rose, he lifted the corpse. He held up the rat and examined it. It spun a half turn to the right, a quarter turn to the left. And then he looked right at me where I stood watching concealed behind my door, and walked down the stairs with no expression whatsoever, I wouldn't even call it a look, Allen, he just walked down the stairs as if he were sleep-walking.

Allen. He never did hear me! He never saw who I was. And it didn't matter if I didn't see it either, in fullness. We'd crossed back to Missouri and in Columbia he thought I was a virgin because I bled for him, but that wasn't it. I wanted Al to be my magician of the normal, to deflect anything abnormal my father had cursed me with. I wanted a magic shield against the darkness in my past.

When Al graduated with his B.S. in business, my artist's life seemed about to begin. Then my grandparents shocked me. They sent us the money for a nice apartment, and then made a proposal, shortly after graduation, by phone. Why didn't Allen and I take over their shop? They were going to retire soon anyway, and they could think of no better way to help us than to turn over the business to Allen. *And* they'd give us a house *and* a car *and* a membership at their country club—how about that? I could hear them smiling ear to ear, thinking this was just what we'd want.

It was what Al wanted. He was effusive and complimented them on the remarkable job they'd done at building up their business and how honored he was to be put in the same class they were—it really was an honor!

But all I saw, again, just as I'd seen it the day Allen went shooting rats, was that my husband didn't understand something very basic about me, and he wasn't going to. He was the deputy of my mother and grandmother, who had plans for me, too—they wanted me to "use good sense." Al was dumbfounded that I'd turn the offer down. "Take it if you want, Al. I'm staying here. I worked too hard to get away from Hannibal and I'm not going back. You be Grandma's daughter if you want. I can't go back there."

I fully expected Al to go by himself and then try to cajole me into joining him. To my surprise he deferred to me—although nearly simultaneously he was offered an executive position at a big food-processing company. So we stayed in Kansas. The corporate ladder—and not love for me—had the strongest pull for Al. I looked good on his arm. I felt good in bed. What else is life, anyway?

When we had first been lovers, I remember we took walks under the spring nighttime sky. From time to time we'd talk about what it would be like if there were no houses and streetlights, no conveniences of modern life—what if there were nuclear war? I thought nobody would be better at surviving it than Al, who reminded me, I told him, of Robinson Crusoe. He liked the tribute. So did I, and I wanted to believe it.

After my marriage to Al in 1964, I went on drawing and painting what came to me from the dream place. I also loved the classes on art history, especially early art and native art—anything that was driven into creation by a strong sense of religion. Egyptian, Indian, even Greek art; early African and Pacific Island art; and, naturally, art of the native people of North and South America.

I was always repelled by the religion of the Catholics, though one of my mother's hopes was that I'd be a practicing Catholic. The "religion" which attracted me—and who but my father forced me to zero in and focus on it?—was about power, any power which brought and upheld, like St. Michael's sword, the power of light over dark, good over evil, me over my father. I found such "religion" immanent in Nature and with the dead.

For pure focused power, no other place on earth could match the graveyard. As a girl, my playmates more than once got spooked by my relationship with the dead. I loved the way the tombstones were. I could hug them and be enthralled by feeling, whereas friends were just mimicking me, their arms full of cold, mossy stone with inscribed words and numbers. Sometimes, when I touched the artwork on the headstones, I could feel how life had been for the dead. Sometimes I'd just put my hand on the marble slab and I'd know the dead woman. I could see her when she was young and beautiful, when she first got married, when she died, when she had her children, I could see what she had worn when she was the happiest in her life.

The dead seemed perfectly natural to me. It was the living who were inscrutable, but to me Al seemed to be a magician extraordinaire at manipulating this alien sphere. He had been hugely successful in college, now a young chief in his company in Kansas City. He was shrewd with money, could plan our security, was a leader to his male colleagues. I also realized many women were drawn to Al. Even the coin of sex for Al was inscribed with success: make love, make money. It was the same. The kind of power I liked was only partly accessed through normal life. So again, as I had in Hannibal, I lived in two social spheres. For security against the unpredictable forces of my own world of magic, dreams, art, the dead, I was *glad* Al had hold of the corporate wheel.

But on the the other hand, Al's possessiveness and fear of what he couldn't relate to or understand began to seriously divide us emotionally. I couldn't help attracting a variety of people interesting to me: artists, thinkers, political activists, cowgirls, mavericks of many sorts. Although I didn't share these friends with Al, whose contempt for "that kind" was obvious, he provided a foundation for my safely meeting them, since I could always retreat to his world.

As the new school year began, I came down with a serious kidney problem. The doctor at the student health center instructed me to go off contraceptives. Twice he warned me that I would become highly fertile during the next few months—even alternative contraceptives might not ward off an unwanted pregnancy. I did not want to get pregnant; I had become very earnest about pursuing a career as an artist. So I insisted that Al and I abstain from sex.

It was two days after Halloween, and we had not had sex for over two months. Allen came home toting a bottle of expensive champagne and a dozen roses. He came right up to me and kissed me passionately, then grabbed my hand and pulled me toward the bedroom. It was dark in the hallway and I struggled, at first politely, to extricate my hand, but he was stronger and dragged me into the bedroom.

"No, Al, I don't want to get pregnant."

"You won't get pregnant. We've waited long enough. You're my wife, for God's sakes. Help me here."

He wanted me to get my clothes off, but I refused. He pulled them off. I ran into the living room. He followed, threw me down, and held me there till he was finished. We lay on the rug afterward. I had my arm across my eyes, crying. Al lifted me up and carried me into the bedroom, telling me how much he loved and needed me, he couldn't stop wanting me. Afterward, I fell into a dark, dreamless sleep, certain I'd conceived, trapped by this man's passion. Several weeks later I came down with influenza. The young doctor at the health center chuckled. "The flu you've got is a baby. You're pregnant."

I'd never heard of the Day of the Dead, in the fall of 1965. But that's when my son, Bobby, was conceived: November 2. Naturally the first thing I did was to run out of the health center to the nearest phone and scream at Al that he'd better get over here right away, he'd ruined my life and sentenced me to the same dreadful life my mother had, I hated him and all men. I ranted and screamed and slammed the phone in its cradle and ran all the way to our house. When he came into the darkened bedroom, I screamed some more at him and threw the flowers he'd brought on the floor. I carried on and on and then ran out the door, got in the car and drove crying into the night.

The baby brought dreams such as I had not had since the days of the Dark Lord. During my first trimester women of long, deep association with Mother Earth came to me. A woman who could hear the voice of the earth, they announced, would always be directed, no matter how lost she might be within the everyday. They did not teach me per se, yet because these dreaming women were with me, I did feel instructed, charged to be vigilant, although I wasn't exactly sure about what. In these dreams, I would be sitting by myself at a campfire in the desert. Sometimes from out of the shadows one of the women would appear and sit down to talk. Other times I was with an entire circle of them. It always started with one woman who'd come out of the shadows and sit down to talk to me. Then I'd notice there were other women and we'd all be in a circle.

If what they were going to show me about was love, the elder women would arrive in a midnight-blue sky. When the woman came who had to do with my son's love life, there was a full moon in which I'd see faces of both Anglo and Indian girls. I saw even before Bobby's birth the pretty face of the Yaqui girl he was to marry twenty-one years later.

My father's mother was one of the women who often came in dreams. Elizabeth Dark Water told me a woman is very powerful when she is pregnant. She should be very joyous. Because her thoughts are so potent, they form the world ahead for both her children and herself. She told me it was good to pray. She told me my desires were bigger than my own personal, egocentric life, and that I should follow these desires. That made me afraid. I didn't think my desires would be compatible with the tidy order my family wanted my life to be. I did want to run free and play in Nature, but that didn't seem possible if I was also to be the kind of normal woman that my grandmother and mother wished. I didn't know how to take the reality of the here and now and have the potency of the dream place as well.

Even though my husband and family accused me of being lost in dreams, the elder dreaming women asserted another level of reality which I should trust—a level at whose center was the consciousness of women. For many centuries, women had let this center get away from them. It was up to us to return the earth to health and abundance.

One by one I grew familiar with the faces and bearing of the women whose human identities I would later learn. The women told me my son was a powerful warrior spirit and that he honored and understood both me and the feminine nature of the planet itself. He would be an instrument in service to the magic and the ancestors, and in conjunction with his birth, the elder women were returning to me power that had been lost or stolen in my childhood.

The month before Bobby was born, in fact, something was already telling me to wake up, but I couldn't put my finger on it at first. I had wanted a garden, so I dug and planted pumpkins and gourds, squash, cucumber, tomatoes—pregnant fruits and vegetables. Being "with child" I returned to stories I loved from childhood, and that is why I selected the variety of pumpkin which would grow big enough for a child to sit within. I planted peas and beans for Jack to climb to meet the giant. I chose wild-colored witches' gourds to grow up on the fence—and promptly began to dream them dancing in their little striped green-and-white trousers, with their bumpy, plump, and homely bodies. In the dreams I could smell the sweet and fragrant blossoms and feel the velveteen leaves on the vines. It was all like a cartoon until I saw a fierce-looking woman whose long hair resembled the silver mantle of moonlight. As she talked to the fruits and vegetables she also manipulated unseen forces.

She would appear over and over doing that till I realized she wanted to show me how the large and small are the same, how the seed and the tree, the wings of the bee and the stars at night, even men and women, mirror one another. Much of what I learned was the result of simple repetitions such as that, until I got the lesson and suddenly was flooded with insights.

Out in the rows of growing things behind our duplex on Minnesota Street after the baby's birth, I began to observe very odd growth in my gourds. By fall, around the anniversary of Bobby's conception, they were huge, ridiculous shapes, so big and unwieldy they pulled the fence off its moorings. They were like vegetable caricatures of the Macy's Thanksgiving parade balloons. On the other hand, the pumpkins were dainty things no bigger than pin cushions or baseballs. The bees had cross-pollinated them, and when Allen noticed it he took his brother and his friend Larry out back and joked, "This is what I mean, boys. Anything Heather touches, something strange goes down. I never know if the house is even going to be here when I drive home at night. Nothing she does is ever normal."

"Well, Al," Larry said, "look at it this way: Heather may have created a special category of food for the state fair: Foods Judged by Witches."

"Right, at the altered state fair."

The raven-like woman in the dreams came often, attended by the other women. In my dream they were a fire-lit collegium who taught simply by being present. Whereas the domestic, middle-class garden of ordinary life increasingly seemed empty, except for questions I had about it, the dreams were a silent and ever-present contact with a reality where explanations seemed highly primitive. Al began to openly resent my weird friends; they represented "the spook shit," as he called their ideas, and by extension, them. I thought I was doing what grown-up people do: pursuing a career and being a parent. Al's insults about the spook shit seemed to imply that I wasn't a good family member, that what I was good at—bringing the dreaming power into the world—would somehow drive me out of membership in the human family because I was not the "good" wife. But being Al's wife had begun to seem like a life sentence to sex and Al's gratification.

When I was eleven, just before the time when the dream of the Dark Lord began, my mother and brother and I had spent a happy month at my mother's family's home in Pennsylvania. When our vacation was over, I pleaded with her to let me live with my aunt and uncle for a year. No, she'd stated, that's ridiculous, and despite assurances from her sister and brother-in-law that they'd love to have me, we took the train back to Missouri. All the way across Ohio and Indiana, as we headed toward the stop in Quincy, Illinois, where my father would cross the Mississippi to meet us, I visualized my father's death.

No one was at the station to meet us when the train got in. A half hour went by, and then a taxi pulled up and my father got out. He had a murderous look in his eyes. "What happened?" my mother asked, trying to head off trouble, "You look awful."

"Get in," he glowered, and to me he said, taking me by the arm to the other side of the taxi, "You little witch—I know what you're trying to pull!" He stuffed me in the backseat and squeezed in next to me. His car had been stopped at a freight train crossing on his way to meet us. When the train had passed, thinking it was clear to go, he entered the crossing only to find that another train coming the other way was about to bisect his path. He'd braked, slammed the gears into reverse, then stalled. He was sure he was going to be hit. The engineer saw him, and, hauling only some empty boxcars from local sidings, had been able to stop the train in time. But my father had not been able to restart the car, so he and the railway men had pushed it off the grading onto the shoulder of the road.

When we got home to the house in Hannibal, he took me aside. "Don't ever try that again. You may think you're pretty smart, but you're just like me, and I know all the tricks!"

I didn't want to, but I kept falling asleep during a lecture course on the Baroque and Rococo periods. I fought to stay with the class, but I couldn't reverse the direction of my awareness, and the professor's voice grew fainter. There was something ahead of me which started in the subject matter of the lecture, but which also lay beneath it, almost literally, like the floor of a forest.

My art history section was taught by Dr. Foss, a small, dandified man with a penchant for walking sticks and expensive clothes. If a student fell asleep during his lectures, the dullard was sternly walloped with the stick. Dr. Foss was an impassioned, witty lecturer. I had moved to the front of his class to hear him better.

This wasn't the first time I'd fallen asleep in his class, either. Though I wanted to, I could never stay awake during his talks, and yet he'd never hit my shoulder or arm, as he did with others. Instead, he'd stand alongside my seat where I slumbered, and continue talking. I was not one of those who slumped over, so to those around me I appeared to be awake. Dr. Foss would let me sleep awhile, and during these narcoleptic states I'd be drawn into dark, medieval forests where sunlight stayed on the treetops high above and the ground around me was covered with ferns. Dr. Foss was there, dressed as a priest of some sort, his black hair slicked back. He wore a ring with a large stone on it, and beneath the stone was a compartment charged with poisonous crystals. Foss was up to business that didn't show—I could see that from the dreams. He was the head of something perhaps like a conspiracy. At other times, I would see Dr. Foss in similar costume at Stonehenge. Dr. Foss was more than he appeared to be in class.

One afternoon I awoke from such a sleep feeling a steady, barely perceptible tapping on my foot. It was Dr. Foss. I'd slipped off my shoes. The toe of his patent leather European slip-on shoes rested on top of my bare foot, occasionally tapping. "Notice," he was saying, "how the cherubim of religious art have evolved into decorative motifs."

The sleeping bouts happened in every class, lasting from a few minutes up to half an hour. I struggled, from a girlfriend's notes, to catch up with the coursework I'd slept through. I managed B's on my papers, took the final exam and, miraculously, got an A. I was startled when I received an A for the entire course because Dr. Foss was notorious for giving out just one A per class. My girlfriend, who was a real scholar, shook her head in disbelief. "Well, I'd heard Foss was strange. He likes boys better than girls—Heather, you didn't sleep with him to get the A, did you?" she teased, jabbing my arm. "Heather, you got the A! Maybe there was a mistake and you should tell him he meant to give me the A." But I took the A, no questions asked.

A few days before the spring equinox, the year after Bobby was born, I was seated on a bench beneath some trees on campus, my eyes closed, the sun on my face. I felt a familiar tapping on my leg. It was Dr. Foss. He sat down next to me. After a few innocuous greetings and pleasantries, he said, "You know, Heather, we've been watching each other, haven't we? I'm sure you must realize in what way I mean that."

I replied that I didn't know he'd been watching me, although, I told him, I had seen him in dreams. I described a general scene in which he appeared during the era of the Druids. "Sometimes you are at Stonehenge," I said, partly disturbed that I couldn't help telling him this, partly because it was true. "Sometimes I see you at the court of Louis the Sun King. You like to plot things," I said with a nervous laugh. "You have a ring in which you hide poison," I said, immediately regretting having said it.

Dr. Foss had a bland smile on his face. "Heather, I'd like to invite you to a special get-together we're having at the full moon at my house. I think you'd appreciate the people who'll be there."

I looked at him in an embarrassed way. "Oh, thank you, Dr. Foss, but I don't think I can come. It's my birthday. Besides, my husband gets home late in the evening and we go to bed early. I'd better say thanks, but don't count on us being there."

"Ah. The equinox—Persephone's birthday. Persephone will

be adjusting her eyes to the sunlight and her husband will be reluctantly keeping his end of the bargain. Poor Pluto will have to twiddle his thumbs while the dear girl presides over nothing but cornfields. When will we leave our mothers, eh? Tell me about these dreams you have about me."

Reluctantly I described my dreaming. He listened impatiently.

"Have you ever had anyone teach you how to use these dreams to get whatever you want, Heather? Let me ask it this way: have things you wanted made their way to you after you first dreamed them?"

I was amazed that Dr. Foss said this. And yet I was increasingly nervous about talking to him. Had he been someone I trusted I would have appreciated the chance to talk about dreaming, to be seen more fully than I usually was. I cut off our dialogue with an excuse about picking up the baby, and went home.

A few days later a male student I knew slightly approached me with a strange offer. If I would come to Dr. Foss's for the spring equinox, I could have a trip to the Bahamas. I don't remember the name of this young man, but I can see him still—he was very slender, all in black, and he had a sweet, girlish prettiness, and I remember he had narrow shoulders. I thanked him for the offer, but said I was busy that night.

After studio that afternoon, I asked David, a classmate in the art program, what he knew about Dr. Foss. A group of us were sitting at the Rock Chalk Café having a round of beers and sodas. David and I had arrived early, before the others who usually joined us there a few times a week.

David's reply disturbed me greatly. Foss, he said, was infamous in campus folklore as a male witch with a coven of other gay men witches. They lived and practiced black magic, the student legend had it, in a big mansion. "I don't know if it's true," said David. "Maybe Errol does."

Errol Butterfield joined us, bringing with him Sarah, a town girl who modeled for our life-drawing class, and Kira, another art student. "What's that?" Errol asked David.

"Heather wants to know about Foss. Is he a witch?"

"Yup. He is. Probably harmless as long as you don't get into his space. But I've never trusted that charm of his. I stay clear of him. Why, what's going on, Heather?"

I said I was just curious, I had him for an art history course and wanted to know what the dreams I was having about him meant.

Although Errol was a professor in educational psychology, his passion was Eastern philosophy and religion. He was popular with a group of us because he was highly respected among the local avant-garde intelligentsia for both the radical and thoroughgoing nature of his mind. Twice our age, he was an amazing storehouse of occult information. There seemed no subject he had not investigated. He liked our attention, but he also was much more than an academic teacher. Errol really did want to challenge us to think. He had a galling knack for seeing through our façades. And he was also particularly drawn toward me.

Errol introduced all of us at our periodic meetings to all kinds of esoteric teachings. Few of us did more than read a little about Zen, Sufism, the Essenes, or Krishnamurti, astrology, Scientology, science, art, hypnotism, drugs. Errol was the first person who mentioned the word "Yaqui" to me. He gave me Carlos Castaneda's first book but warned me not to take hallucinogenic drugs. "You shouldn't take acid—you already are experiencing what everyone else is trying to accomplish with it. Stay away from it."

There was a strong attraction between Errol and me that went beyond the simply physical. He was born on All Souls' Day, and I saw in him a mystical connection to deeper things. Whenever we talked together and discovered insights about life or ourselves, Errol would say, "That's because we've been through this before." He felt that we'd been students of the magical arts in former lifetimes. I both admired and envied his knowledge of esoteric disciplines and the tools of magical art, numerology, astrology, the I Ching, tarot. I both liked and resented his having an inside track on magic. Like me, Errol was not without some arrogance, and he was full of himself that Friday, his rugged, lined face strong and handsome. He wore his hair swept back over his head, pulled into a short ponytail. His eyes twinkled behind his steel-rimmed glasses.

Errol had brought with him a beautiful deck of tarot cards in full color. It was the Rider-Waite deck, one of the first tarots to be distributed in the United States after the ban on tarot cards was lifted. I myself had seen only the Brotherhood of Light deck, which my friend David in the design program had given me. The Brotherhood of Light tarot, in stark black and white, was nonetheless powerfully mysterious to me, and I was instantly taken with tarot. I used the cards as a formal way to channel what I felt about people or questions, reading the cards, perhaps, as some people read poetry—I looked at the cards; images already present in my mind were drawn forth into the light of speech by the provocation of each card.

Sarah and Kira both asked lots of questions about the cards and the deck, and about tarot in general. I was too arrogant to ask anything—I thought I should know everything about esoterica, and I especially didn't want Errol telling me anything about tarot. I didn't want to appear a fool, but I had never seen anything to date to match the new pack of cards, which were more impressive than the deck I had. I listened intently to pick up information, because I really didn't know much in a formal way about the cards and their traditional significations. Obviously, Errol had something I wanted that the new deck represented. He knew it, and he took advantage accordingly.

Errol cleared away the beers and soda pops and spread out the major arcana faceup on the table. "Okay, ladies. Pick the card you identify with." The other women selected "The Priestess," one of my favorite cards. "The Priestess," Errol said. "She is the void, the woman behind the veil of appearances. What better place than the void, eh, ladies, from which to look into the future? That may be the ultimate feminine mystery."

I nodded my agreement. The Priestess was the best card for a woman who was an oracle and seer, and I took what he said as a confirmation about my growing sense of myself as both those things. Errol looked at me, "Is this the same card you pick, Heather? Or not? Go ahead—which one?" I felt that my girlfriends had preempted my selection, and I wasn't about to be outdone. So I selected a different card, just for fun. I looked at the offering again and picked out card 21, "The World," because I liked the woman who was posed in the center of a garland of green leaves and roses, dancing with only a veil covering her breasts. I liked it that that was what the world was. In many of my dreams that was just how the Indian women appeared, dancing unclothed, free.

"Ah, Heather. How apt you should pick this one."

"Well, tell me all about it, Errol. You seem to know all about women tonight. Who is she?"

"That's the World card"—he moved his eyebrows in a bemused and quizzical way—"a.k.a. The Great Whore of Babylon."

My girlfriends laughed at my selection, and I felt myself flush with annoyance. Errol looked at me a moment, and then we moved on to another subject, which I attempted to look interested in, but I was disturbed by what Errol had told me. He had a way of provoking me so that I wasn't sure whether he was mocking me or showing me the truth. My self-importance stood in the way of asking Errol to explain more. Nevertheless, I thought about this card and his words. Had Errol seen something I couldn't? Could a man see more than I could; or could I see more than he did? I began my own informal studies of her. Ishtar, Astarte, the woman dancing on the card, was both queen of heaven and queen of hell. But of all the goddesses and heroines I encountered, I was most interested in Persephone. First, we shared the same birthday. In addition, her dark magic scared men—and attracted them, too.

But over and above all, it scared and amazed me that the first real glimpse of Persephone I had was in Dr. Foss's art survey when he showed us Bernini's marble statue of the rape of Persephone by Pluto. My reading had turned up an alternative legend of Persephone in which she willingly agreed to serve the dead upon hearing their sorrowful pleas. The tension within me was over the nature of the man with her: was she his consort or his victim? I didn't know yet how to make everything cohere into a usable form against men who kept wanting me. Meanwhile I replaced St. Michael as my primary protector; the Woman Who Dances the World—she who does as she pleases—became my inspiration.

The first semester of my graduate work, I ran into Dr. Foss on the way to the parking lot from classes. He said hello. I told him I had loved his class. He thanked me. "We missed you at our party. I hope you can appreciate what your presence would mean to these people who've been waiting for you to come. They all know who you are, Heather—even if you don't!"

I laughed involuntarily and thanked him for the compliment; I supposed it was a compliment. "Heather, I could easily lose patience with you. A woman of your talents, pretending not to know—it's a real crime against yourself not to be aware and proud of what you are.

"Let me ask you something. If you could be granted any three wishes, what would they be?"

"Oh, gee, I don't know, Dr. Foss."

"Humor me, Heather. What would you wish?"

"Well, I'd like a white Lincoln Continental," I said in a nervous way. "And a white fur coat. And a trip to New York with tickets to Broadway shows. How's that?"

"That's all you want—trifles?"

I didn't know what to say. Dr. Foss answered his own question. "These are such insignificant wishes compared to what real power is all about. Why does it scare you to ask and receive whatever you want? You want fine things; you want a good life for your little boy and husband. What about yourself, Heather? I take it you are a woman who has, perhaps, ambitions about power?

"Do you recall that quaint little saying from the Orient that liberals love to quote? 'Give a man a fish and he'll eat for a day. Show him how to fish and he'll never be hungry.' Come over to my house next week for our meeting. We are a group of fishers, Heather, and what we angle for, if I may say so, is nothing less than everything. Nothing comes of nothing, isn't that right? What do you have to lose, Heather? Why are you denying yourself?"

"Dr. Foss, why are you being so insistent about this? I have a son now. I just can't be away from my family in the evenings. I have responsibilities to them. I have classwork to do. Thank you, but I can't come."

"Heather!" Allen yelled one night. "Guess what, babe? One of my vendors comped us two round-trip tickets to New York, with a week's accommodations and expenses!" It wasn't unusual for Al, as one of his company's top young managers, to be given food and gifts by various vendors, but this was extravagant. We decided to go and stay with my mother's relatives in New Jersey, where my mother's sister could take care of little Bobby. We were both eager for change and adventure, and I picked up Al's excitement.

Just before we left for the vacation, we went down to Hutchinson for the county fair. Allen was standing with his father, talking about the trip. I was holding the baby, rocking him from side to side. Miss Kansas rode by in a big white convertible. "Look, Bobby," I said. "It's Miss Kansas."

"You're prettier than that girl, Heather, and you certainly have a better figure, even after having little Bobby here." My father-in-law chucked his grandson's chin.

"I don't need to be Miss Kansas, Dad. But I'd take that Lincoln she's riding in."

He looked at me and said, "Come on, Allen. We're going to get you and Heather that Lincoln." Mr. Hunter called up the Lincoln dealer, talked to him, and we met him at the dealership, which he opened especially for Allen's father. They'd recently gotten a used, low-mileage white Lincoln Continental convertible from an estate sale. Within an hour I was driving the car.

Because it was late in the day and I was tired, Al took Bobby home to Lawrence in our little sports car. He had to work the next day. I spent the night in Hutchinson and drove the new Lincoln home in the morning. When I got in the house there was a package from my grandmother's shop. It was a beautiful white fox fur coat, "For your trip to New York," the card said. I was breathless—this wasn't just a nice fur coat—this was a *beautiful* coat, lined with silk and of the best white fox fur I'd ever seen. My grandmother was truly a contradiction: she really did want the best for me; on the other hand, I also saw the ploy of rewarding my good sense at having joined the "real world" Al represented to her.

Neither Al nor I had ever been to New York. From start to end, the week, for me, was like living a vision. I felt I was surrounded by conspiratorial winks of the eye from the universe. Small, wonderful things happened that took on the aura of magic: food vendors gave me hot pretzels, bagels and cream cheese, the first I'd ever eaten. We took a ride in a hansom around Central Park and it was as if we'd driven into some Camelot of the future—what may actually have been grimy, gritty old New York to others, I saw as bejeweled, an alabaster and ebony kingdom with entrances and tunnels of lapis lazuli and carved stone daisies.

Outside Rockefeller Center a chauffeured stretch limousine was parked. I'd never seen one, and was so excited I ran to the curb and sat on the fender. "Take my picture, Al!" I yelled, striking a starlet pose. But Al was embarrassed and started to come up to have words with me, when a man in sunglasses and a well-tailored suit offered his hand and helped me down. "Please," he said with a Middle Eastern accent, "I would be honored if you and your husband would join me. Anywhere you like to go, I will show you."

"No thanks," Al said brusquely, tugging me along behind him. "Let's go home. I've had enough of New York and I've had enough of you making me feel like a jerk. Did someone put LSD in your food or what?" For him the city was only a big, hurried, monolithic force. The shows he had enjoyed, but when we crossed the river each night and returned to my aunt's house in New Jersey, Al was relieved.

A few weeks after our return to Lawrence, I dreamed that Al had been killed driving the Lincoln. I said nothing about it because Al didn't put any faith in dreams, and besides, he always drove the sportscar. But when he told me he was taking the Lincoln that morning, I was alarmed and told him the dream.

He puckered his face as if to kiss me, but then, exaggerating the sound of each word, said, "Sss-poo-k shh-ee-it!" He grabbed the keys from my purse and said he was taking the Lincoln from now on. It wasn't my car. He walked imperiously out the driveway and disappeared, leaving me the little red Sunbeam.

An hour after Al left, there was a knock on the door. A Lawrence police officer asked if I was Heather Hunter. I said yes. "Your husband has been in an accident, Mrs. Hunter, but he's okay. He's down at the emergency room being examined now, but like I said, he's just shook up. Unfortunately, the people in the other car weren't so lucky."

The policeman continued his story. The Lincoln had been

passing across an intersection with a green light when from down a hill to Al's left, a black Corvair occupied by four nuns careened broadside into the Lincoln. They'd lost their brakes, and the impact was so intense that the front end of the Corvair had been folded all the way over the passenger compartment, crushing to death all four women.

The accident shook Allen up, and I couldn't stop thinking about it either. I probably shouldn't have told this to Allen, but I was frightened that Dr. Foss was after my blood. I wanted Allen to tell me he'd protect me, or that he'd look into it, at least. Instead he told me I was crazy, that this was what he couldn't stand about me, more spook shit, and what the hell was I doing with these weirdos, didn't I care about him and our baby?

What I recognized was the handiwork of witches. Suddenly it all came back, the wishes I made! Dr. Foss was showing me that what was given could be taken back, and this message was underscored one Friday night when Al and his fraternity brothers took several rows of seats at a Kingston Trio concert. I had worn my beautiful white fur coat and draped it over the back of the seat. We were surrounded on all sides by Al's fraternity. The trio was well received—people jumped to their feet and applauded them. After the final encore we got up to leave. My coat was gone. I looked everywhere around the seat, and then asked people behind and in front of us. "Heather, you didn't wear a coat to the concert. You had that on," Agnes, one of the fraternity dates, said. She was right; I was wearing a shawl. But nevertheless I knew I'd had my beautiful coat on. I searched high and low at home for it, and I never did find it again.

I felt a kind of exposure from Dr. Foss and the witches that I hadn't had since the years when my father would terrorize me. I told Al my fears, but Al wasn't interested in being consoling because to him it was all childish nonsense.

I had a very practical reason for giving in to Al's insistence that I quit my teaching assistantship and take a "real" job. It wasn't money—I was scared that my father was right about me. Maybe I was a witch. Maybe Al was right, too—my friends were just spook shitters. Maybe only witches and kooks could see me accurately. "Takes one to know one," my father loved to tell me. Now I was going to have to figure out how to protect myself all over again. I had to get out of Lawrence, and I wasn't going back to Hannibal.

The opportunity appeared immediately. A job opened up at the Jefferson County Welfare Department north of Lawrence, for a caseworker to work with Indian clients. I applied for it and was hired. Al, Bobby, and I moved out to Oskaloosa. Shortly after our arrival, one of my co-workers was showing me around the region. We drove by a big, handsome mansion, and I mentioned out loud how nice it would be to live in a house like that. Beulah, who was driving, stopped the car and said, "Why don't you go up and ask him if he'd be interested in renting? It belongs to old Neil Curry and he's gotten pretty invalid since his wife passed."

I went up to the door of Neil Curry's house and knocked. An old man who must once have been the spitting image of John Wayne came to the door, leaning on two canes. I excused myself for interrupting his privacy, but my family and I were looking for a nice place to live, and I wondered if he rented rooms.

Neil Curry thought a moment, and said, "Heck, I have so much room here, and I can't even climb upstairs to see the other half of it. When do you want to move in?" With that began a warm friendship between me and Neil, who soon refused even to take money as payment. Instead, in exchange for the master bedroom and the run of the house, I bought groceries and cooked for him. There are few things I can cook, but if it's straightforward and simple—well, all Neil liked to eat was fried liver and vegetables, right up my alley. Neil, who was in his eighties, indulged me in sweet ways, none of which made me happier than when he let me ride his old mare, Lady. Though she was ancient, she brought me the singular happiness of riding through the wooded country along Buck Creek.

After breakfast one morning Neil beckoned me out back to the corral behind his house. His nephew had brought over a beautiful red mare named Princess for Neil to board. The nephew had to give her up, and didn't know what else to do with her while he was waiting for a buyer. To his nephew's consternation, Neil immediately turned her over to me to ride. I was off all that morning, forgetting everything but how the world looks from a horse.

When I returned, Neil took me and the horse into the barn. "Pity," he said cryptically. "Nephew's got to get rid of this beauty. Wish I knew someone who could use Princess. Besides, they'll never get what this lovely's worth. Heather, you know anyone who's got fifteen thousand dollars and needs a horse?"

"I need a horse, Neil, and I love Princess, but we sure haven't got that kind of money."

"You? You'd be interested in this horse?" Neil said with feigned surprise. I smacked his arm for teasing me.

"Give me a hundred and fifty bucks and she's yours," he said bluntly. And he wasn't joking. I practically knocked him over with hugging.

"You know who George Allen is?" my case supervisor asked. I did—his ceremonial dancing was famous throughout the Indian reservations of the region. He lived just outside Oskaloosa. I'd gotten personally involved with some of his grandchildren in a dispute with the local school board concerning the teaching of Native American history.

"Good, then you're the person I'm looking for. I want you to go out to his place and see if he's flipped out or what." Mitch related the background: at the request of George Allen's children, their mother and George's wife, Quashnay, had been hospitalized for cancer. George, who had refused to let her go to the medical center in Kansas City, was away at a powwow when the children came and took their mother with them to the university medical center. When George returned from the powwow, Mitch continued, he'd taken a gun and forcibly removed his wife from the hospital. He'd driven her back with him to Oskaloosa.

"If he's gone over the edge, the sheriff is going to have to get involved. The old man doesn't speak English, so work with the wife. And, Heather, if it looks like trouble, just ease off and come back to the office. No sense in being foolish, right?"

When I drove up to their small house about a mile out of Oskaloosa, I parked next to one of several vintage reservation cars—its windows were rolled down and I assumed this was the working car—an old '58 Chevy Bel Air with several different

shades of paint and rust showing through. I walked up to the
open door and called. A high, sweet child's voice, the kind that
belongs to an old woman, told me to come in. I entered and
turned to the left and went in the front parlor with its bare board
floor. Underneath the front window a doll-like woman was
propped up on pillows in a narrow iron bed. Though I'd never
seen her until that moment, her eyes warmed and she smiled
when I came over and introduced myself. "Yes, sit down. You
have come to see the Chonukuk." She gestured to a painted
high-back chair next to the bed. An old man sat in a rocking chair
by the north window, his face in profile. He didn't seem dangerous, and he didn't seem interested. He just rocked and, from
under his red Cardinals baseball cap, looked out the window at
the apple trees in front of the house.

Quashnay glanced down at some beadwork she was doing,
then looked over at her husband and pointed with her chin.
"That's him." She giggled and shrugged. "He don't look like the
Thunderbird. But he is."

"You are Quashnay," I said.

"I have seen you before. What's your name?"

I told her. "Are you feeling okay?"

Quashnay pursed her lips and shrugged. "You look Indian,"
she said. "What tribe?"

"Cherokee. But just part, on my father's side." I joked that no
one in my family liked to admit it.

"Why don't you register with us? Potawatomi. Georgie will
help you."

Chief George Allen was still looking out the window, his classic, handsome face impassive. He didn't appear to be the least
bit interested in anything except the world beyond the window.

I said my grandmother, who'd died giving birth to my father,
had been a full-blood Cherokee, but that my father had been
raised in an Anglo family.

"You know where we met?" Quashnay abruptly changed the
subject. She looked at me as if I was to answer the question. So,
almost involuntarily, I answered.

"Yes. We've met in dreams."

Quashnay smiled broadly, revealing her few teeth. "I saw you in my garden when I was pregnant a few years ago, over in Lawrence," I said. Quashnay took my big hand in both of hers. She didn't exactly shake my hand so much as weigh it, sensing as she gently shook it. She was checking me out, not because she didn't trust me; she was seeing how I had been. I could feel that in her hands. Our eyes met a moment, then I closed mine and told her this house, the tree outside, the kind of day it was, I knew these things. I remembered Quashnay singing and dancing. I saw both of us together, first when I was younger, then much later, when I was an old woman.

I opened my eyes and Quashnay started to talk to me in her elfin, lilting way, as if picking up a conversation we'd dropped earlier. She chattered about how nice it was to be home with George—how about some coffee?—she had a daughter, about my age, who was born when George was making sausages at a factory in Topeka, back during the forties. Then they took him off to war. She said something in her language to her husband, and he got up and went to the stove at the far end of the room, which doubled as a kitchen and dining area.

He started boiling water for the coffee, his back to us. He was in excellent shape for a man his age, his cowboy shirt tightened around a trim, still well-muscled torso. His long, steely ponytail was pulled through the adjustable loop at the back of his baseball hat. Caps from other ball clubs hung on pegs, some on top of other caps beneath, along the same wall he faced.

"What are you beading?" I asked her.

She looked at me as if just figuring something out. "You know where I seen you. I seen you coming to us in the sky. Do you know what this is?" she asked, holding the beadwork up. It was a medallion of a Maltese cross in black against two shades of red, a starburst of scarlet and sapphire behind it. It reminded me of something—I couldn't quite hold whatever it was long enough to make a complete memory or image. Years later I would remember Quashnay's design when I saw the pascola masks at Yaqui.

George brought over two white glass cups and handed one to each of us, then went back to the window and sat. The coffee was terribly sweet, I was thinking, when Quashnay accidentally dropped a bead on the floor. From the other room a blue pigeon waddled in and pecked it, jumped up on the bed and put it in Quashnay's hand. I giggled, and Quashnay said, "Do you know how dreams come down into this world?"

"I'm not sure I do."

"Nobody can be sure. Watch what those apple trees out front are doing."

I suddenly realized that the trees that were full of ripening apples were also blooming big clusters of white flowers. I got up, exclaiming, "Oh, they're blooming! They're blooming!" I noticed George looking at me with curiosity. His implacable face melted into an entirely transformed, humorous mug. His eyes were shiny and merry, as if he'd pulled a practical joke on me that I was almost on the verge of getting, and now he couldn't help betraying his mirth.

"Oh, just ignore that old fool, Heather," Quashnay said, clicking her tongue. "Aren't the trees beautiful? I love the big storms we get out here in the spring. You like clouds. You come back here when the storms bring them from all over to dance for George. He's the Chonukuk.

"Cloud Dreaming Woman is the grandmother of all people. We are her children. The clouds are Grandmother's dreams. She dreamed all of us. The Chonukuk danced around up there and made all those clouds come to earth and get solid. That's how her dreams show up—you look up and there's a story for everything. You don't know what you are going to find out because every day and night she dreams again and it is never the same even two times out of all those nights and days."

George winked at me, entirely transformed from the stoic Indian of only minutes ago. He nodded several times. George reminded me of an Indian Harpo Marx.

"You know your Indian name, Heather? Heather—that ain't Cherokee." I laughed and told Quashnay I didn't know what it was in Indian.

"Have you ever seen the spring lightning? It's different than other times of year. It comes from high up in the heaven, like white tassels on the corn. High white lightning. Snake lightning. That's you. I saw this in my dreaming. Grandmother pointed you out to me. She told me you are one of my children. In my language I would call you 'Onamwashnatena.' High white lightning. Because you fly through the clouds. You fly through the grandmother's dreaming and see what's on the other side. Then you come back again. Like spring lightning. You know the story of our grandmother?"

I said I was embarrassed that I did not, but I'd love to hear it.

Quashnay straightened a little, and then relaxed back into her pillows. She seemed very tired. "Grandmother loves you because you are the daughter who brings her joy of spring rain. You dance with the Thunder and carry her ideas straight to earth. That is what you have to do. Dance with the Thunderbird and refresh us with rain. You know it is hard for a woman. No," Quashnay smiled, "not just because we have to put up with these old fools." She chuckled weakly. "We are part of Grandmother's dreaming power. We make our little part of her cloud story. But who can remember everything we dream? You must pay close attention to all the details Mother Earth reflects.

"This earth is a shiny glass where the daughters can see Grandmother's wishes, all her ideas and thoughts, all her feelings. It is hard to catch it all.

"You have a big dreaming medicine. Be careful! Whatever you dream, it's going to be brought down to us by Chonukuk. He will give the dreams their life on earth. Be careful what you dream! Lots of the women who dream don't pay attention and get lost. They can even create trouble for Mother Earth.

"Are you married?"

I said I was, and Quashnay looked at me for a moment without saying anything.

"You happy? No, I can see it's wrong." Quashnay laughed like a little imp. "You too much for him, eh? Your medicine, it's not good for him!" she tittered. "Medicine won't work with the wrong one. It's easy to go off with the wrong man and get yourself in trouble!

"This one." She gestured weakly to George Allen. "Good medicine. He makes lot of folks upset—" She interrupted herself with a soft peal of laughter. "Should have seen them at the hospital! Oh, Georgie can be wicked.

"That's medicine, Heather. You have it, you can't never get rid of it. If you got taken in the whirlwind and dropped in the middle of the desert the medicine people would still find you. That's how medicine is.

"That's why you scare your husband."

Her voice trickled out. Quashnay dozed. I hadn't remembered getting up, but I was standing in the front room with George, staring at Quashnay in bed. "Take all of them you want," George Allen said.

I didn't know what he was talking about because I was amazed he could speak English. "Go ahead. Plenty of them," he said without cracking a smile at my bewilderment. "You can call me George," he said as he crossed the room. "Take all of them you want," he said, winking at me.

I wasn't sure what he meant at all. He pointed to my arm. "You like those, huh?"

I hadn't realized it, but my left arm was aimlessly stirring some strange-looking dried potatoes in a big barrel by the door. I immediately pulled it out and laughed. "Oh, no, I mean, what are those, Mr. Allen, potatoes or something?"

"George," he said. "Call me George. Potatoes? Mmm, yup, special potatoes. So you're married?" I nodded. "Maybe your husband will like this kind of potato. Take a handful, fill your pockets. Fill your pocketbook. Fill your car. Make you drive like a tiger!" We both laughed at the thought of my car filled with these funny potatoes.

I was examining two of them closely as he continued across the room and took some rolled things from a drawer. The potatoes actually didn't look like potatoes—although they had bristly little eyes, but they were brown and dirty-looking.

"These are Chonukuk," George said as he unfurled two beautifully beaded dancer's loincloths. "The Thunderbird," he said, his eye twinkling. "That's me. You must of heard of me, huh? They named a wine for me."

We both laughed loudly and Quashnay muttered George's name. She motioned for me to come back. She said to come again, George had liked me. She saw the little potatoes in my hand and looked at me, as if surprised. "You know peyote?" she asked quizzically.

"Is that what these are?" I said, looking immediately at George Allen in the other room who was laughing merrily at his joke.

"Is he always like this?" I asked Quashnay, who had pursed her lips in mock disapproval of her husband's humor, which the old guy was still enjoying.

"Mr. Allen—George, I hear you held the hospital at gunpoint the other night. I've got to tell them something back at the office. Is it true?"

"You tell them it must of been the Thunderbird. Tell them it was Mr. Potato Head. Tell them whatever you want," he said, getting riled. "I'm just a Indian. You're the one with all the college."

"Don't mind him," said Quashnay. "He's not just an Indian. He's crazy." We laughed. Quashnay had my hand again. She was pressing the mandala in it. As she let go of my hand she folded my fingers over the Maltese cross in the center of the design. "You are a good dance partner for the Chonukuk. Look up there now," Quashnay said, gesturing ever so slightly toward the long thin clouds scudding across the sky.

"Our ancestors are coming up from the south in those clouds." She stared out the window and we sat quietly. "You know Yaquis? They were neighbors of George's people. Kickapoo. My people come up here with them dream clouds, too. People with big dreaming. Somebody's looking for you!"

I felt hypnotized by everything that was happening, especially Quashnay's voice. She seemed half out of the world, but every time she said something more it was like a kite dipping down to ground awhile. Then she would drift away.

She opened her eyes a minute, seeing me finger and look closely at the beaded mandala. "Come again soon," she said. "Real soon."

On the way back down Route 1, passing fields of high green corn, I saw shimmering upon the tilled farmlands expanses of thick tall grasses flowing from horizon to horizon in a seamless river, grass that was no longer of this earth in 1968, but that had been here hundreds of years ago, before anyone had ever pushed a spade into the grass and opened up the earth to the air. I could smell that, as I drove away from Quashnay—something unbroken, something newly exposed that was nevertheless familiar, simple, strong as the old fertile plains when the woodland Indians from the East were forced across the Mississippi on their own westward journey to the part of Mother Earth that would be their home.

Something deep and rich was on the land and in it, and in me. A feeling of happiness warmed my solar plexus, as if Quashnay were still with me, and as I drove along there was no "as if"; she was with me as the ancient grass, also shining every now and then through the modern corn. The impression she made on me inhabited me for many days, and I had the illusion—or hope— that it would be permanent, like grace.

Back at the social services office, I quieted things down for George, and no charges were pressed. Several busy weeks went by; then word came to the office that Quashnay had died. I felt sad that I hadn't gotten to return to talk to her.

"Heather." The receptionist was at my office door. "Heather, the Chief is here to see you. Do you want me to—"

George Allen suddenly entered the office and sat down beside my desk. He looked oddly serene. He had a black scarf tied around his left arm, and he just sat there. I said I was sorry to hear that Quashnay had died. He nodded, and as there was nothing to say, I let him sit while I finished my dictation. After an hour he got up and just left.

I contacted one of his children listed in his case file and she explained that he would be mourning for six months and abstaining from talk. About once a week George came in and did the same thing each time—walked right past the receptionist's desk, past the secretarial pool, down the long hall to my office. He'd sit with me while I did my work. He'd never look directly at me, but I could feel his attention on me nonetheless. Bit by bit I got very comfortable being around George Allen.

One weekend, as I frequently did, I went riding my red mare. Al had two favorite suede jackets that he'd worn all through college. Sometimes I borrowed one. It had been chilly that morning as I rode down the dirt roads of Jefferson County out into the hill country, but now it was warm. I took off the jacket and tied it to the saddle and continued my ride. When I got back to the stables, the jacket was gone. I rode back over the roads I'd traveled but I couldn't find the jacket.

A few days into the work week I got in to the office and saw

George sitting by my desk. He looked mournfully at me, and I went over to the chair and put my hand on his shoulder. I felt so bad for him during his time of grief. He put his hand on mine in a rather ardent way. I withdrew my hand, and walked back to the desk, flustered. I pretended to be absorbed in one of the client files on my desk when it hit me—wait a minute! That jacket George has on—that's Al's jacket!

I didn't know if I was supposed to laugh or yell at him, or what, but that was Al's jacket, although it looked like it was meant for George. George was lost in thought, looking at the ceiling—with a little smile on his face. I let him keep the jacket.

My supervisor at work was a Scoutmaster. He'd noticed I got along very well with the old man and wondered if I'd ask George to dance at the Boy Scout jamboree. The period of mourning long since over, I said I'd ask, but no promises.

I drove out to George's farmhouse on a beautiful October day. The air was thick and ripe, full of a harvest of slow flies and little mites, of golden particles of grain or grass, as if the sun had threshed the morning into afternoon. I parked my car. The door was open, but nobody was around. There was something very still about it. I called his name, waited, looked around again out in the yard. Suddenly the apple trees caught my eye. They were loaded with big fruit—and they were also filled with blossoms just as they had been that first day, with Quashnay.

"George?" I poked my head into his front room, walked through the door. I felt a chill pass up my spine, I turned again, but before I knew what was happening I was being grabbed and swept off my feet, all in one motion. When I got my bearings I was lying on a white buffalo robe inside a teepee. George Allen was making love to me with all the power and fierceness of a young man. He *was* a young man! We were making love in the middle of a buffalo skin, a fire burning, in the middle of a teepee in the middle of another century—I remembered the apple blossoms, I knew this had something to do with them . . .

George's lovemaking was full of some kind of spirit fire—he gave me so much pleasure I couldn't resist his caresses even though my heart was accelerating with anxiety at the thought of what this all might mean to my child—and then I remembered I was in another century, another place. Bobby—where was Bobby, which place, which world was he in and how was I ever going to find him again? Then I forgot about those things, because George was so—unpredictable. How did he get so young? How did I get here with him? I tried to ask him, but each time he'd answer by giving me more pleasure. We stayed in that place for weeks, either riding horses or swimming and fishing in streams, or eating the most delicious meat I've ever tasted. We quaffed down draught after draught of a mysterious cider from a big seashell. George sang beautiful songs in the language of his people and I understood them.

Then one day I woke up from the dream place and was lying in the little narrow bed where Quashnay had died. I was under a brightly patterned blanket. My clothes were neatly folded off to the side of the bed, on a crate. There was no one in the room. "George?" I called. "George?" The door was wide open.

I jumped out of bed, practically leaping into my clothes like one of those cartoon characters who jumps into the waiting clothing as if the costume were a taxicab, and I was out the door. I didn't have a watch, but the sun looked like about four o'clock and I drove with alarming speed, alarmed that I had abandoned my child for several weeks, who knew what my husband was thinking or doing, or my boss at work. How had that happened, how could I have so completely lost my head as to be seduced by that old George Allen? What had he done to me—nothing short of ruin my life! Except my body and being were fired with such lingering, sweet pleasure!

I pulled into the lot next to my office and walked briskly into work. And of course the first person I ran into was my supervisor, Mitch. "Well?" he said expectantly. "Well, what?" I asked tentatively.

"Well, how did it go? Everything turn out okay?"

I wasn't sure what he meant, so I just said, "Oh, yes. It was no problem."

"Good. The boys will be thrilled to see the old guy dance. Thanks, Heather." I gathered up my papers, picked up Bobby and went home to my family life. I reheated some macaroni casserole. I was suddenly famished.

*   *   *

Inevitably, George began to come over. Sometimes he'd bring a twelve-pack of Coors, sometimes some donuts. Now and then he'd take me and a girlfriend out to eat. To be honest, he was great company when I was with him without my family. But as soon as I'd get in the door of my house, I'd feel an overwhelming obligation, and then a panicky sense that I must do for the family. I had a duty to give my child an upbringing that was free from the burdens of the spook shit—and I couldn't believe that I was even calling it spook shit. But I was, and I knew George Allen was ruining it, that he was going to somehow destroy my normal family life just as Professor Foss had tried to do before him.

No matter how often George Allen came over, Al could never act on his wish to get rid of the old man. He blamed me for encouraging George, but I told him I had nothing to do with it. "Maybe he likes you, Al. You keep saying you don't want him around the house, but each time you end up being courteous."

For nearly the entire winter we saw George Allen several times a month, and then, with the return of spring, I lost track of him. Early in the summer, I got a message at the welfare office to please come out to Buck Creek and see George Allen.

As soon as I parked my car, I wondered what in the world I was thinking of to be coming out like this to see George. I had secretly missed George. He did upset and scare me; yet he was exciting to be around because he was unpredictable. I had to admit to myself that I thought often of George, he fascinated me, whereas my life with Al never went beyond the bounds of predictability.

George was, like the joker, a man capable of many faces. And I knew that he was showing me something about life, and mine in particular. I felt in an open mood, so as soon as I saw him, I gave him a hug. "Does this mean you'll marry me?" he asked with great melodrama.

"No, George, you old lecher. I'm already married."

"Why you want to waste yourself on Allen? You can have a better Allen." He lowered himself onto one knee by the peyote barrel, and knelt there in the doorway. "I, Chonukuk, promise you, Onamwashnatena, to honor, cherish, and show you a good time." He was hysterical, his right hand over his heart, his head raised moonily to the heavens. He extended his left hand toward me, encouraging me with a jut of his chin and his eyes to take his hand. "It would make a old man very happy."

George began to sing, his face suddenly serious. His voice was a strong baritone, and as he sang he looked off into the distance.

"Tell me what you sang, George," I said when he finished.

" 'I saw you walking in the forest. I want you, if you want me, you better come now. If you don't, see you later, Baby!' "

I was laughing with tears in my eyes. "Oh, George," I said with mock passion. I turned my head aside like the maiden in the silent movies, overcome with feeling, and grasped his hand. He had something in it: three peyote buttons.

We walked out back and down toward Buck Creek, which at that time of year was little more than a trickle. Everything was warm, green and gold, pungent, a myriad of wildflowers still poking through the taller grasses and shrubs. We sat down on the banks of the creek. George told me how to take the peyote. I chewed two of the buttons slowly. They had an indescribably strange taste. Sitting next to George, I felt at ease, detached. After I had chewed the buttons he gave me some grapefruit sections to eat. We continued to sit there quietly, letting the shadows of the big cumulus clouds sink in, dazzled by the shivering, quicksilver green leaves of the oaks. There were thousands of dandelions, some tiger lilies in among the grasses. Suddenly we were in Buck Creek, which had become much wider, green, shimmering gold. We were on a boat made out of paper, but it seemed we were on a leaf. A big bubble came up and George got into it. I got into one. We went down the water and over some falls—it was very joyous. We played in these bubbles and then mine popped and I was back on the leaf. Something big and green as the water moved like the water. As I watched, it turned shiny and the shinier it got the faster it moved. Then it changed direction and showed its huge head. It had golden eyes and a ruby tongue which felt the leaf I was on. It almost touched me. It was a serpent so big I couldn't have put my arms around it. I wanted its tongue to touch me, but when it did, it was all over me and it woke me up and I was lying on the bank.

I felt exhilarated. The hair on my arms and the back of my

neck stood up as if in anticipation of lightning. "Look at my arms," I said, delighted, holding them out for George to see. I told him I had just been with the most incredible serpent and that I wished it had stayed.

"It was like being with my name, George, like almost getting my arms around my name!"

I think George was laughing both at my naïveté and out of pleasure and gladness for me. "Yep," he said. "Onamwashna-tena. God's voice." He laughed harder, as if at some personal joke.

"What? What's so funny?"

"I was thinking where good Catholics end up for naming their children 'God.' You don't hear of too many God Smiths or God MacNamaras. How about you change your name to God's Voice Hunter?"

I laughed with him. I wiped the tears from my eyes with an edge of my shirt and caught George looking at my bare midriff. I clicked my tongue.

"Don't you ever stop? Seriously, George, I thought Onam-washnatena meant 'the spring lightning.'"

"You *are* the great, high white lightning, and when it thunders and lightnings, it is the Creator." He looked at me a moment. "You're young. And you have been too long with the white people who are cut off from God by the arrogance of their thinking. We have never separated ourselves from the Creator in any false ways of thinking. At least not until recent times."

I told him I'd rather be bringing something to the earth and the people, like rain or the cosmic weather report, if that was the Creator's wish. George chuckled and smoothed my arms, very gently, the humor receding to the background and his sweetness all in his hands, kindness in his eyes.

"For me the only real thought comes from the heart. We Indians don't cut our tongues off to spite our face. Our face is the Creator's face. It is a very great thing to be the voice of the Creator. And the Great Serpent has truly shown himself to you, he has come for just you today!" I felt so drawn, suddenly, to George. I wanted him to change the subject because I didn't know how else to shift the mood away from the confusions of romance.

He made his eyes wide. "Maybe," he said somberly, "he's gonna take you with him. Make you Missus Serpent." He couldn't control his mirth and burst out laughing. "Listen, Miss Heather. I'm gonna save you some trouble, so listen good. You're gonna marry an old chief. One of these days, you'll go off to his reservation and live in a dream house. Beautiful house of dirt. You'll plant your potatoes right in them dirt walls."

I smacked his arm for teasing me. "Here's the timesaving part: I am one heckuva old man—and I got a wood house! You should come marry me!" I was too young to think George was much more than an eccentric, lascivious old man. I thought everything he told me—which was a substantial teaching in and of itself— was an elaborate seduction designed to get me into his bed. Which, of course, it was.

"You laugh now, but like I told you, save time. I got a house with wood floors, an icebox, a stove, a barrel of all the peyote you want—and a great big bed. My big snake will visit you every night!"

I groaned with laughter. He laughed, too, and shook his head. "I see you are going to have to learn the hard way. Onamwash-natena.

"Ah, the beautiful white lightning, high up in the dome of heaven . . ." With practically every word or phrase he added a flowery gesture. "The beautiful high white lightning, which is so welcome, especially in spring, the time of love. That's what Onamwashnatena means, Heather Helen Hunter, you who are too young to realize what you are turning away."

George Allen was right. I didn't know what I was turning away. In order to get on with my marriage to Allen, I gave up the better Allen, as George would have said. In a way, they were competitors for me, and by far, George saw me better than Al did—but then George saw me better than I did. I wasn't ready to find what was waiting for me. I was scared that I was getting only the dark part of what I wanted, and that power was playing a dark trick on me and I'd become like my father. I didn't really *see* George. He enjoyed himself at all times, and therefore he wasted no time worrying. But the depth of his brand of magic wasn't apparent to me until I sent him, along with Al Hunter,

Errol, the witches, and my father away to some Lethe that flowed in the opposite direction from the river I hoped I was following. I couldn't see what George could—that the river doesn't have a past or future, a start or finish, it has no perspective—it moves, like the Great Serpent, and as it moves it finds.

One time before I left Kansas, George took a girlfriend and me to a little restaurant for some supper. He ordered Kickapoo Joy Juice all around. Kickapoo Joy Juice was a chocolate carbonated soda I'd loved as a little girl. The soda came, three bottles, with the red-and-yellow label of the Indian and mule kicking. I hadn't seen it in years. And the reason I hadn't seen it in years, as I found out days later when we went back to order the same sodas at the same restaurant, was that there was no more Kickapoo Joy Juice and there hadn't been for years since the company folded. "Coke or orange," the waitress said to us. "All we got." She'd never heard of Kickapoo Joy Juice.

That was what I turned away because of my fear: joy. George's unbridled joy at creating entertainment for us. That was how he lived and loved: he just expressed his happiness by manipulating seemingly minor details, tangential, sideways things like soda and apple blossoms. But he understood how to part the waters and make way for the even more substantial magic to come into the world, and he did it not for his own gain but to show me. Many years have gone by, and George Allen is no longer the splendid man he was in this life. But he is still a magician. Kickapoo Joy Juice. Not much for a girl from the Show-Me State, stubborn mule. Yet how true to the spirit of life he was! Not just the trick of getting that soda for me. The far greater magic of love: to keep showing me what I was, kicking me to wake me up.

3 ⌘ MEN AND DEATH

When I woke up one morning I could see blue sky through the roof. During the night a tremor had shaken Central City. I was lucky to escape with just my roof slashed along the ridgepole. I even liked the way it looked—a forty-foot-long blue lightning slice! My neighbor the druggist wasn't as lucky—from my back door I could see his porch hanging precariously off its footing. That freak tremor was the beginning of a brief but intense period of inner seismic shakings that changed my course.

It had been months since I'd seen my husband, Al. I'd fled both Allens, although, there in the Rockies of Colorado I felt I was continuing George's spirit journey. It was George who had called the Rockies the "Mountains of the Silver Ghosts." He'd always wanted to go there to be among his ancestors. But, it was I, in 1972, who went, alone with Bobby. I was glad to be rid of men in my life—that was the brave image I preferred. After separating from Al Hunter, I threw myself into a career. The little house in Central City had been a retreat Al and I owned where we went on weekends. After the break with Al, I went there permanently and Al stayed in Denver where his job was. At first I took a part-time job in an antique store. Though we had the house free and clear, Bobby and I had living expenses to meet, and the meager wage I drew at the shop, supplemented by money earned from occasional tarot readings, was inadequate. I ended up taking a managerial job back down the mountain in Denver as a designer for a large Denver retailer. I spent long days driving from the natural haven of the Rockies to the bustle of retail merchandising. All day I oversaw how the general merchandising departments of five metropolitan stores would look to shoppers—where to put the camera department, the ladies' apparel, the cigarettes and tobacco.

The "career" was an opportunity to prove to myself that I could make it in a man's world, without a man, to draw a big salary and care for my son, and to be a productive member of middle-class society. I conveniently ignored how much like Hannibal, how much like Al's corporate world, my brave new retail world was. I hurled myself into color schemes, traffic flow, square feet, square inches, into chrome and glass and plastic, into plated jewelry, clocks, shoes, tennis rackets and fishing poles, into cartons and dollies and swinging doors and fitting rooms with sliding gray curtains, polyester, nylon, nostrums, aisle seven and aisle eighteen, into scuff-resistant wax and cash registers, into buying, selling, and displaying, into eight-, ten-, twelve-, fourteen-hour days, bringing home a new little Fiat sportster (better than the one Al had had in Kansas), bringing home toys and records, new clothes with designer labels . . .

I'd get back home to the mountains well after sunset many nights. Bobby would still be at the babysitter's or at friends' and I'd hastily go up to the Knights of Pythias cemetery, the prettiest of Central City's three graveyards, and pray to the forces in the earth and stars. Sometimes I'd go in the snow in my high heels, just to break the spell of merchandising. I began dreading going down to Denver, but once there I'd lose myself in work, drag myself to the parking lot, drive fast back up into the Rockies, pray, get Bobby, fall asleep half-dead . . .

And when I slowed down out of weariness I looked around and realized my son spent nearly all his time with Kelley, the young woman who babysat for him after school, and her easygoing, unemployed, dropped-out friends. I saw the emptiness of the house, the disappearance of the high white lightning of magic, the loneliness, the confusion, and, finally, the crack in the roof, and I woke up as if from a fever. What was I trying to prove? Here was the lightning, not just on the wall but in the peak of the house itself!

Even though there weren't men in my life, at first a welcome relief, I still was accustomed to thinking, in those days, that the key to magic was a man. I was working long hours to conquer the man's world of money, and I was succeeding. Yet in playing a man's game, I had no magic left in my life. Worse, I had no guide, no teacher, no George Allen. George had long maintained I had an unusual effect on men. I never could figure out how to take George, and in the end I left him, too, because it was easier than trying to understand.

One day in 1969, before my family and I moved to Denver, George and I had been walking down a street in Lawrence together, headed toward a restaurant. "Watch," George had said, pointing at a middle-aged man across the street. The man, raptly observing our every move, had not noticed where he was walking. Suddenly he collided with a telephone pole and fell on the sidewalk. It was all we both could do to keep from howling.

George kept telling me I had power over men. This seemed to me one of his tricks—to butter me up and make me think he saw all these things about me, and then manipulate the environment to make me believe him. Back outside after dinner, he gestured ahead to a good-looking young man. George was right: he was giving me the once-over. Just as we were approaching each other, a shop door swung open; the man was unable to avoid it. George roared and I couldn't help laughing, too.

But I never could figure out whether it was George or I who was making men fall over.

After the roof cracked from the shaking of the earth, I gave notice at work. It was at the end of a gray March afternoon in 1974 when I realized I hadn't seen Bobby for several hours. I called for him, but there was no answer. I looked out the window. Snow was falling, but I saw no Bobby in the yard, no footprints. Bobby had talked to me about seeing "dwarves" down by the old Sleepy Hollow Mine. I'd seen those ghosts of miners myself. I began to get fearful that something had happened to my child. I was going to call the sheriff, but before I did I thought I'd take one more look through the house. Maybe he'd fallen asleep in some nook I hadn't looked in.

I checked everywhere in his room, my room, the bathroom. Our living room was a large, open-beamed space with a big fireplace off to one side, and he wasn't asleep behind any of the chairs or pillows along the walls. I was really worried. Then I looked up; Bobby was sitting upright on one of the cross beams, grinning, waving at me. He'd waited up there without moving to play his trick on me!

"How did you get up there?" I asked, amazed that he'd been so silent, so patient. "How long have you been up there?"

"I don't know. Awhile. You were funny, Mom."

"How did you learn to get up there?"

"Alex showed me how to."

"Alex? When was he here?"

"No, Mom, Alex and Roger showed me how to climb up rocks. You know, with ropes and pitons."

I was doubly amazed. Pitons? After questioning him when he sauntered down with remarkable athleticism, I learned that Bobby had been cutting kindergarten to go uptown where Alex and Roger, two sweet, pony-tailed young men, had been teaching him how to scale rocks.

After that Bobby would often play hide-and-seek with me. It was *his* game, and I never knew I was playing it. He had become so adept at making himself invisible by blending right in with trees outside, or inside by standing so still I never noticed him, that as often as he annoyed or scared me by disappearing, he also impressed me. He wouldn't play his disappearing act every day but would wait until I'd forgotten the last time, so that I'd be worried about him in earnest. His ultimate achievement during this phase was the morning when I got up to fix his breakfast and couldn't find him. I looked high and low, in the rafters, out in the yard, under, upon, behind. I opened closets and cabinets. I heard a muffled "Over here," and went into the kitchen. I heard laughter by the sink, opened the cabinet, and there, like a blond snake, my son had wrapped himself around the plumbing.

*   *   *

Bobby was asleep early one evening when his father, Al, waved in the window after rapping on the door several times. I came from Bobby's room to see who it was.

"Al! Hi, babe." I was glad to see him, and went to hug him. Suddenly he burst into tears.

"Al, what's wrong?" I walked him over to the kitchen table and we sat. I held his hand. He wiped his eyes with the wrist of his other hand. "My uncle just died of Huntington's chorea. It's hereditary. My mother has it, too. So it's in the family, and you know me, I've never been sick, always been healthy, I don't know why but it's just frightened me all of a sudden. I can't stop thinking about *my* nerves disintegrating—I thought maybe you, maybe you could *prevent* me from getting it, too."

He covered his eyes with his arm and sniffled, then looked straight at me. "I know I was very disrespectful to you. But would you? I know if you want to, you can keep me from getting sick."

"Allen," I said, reaching for his cheek. "That's not how the magic works. If I could protect you from sickness, of course I would, of course I would. But I can't. It's not within my power."

I moved next to him and he put his head on my shoulder and I held him. In a while he brightened. "So you want to get back together anyway? I'll take better care of you . . ."

"No," I said quietly, "we have to go forward with our lives. I'm scared, too, Al, but I know this is the right thing and for Bobby, too. I have to follow my path. We had some great times together, babe, but you need to set them behind you, too."

"Well, I thought I'd give it a try," he said, and sighed. We got up and walked together to Bobby's room. I put my arm around Allen. He'd gotten thinner. He put his arm around me and we stood there together looking at our child sleeping.

I have a dream in which I am in a torrential river in a dense storm. The man I am with—I cannot make out who he is—is desperately trying to keep the boat we're on from being over-powered by the tempest. Maybe we are at sea. We might as well be, because there is no shoreline to the river that I can see. I am scared that I will be thrown overboard, that he won't be able to hold on. I hang on to the bow of the boat with all my strength at the same time I pray we will make it through. Suddenly I know some deep secret for our survival. Just then the man yells through the torrent, "Heather! I'm not the storm, I'm the boatman, I'm the boatman! You are the—Did you hear me? You are the—!"

But I can't make out what he says. I just can't hear the last word that told me who I am.

Allen sent me the divorce papers to sign. I took a deep breath and put my name to them, licked and sealed the envelope, walked to the mailbox and posted it. And then felt simultaneously exhilarated and unhappy. So here was "freedom," I thought on my way back to the house. Spring was coming, the darkness was lifting the way you can feel, after illness, your spirit lift itself when you first step into the clean, fresh air. Nature's new season buoyed me, but, looking around Central City, this little island of dropouts, I remembered my mother's and grandmother's first impression when they'd visited at Christmastime: "You live in a ghost town!" There were only about a thousand people in all Gilpin County. My mother especially was most disapproving of my decision to end my marriage to Allen, whom she and Grandma still viewed as the ideal mate for any girl with sense. I couldn't explain it to them; I myself sometimes wondered if I was a fool.

But all in all I did know something important to me was missing with Al. I didn't love him, not as I had loved the Dark Lord of the dreams who still seemed as real and bright as the gleaming air of the Rockies. Wasn't there a man *and* freedom in my future? I was beginning to doubt the two were compatible.

My birthday, always a powerful time for me, came and went. The battle for spring wasn't won easily. Into April 1974 the weather tramped back and forth from clear to stormy. A sense of meaninglessness had begun to cling to me like spider webs. I went out riding one overcast, chilly morning, after Bobby was off to school. I rode Princess hard up onto the ridges outside Central City. Ever since childhood physical or emotional exertions had upset me. The presence of my father at meals could often send me scurrying to the bathroom to throw up. The motion of riding a horse brought on the old effortless response—I leaned over Princess, and my undigested breakfast came up.

I didn't know what I was looking for, but over the next few weeks and into early May I took to riding my horse after Bobby went to school, leaning over, throwing up, riding on all morning around Central City. Before long a bunch of ravens began to follow me as if I were their raven-mama. I'd lean over and vomit; the ravens would dive down and breakfast on my breakfast. In my long black cape, the ravens following along behind, as soon as I hit a certain place on the ridge they'd swoop down—from the town below it must have looked like a witch was riding, attended by Hecate's mob of birds.

As the ravens followed me they'd chatter in what sounded like an Indian dialect. Sometimes I heard George Allen's voice, heard his little love song. I began to go to the Knights of Pythias cemetery. I'd get off and let Princess graze on the tender grass while I'd sit on the graves. The crooked, soft limestone head-stones belonging to three miners from the Sleepy Hollow Mine cave-in were my favorites. All three had died on All Souls' Day, November 2, 1894.

Sometimes I did feel like a witch spurned by the world. On other occasions I saw it was the world that had bewitched itself. Either way, I wanted *my* life to begin anew. Every morning and night, as spring haltingly came, I'd go to the cemetery and make my prayers for guidance. Day after day went by—no sign. I began going there in the evenings, too. My prayers were very serious and solemn. I felt very much at risk, having given up my design job in Denver, along with my marriage to Al. I knew I had to trust I would not be abandoned by the life forces, but I was afraid.

That year the comet Kohoutek was low in the southwest; I liked its Indian-sounding name, even though it was named for someone from Eastern Europe. All I knew for sure was there was medicine in it, and like Mark Twain with Halley's, I wanted to ride my comet out of the mountains, away from the ghosts living and dead. Kohoutek became the visible tail of my own dream fire.

*   *   *

Another lightning strike from out of the blue came by mail: my childhood friend Della Wells was enrolled in a master's degree program at the University of Arizona in Tucson. She'd love to see me anytime. I leaped at the offer, arranged for Kelley to look after Bobby, took some of my savings and flew to Tucson.

I was instantly in love with the desert. Between her classes we drove miles in all directions, exploring the mountains that surround the city, the water canyons where streams were flowing down from the higher elevations, the amazing blanket of wildflowers and cactuses blooming. There was a pungency in the air, and birdsong, and the light had a particular weight to it, as if it were actually a physical creature.

At the end of my last day with her, Del drove us south to Madera Canyon to watch the sun set behind Baboquivari on the Papago reservation, fifty miles west. The warm air made me feel both secure and alive, awakened, ready. The mountains were like black lace agate, the sky gold and yellow and pink. We were standing on a high foothill. I had asked Del to stop so I could look one more time at the western sky. To my right, down a little slope, a sandy wash seemed inviting. I went down into it. In the fading twilight there was a shiny spot, as if light were striking a little hand mirror. But there was no light for a mirror to reflect, and I went to see what it was. It came from a small, lavender rock half buried in the wash. I took it in my hand; it was icy cold. I felt other rocks in the sand. They were all quite warm, as was the sand itself. I took the piece of sandstone and carried it back to Colorado with me in my suitcase. Unpacking, I noticed the rock seemed to have gotten smaller, but I couldn't tell for sure. I put it in a cedarwood box I had on my altar in the bedroom.

When I went back to do my prayers at sunset in the Knights of Pythias cemetery, I was both bemused and puzzled by the raucous noise of the ravens. Had they always been this loud? They reminded me of a cowboy bar when everyone gets to talking and laughing together. They seemed the most boisterous at the end of my prayers to the Ancient Mother. And then the smart-alecks would holler and caw. The big raven who liked to sit by the gate kept looking at me. He didn't budge as I walked up to him. I began to talk with him because I was sure he was George Allen, shape-shifted into a raven. "Well, Chief," I said, as the bird rocked back and forth from one foot to the other, tipping its head as it looked at me, "I still don't know if it was you or me making men fall over, and I wonder what I'm doing alone up here in these mountains with you." The bird sat there; we looked unblinking at one another, and then the raven made a strange, almost burping sound, waited for my reaction, which was to laugh, and then casually flew off until it was lost in the twilight.

I went home and fixed supper for Bobby, curled up with him by the fire and fell asleep while he watched television. I dreamed that I was a raven and George Allen and I were flying low over a desert. It was warm and the light drenched us like water. We seemed to absorb it instead of reflect it. There were long-armed cactuses and shrubs and small trees. We flew through a dry riverbed and perched on phone lines that went into a town ahead of us. I could see the headstones of the graves in the town cemetery. I awoke thinking of Tombstone, Arizona.

The next evening, sitting on one of the graves near the top of the upward slope of the cemetery, a shiny object caught my eye from near an aspen tree in the grove next to the cemetery. I got up and walked through the gate and into the trees. The light came from a small piece of rock that was sitting on top of a large, smoothed outcropping of granite. It was as if it had been placed there. It reminded me of the rock I'd found with Della in the dry wash, and I hefted it. It was very hot, and I wondered if perhaps it was uranium or some radioactive ore. But I didn't know. I wrapped it up in my scarf and took it home. When I opened the cedar box on the altar to compare the two stones, not only were they the same color and texture; they fit together like puzzle pieces. Two weeks later I had tidied up all my affairs in Central City and left the Rockies for Arizona.

I arrived in Tombstone in June 1974, just before the annual monsoon season. I put my house and property in Central City on the market. I didn't know what I'd find in Arizona, so I decided I'd better part with my beautiful mare, Princess. The horse to ride had become increasingly invisible, like destiny itself. With my sizable tax refund I wasn't worried about having to work at a job for a while yet. I rented a shop and living quarters in the historic Nellie Cashman Hotel. Bobby slept in the Wyatt Earp Room, I in the Doc Holliday Room. A few weeks after I settled in, a real estate agent approached me to see if I'd be interested in becoming part of the hoped-for revival of Tombstone. Would I like Opra, the realtor, to make inquiries of the out-of-state owner about negotiating? I told her I had property back in Colorado, in the Rockies, in Central City. Opra knew a little about Central City and she thought maybe a deal could be suggested that involved a trade of properties, some cash. What did I think, how about letting her at least find out?

Opra proceeded. She'd come from out of nowhere and that seemed a medicine sign. But then my interest in realty deals faded. I began to feel exhausted all the time. At first I believed it was the heat which was debilitating me. But after a battery of tests, the local GP diagnosed lymph cancer. He wanted me to go to Tucson for more tests and a second opinion. He didn't mince words about the prognosis: "bad news."

I ran from the doctor's down the boardwalk. Johnny Ringo's Casino and the Crystal Palace seemed like stage sets and the sound of my feet drumming on the boards made me think, briefly, that all this was, as my mother used to say, only a dream.

But it wasn't a dream. That was the problem. There wasn't anyplace to escape the failure that apparently resided deep within the cells of my body. I may have felt at home with the dead, but I certainly did not want to join them, and my heart was devastated. Had everything, everything in my life, raised me up, like St. Michael's sword, only to be struck down like this? I ran to a small drainage wash that fed into the San Pedro River and sat by a chaparral bush. I cried. I watched the sunset through eyes that felt very old, weary from disappointment. I felt at the edge of giving up. It would be easy. Finally have it over with and not have to run anywhere, choose anything, take care of anyone, even myself.

In the dark I walked over to my rooms at the Nellie. Bobby had gone off to a friend's. I climbed the wall in back of the hotel and then climbed into the big branches of a chinaberry tree. I sat there, watching the full moon turn to water when I cried, then rise and disc the sky. Then I stopped feeling sorry for myself and just prayed. It was simple; I wanted to live, and I'd do anything

I was directed to. My son needed me. My destiny still seemed to need me, too. I just needed a sign.

Someone knocked loudly at my door a few hours later. I was so exhausted and emotionally spent that I felt separated from my body, as if my spirit were forced to drag my flesh and bones to the door.

"Yes," I said, "who is it?"

"Heather? Are you Heather?" A man was practically yelling my name.

"Yes," I said again. "I'm sick today."

"I know," the voice said. "I need to talk to you. It can't wait."

I opened the door. Standing there was a tall, gaunt man with a shaved head, piercing aquamarine eyes and a trim, severe goatee. He looked like something burnt raw and then cooled down, toughened, aged, crazed. I took in what I was seeing, aware that I was not precisely in the world. I had no idea whether this man at the door was real or not. At first, as I sort of gawked at him, he seemed to be wearing a turquoise shirt made from a material I'd never seen before, some sort of woven, shiny tinsel, perhaps a new high-tech synthetic metal. The man's bare head had a thin, filmy glow of white around it.

"Can I come in?"

I excused my appearance, and motioned him in. "Do you want a reading? I'm pretty tired and don't know how effective I'll be. Maybe another day would be better, if you want to make an appointment." I reached for my pen and my datebook. "Let me see when would be a good—"

"Stop," he said. "I do want a reading with you, I know you're an extraordinary reader. In fact, I've been told you are the best reader in the western hemisphere."

"Who told you that?" I asked. It was true that I had given many tarot consultations, but never in any ostentatious way, certainly not so that I'd have been well-known.

"Who are you, anyway?"

Having gotten my attention, he became refocused. I now saw he was wearing an immaculate white T-shirt and clean but well-worn Levi's. He was considerably older than I—in his forties, at least, and in excellent physical condition. He had long, slender hands, one of which was holding a green-and-white Coleman thermos. "Could I ask who you are? I've been so sick. I've been praying, and I need to know what you are." I didn't want to be alone with some weirdo, but, on the other hand, I'd prayed hard for a sign, for a miracle, and this man, with his unearthly look, had the aspect of the miraculous to me.

"We've been looking all over for you for the last three months. The space beings told us about you. I know you're sick. I've brought the medicine you need," he said, gesturing to the Coleman jug. "So don't worry. What I need to know is if you're as good as they say you are. I want a reading now, and then I'll help you get better."

"Look, just tell me who you are. Then I'll give a reading."

"I'm Bennett D'Angelo. Ben." He was suddenly awkward being social. But everything seemed weird to me. I was facing my death, and if the space beings had told him I was in need of healing, that was fine with me. I'd take any cure. So I gave Bennett D'Angelo a tarot reading.

It was an unusual reading, to say the least. Bennett D'Angelo's cards were all major arcana—long odds that of twelve cards all would be picture cards and not the suit cards of the minor arcana. To this day that is all I can remember, I was so ill—except whatever I told him convinced Ben the Angel that I was what he was looking for.

I took Bennett D'Angelo's cure the way someone hungry takes the offer of food, and that was the first thing he inquired about. "What *have* you been eating? Wait—let me tell *you* what you've been eating: garbage. Your body's been turned into a garbage can." If I'd been stronger, I'd have at least giggled at his sternness. He was right. I'd been eating junk food for many months.

"Ben, I hate to cook, what can I tell you?"

"For starters that you swear to God you will never, ever eat a hamburger or French fries again!" I laughed, and then I swore to God I never would. Ben the Angel wasn't going to be a barrel of laughs, but I didn't need a stand-up comedian. I needed a miracle. And Ben was strange enough to be just that.

I had to agree to three rules. I would stay celibate for the course of the treatment. This I easily accepted—I was still sick and tired of men. Second, I would eat only food Ben the Angel personally prepared or sanctioned. Finally, I would do as he instructed in matters regarding my health.

"Fine," I said. "Just so you don't ask me to shave my head or start worshiping goats."

Ben didn't even smile. He looked at me severely and said, "You don't appreciate the seriousness of what you've been do- ing to your body. We're talking about doing what it takes to depossess you of death. You're dying. I can reverse that. It's in your interest to trust me. All or nothing. All or nothing."

Ben was right. Even though I was no longer eager to have the benefits of "normal" American social existence, my life seemed to be ending one way or another and "normal" medicine already had admitted it could do little for my cancer. So, I thought, I'm already dead to that life.

The treatments began immediately with a vile cupful of a black slimy herbal mix. As I gagged it down by the sip, I consoled myself—what could be more magical than slime that looked like it was brewed by medieval alchemists? I drank a cupful morning and night, and within an hour of drinking it, my body would be in sharp, painful spasms that I endured by curling up in a ball and hugging my knees. Hours seemed to pass before I would feel any relief, but within four or five hours of drinking the black slime, I'd start feeling more energetic—until the next cup.

Ben the Angel went to northern Arizona for a week, to get his followers. The next time I saw him, he noticed immediately that the black slime was having the effect he'd desired. He came into my room at the Nellie Cashman, trailing a group of five men, of various degrees of size, height, and hair length. He introduced them and I thought of the dwarves in Snow White. One of the men set up a portable massage table. Ben was all business—he ordered me up on the table, and they all surrounded me, two on each side, one at the head and Ben at the feet. They adminis- tered a very deep massage the first morning, followed by a cup of a new potion, much better tasting than the black slime. It was a fairly innocuous blend made from green vegetables, and after a week of the kiss of death on my tastebuds, the new, fresh juice tasted like ambrosia.

That afternoon, however, Ben and his group put me back on

the massage table and this time he began poking me with the sharp end of a deer antler, starting at my feet. Ben told me to stop him if the massage got too painful. He also warned me it would hurt, but to breathe through and not try to suppress giving voice to the pain.

He said that he had cured many people of cancer. As far as he was concerned, cancer was a form of possession that was not from within me, but from what I had allowed into myself because of others and their hypnotic belief system. Being an open and trusting person, Ben said as he worked on my neck, I had taken in their demon, so to speak, lock, stock, and barrel.

The entire hour of this treatment seemed to me a constant repetition of beginning the same sharp pain, time after time, starting with the arch and instep of my foot. It was easy not to censor myself—I quickly went from "Ow!" to yelling and screaming at the top of my lungs. The people at my sides had to hold me down when I began to thrash about, but still I would not say stop. I wanted to get better. Perhaps Ben was right—I did feel that something that didn't belong with me was leaving the very muscles and tissues of my body.

I was so exhausted from the antler treatment that I slept from late afternoon until the next day. When I awoke the next morning I was surprised to find Ben still there. I heard him in the other room. He came into my bedroom and said that I would be feeling better and to expect a real burst of energy soon. He told me that during the next period of weeks he would be staying close by during the period of transition back to full health. I had been such a self-abusing person in the past he was going to watch me like a hawk.

By September, after two months of massage and herbal treatments, I began to eat fresh, finely grated vegetables specially prepared for me. I still lusted for hamburgers, but there was no denying the miraculous effect his work had on me—by October I lost my desire for cooked food altogether. During the treatment, at Ben's instruction, I had been sleeping on a thinly padded plank elevated twelve inches off the ground, oriented north and south, barely wide enough for my body to rest on. Even if I'd had any sexual energy, no man would have enjoyed spending the night with me in such a bizarre arrangement. No one except Ben, who began to sleep on the floor in my bedroom.

The treatment had progressed well, Ben declared. Now I was at a critical point—nothing less was at stake than the future of my health. As my strength and stamina returned to normal I noticed Ben the Angel's interest in me was more than patient-physician. After a few nights on the floor, one night I heard Ben rustling in his sleeping bag. Suddenly his head was next to mine. "Ben," I said, "is this about to be the romantic part of the treatment?" He didn't laugh. He confessed he'd been without a woman for nine years, and he apologized for being human, but he was no longer able to hide his powerful attraction to me. He knew, he said, that I was a remarkable woman, and he hoped we could create something together that night that would lead to a harmonization of the planet and ourselves, too. He hoped I'd understand how special this decision of his was to break his sexual fast with me. I was less than consoling, however. "No. No. Ben, get out, get out right now. Thank you for saving my life. I can never repay you for that. But this isn't the best way to thank you. So out, out you go!" He left. After that I seldom saw him.

I stood in my doorway in Tombstone, Arizona, in 1974, the year I was twenty-nine, thinking of all the men who had tried to kiss me, just as this man was trying to do. The man, whom I will call Jack because he told me his card was the Jack of Diamonds, was a newspaper editor, new to town. Not long after his arrival, following my recovery in the fall of 1974, I had called him angrily about a mention of me in the local weekly newspaper, which he had just taken over. Each issue featured a clever column of gossip called "Random Shots," and within each edition of "Random Shots" was a subheading that wittily played off Tombstone's undying love affair with its image as the "Town Too Tough to Die." This subsection was titled "Madame Ladeau's" after the madam who ran the local bordello during the 1880s.

"Rumor has it," the writer had said, parodying the style of Madame Ladeau's era, "a member of the fair sex, new to our town, is staying at the Nellie Cashman. Word has it she has recently been engaged while yet married to a second and has come to Tombstone Territory to run off with a third!"

I called the newspaper and demanded to talk to whoever had

written such drivel about me. The man answering the phone said, "You're speaking to him."

In a polite but annoyed way I castigated him for printing the gossip about me. "Ah. So you're Heather. I hear you're an incredible card reader."

"Didn't you hear what I said?" I asked him. "Thanks to you, I'm going to have trouble buying the hotel and trouble with half the crazy people in Cochise County. I want you to print a retraction."

"How about if I come over and talk to you about it? I'll see what I can do."

And that was how the evening in the fall of 1974 I stood in the doorway in the arms of a man who was so grateful for the tarot reading he tried to kiss me. I averted my face and put my cheek against him. Just then a purple shooting star fell as if it had been poured, poured as if in the blackness all along had been an amethyst bridal fall that was part of the river invisibly carrying me along.

I shrieked, and Jack joked, "If that excites you, may I ask you to dinner tomorrow and—who knows?"

I stepped back into the room and laughed. "I just saw the most amazing shooting star, Jack."

"So let's celebrate! Let's go down to Bisbee tomorrow night for dinner. Bring your crayons and we'll color the sky!"

"Not after you painted me as some kind of madam. Jack, please fix it. I mean it. I don't want any more loonies in my life. Fix it and I'll go with you Friday night."

"Deal." He took my hand and held it. "Thanks for the reading. You're welcome for the star."

The Jack of Diamonds drove us from Tombstone to Bisbee at sunset. The desert lay pink and orange to the west where the sun got in my eyes. The sun came flat through the window. Jack had been talking nonstop since picking me up, first about the town gossip in which, as editor of the newspaper, he was well versed. Listening to him talk about the town, about newspapers and writing, I was impressed with his ability to articulate ordinary life into a larger framework of meaning.

The sun was like the tip of a wooden match, igniting the

western range for a moment, exploding the sky around it. I couldn't look at it for long. Then the light on Jack's face started slowly to drain. Knowledge, Jack asserted, matters only when people have some ability to understand what to do with it. This was true whether you were an auto mechanic or a cook, a writer or a teacher of esoteric knowledge. The Jack of Diamonds wanted to be the latter, though he made a living in other ways.

For many years the Jack of Diamonds had followed the teachings of G. I. Gurdjieff, the Russian mystic. Actually, as Jack pointed out, Gurdjieff was far from mystical. "He had a great clarity when it came to what human beings were like. He wandered the Middle East looking for answers to questions he couldn't stop asking. His travels and studies convinced him that human beings see things from almost total sleep."

We arrived in Bisbee and pulled around the little grassy square above which the Copper Queen Hotel sat. In the dining room we sat by the windows looking out at tourists and strollers, people lounging in the grassy park, couples holding hands, some panhandlers.

"The genius of Gurdjieff was in how he woke up his followers: he made them *do* what they had been doing all along. He didn't *tell* them to wake up; he showed them just how mechanical they already were. He was a master of confronting people not with what they *should be*, but with what they were.

"Real teaching always has to first undo all the harm our upbringing has done." Jack looked straight at me. I liked his self-assurance. "How can we find out who we really are in a culture like ours that's hell-bent on "socializing" us? This culture prides itself on the quality of its education, but we're so thoroughly educated that we've taken upon ourselves all the rote teachings that make it next to impossible to learn what's really outside our minds. What's really within us? How can you tell? By the time we leave home and grow up and replicate the old ways—even if you want to be different from your parents, how easy it is really, to be your own person?—by that time we have to worry about making a living to support ourselves, our wife, our kids. So when is there energy left over to stop the world, and if we could stop the world, where could we go to get off and try something completely different?"

Jack smiled. "Too bad we can't live four or five hundred years before we die. Life itself would allow us to come to our senses and know what's real, what's true, and what, above all, we're here to do. But we only live a little while, so we need help. We haven't got any tradition left, so we have to follow paths where we can find them."

"What about former lifetimes?" Wouldn't it be possible, I wondered, to remember what we'd learned once before on earth in previous existences?

"Maybe. I don't know. The voice of this world is the one that's loud in our ears. And something seems to happen at death that puts a barrier between past knowledge and present life circumstances. Have you ever thought about what happens to those who tell the truth about what's really real? Socrates, Christ, Gandhi, Martin Luther King. You pay a big price for speaking out too directly. That's one of the amazing things about Gurdjieff. He was smart. His way of teaching he dubbed 'the Fourth Way,' the way of the sly man. He had a school for many years; he even got to write his own bible, his own teaching."

I told the Jack of Diamonds about how my family and upbringing had affected me. I told him about my first husband, how I knew I had to live in this world, but that I had to listen to and honor what came to me from the dream place. Without a form to accommodate both, I said, it had been painfully hard.

"Of course it's painful! That's how you start to wake up, to find out what's really going on. You have to break the grip of fear that has been used to manipulate you."

Jack's intelligence appealed to me, although, honestly, I couldn't keep up with his ability to theorize. He launched into a long description of Gurdjieff's method of Work on Oneself. What I remember now is his excitement and passion for the ideas—the rest seemed very abstract. After awhile my eyes began to unfocus.

"I'm boring you—or else illustrating what I mean about how hard it is to wake up to what's real."

I laughed. "No. It's boring, Jack. It's too abstract for me."

He laughed good-naturedly. "Touché. I do have a tendency to like the sound of my own words." He asked me to tell him how I'd happened to come to Tombstone. I told him my story.

"So how did *you* end up here, Jack?"

"I needed some time to make a transition," Jack replied, confidently, "to create time for whatever is going to happen next to become fruitful. I also like writing and editing. I'm good at it. This opportunity at the newspaper came, I took it. But I think before long I'll need to start my own teaching group to give my ideas a chance to grow into practical outcomes.

"Besides"—he grinned—"I can't wake up without the reminder presented by friction from others. Tombstone is impossibly asleep. Hell, those folks are still living at the end of the last century. But it ain't just Tombstone, babe. It's not just the conspiracy of the billionaires and the military who run the circus of America. It's the earth itself. The planet itself wants us to be asleep. Earth needs to eat too. It is a dog-eat-dog world, they've got that right. If we eat, why shouldn't earth need to eat, too? She wants us to be happy so we are lulled into the life of sheep who become her source of nourishment."

I was disturbed by what he was saying about the earth. "You make waking up should like a dulling task, as if anyone on that path would be in for a life sentence on a rock pile. I don't think Mother Nature intended for us to be asleep. She wants us to have the best, as any mother would. She wants us to be joyous and happy."

"Let me ask you this," Jack argued. "Are you always joyous and happy?"

"No!" I laughed. "Certainly not. I'm only objecting to the systemization of it. It sounds heavy and ponderous, controlling. Only a man would devise such a system! You're right that there's more to the universe than the Mother alone. And real magic is always outside the laws of society and thought. But if our task is to wake up, like you just said, we have to wake up to earth first, to what we are as Mother's children. That's the Native American teaching. There's more to Mother than you realize. You can't skip over her like that and hurry along to God. I'll tell you something, Jack, something I learned from Bennett D'Angelo—"

"Oh, my God," Jack interrupted. "Not *that* guy. Old Lightning Bones actually *touched* you and you're not seeing visions of space critters?"

"As a matter of fact Old Lightning Bones saved my life, strange as that may seem. Strange as he may seem to you. Whatever you care to say about him, he had the magic to heal me. But he's also just an ordinary man. Of course, I don't know how strange you might be. Or ordinary!"

I laughed, but Jack only smiled. He twirled the water in a glass, listening.

"When I almost died and old Angel Ben healed me, he told me his treatments were depossessions. What possessed me was belief in death. When Ben treated me, he did just what Gurdjieff was doing: he forced me to experience for myself just how mechanical I'd become. All the fear and all the part of me that wanted to do the right thing for my parents, my town, my school, my career—it had all become manifested deep in my body.

"When he and his merry crew worked on me with their deer horns and their slime-ade, it hurt. I screamed so loud neighbors sent their kids over to see if I was okay. But what happened was nothing. Once Ben the Angel took away death, which was only my mechanical belief, I was the same, absolutely the same as I've always been.

"That's the Mother's teaching, Jack: there is no riddle, because there is no death, even though we have to express our immortality in forms that are subject to change."

Jack's face had lost that square-jawed edge. He was quiet, smiling at his glass of water, which he twirled gently, creating a little whirlpool in his glass. "You've taken peyote, haven't you," he said suddenly. "I can see you have from your eyes. I can also see you are someone—" He paused, looking for the right word. "Someone gifted. There are people on the earth who don't have to work for knowledge, who are already much more awake than even the bulk of those who would like to awaken. It's as if there are holy centaurs, you might say—" We both laughed at the idea.

"No, really, creatures born half human and half something different."

"Listen, I've always loved horses, but could I be a mermaid instead?"

He laughed. "Absolutely! Be an angel. I'm eating dinner with an angel. Dear angel, are you an angel of heaven, or hell?" He raised his eyebrows up and down suggestively. We laughed, and he stopped talking.

Jack wanted to see me again; we became lovers after a while— I was drawn to him by sex and wonderful conversation. Still, I felt a distance. It was like one of those irresistible algebra problems from high school, in which, for the sake of creating a problem to work on, you imagined traveling half the distance between two points one day, then halfway again the next, and so on, but the more you traveled, still there was always a distance, however small, that remained to be crossed. I did not feel that passion that causes a person to break out of the algebra and leap beyond the rules into the unknown. And the reason wasn't hard to understand: I'd never really loved a man in my life. I seemed to pick them for what they could do for me in exchange for what I could do for them. Well, that was why you had sex—it was what women could do for the men they were with. That was how I'd been raised, and except for the man of my dream, nothing in experience seemed to give me reason to modify that perception.

When I walked into my house one day early the next spring, Ben D'Angelo was sitting restlessly at the table, waiting for me. He'd been looking at a spot on the ceiling. "Come to Tucson with me this weekend. It's Yaqui Easter and I have some friends up there I'd like to introduce you to. It would be a great favor."

For some time I'd known that Ben was telling various people he and I were lovers. I'd found this out from a girlfriend in Tucson, where Ben was spending more time. She'd met Ben at a gathering at which someone had asked where his girlfriend was and Ben had replied she was down in Tombstone. Well, the other person asked, I thought you were going to arrange a card reading. That was how my friend realized I was the mysterious girlfriend none of Ben D'Angelo's friends had ever met.

"I'd love to see the ceremonies, Ben, but I'm afraid I'm tied up this weekend," I lied. "Bobby's going to be home soon and we're going to a Cub Scout dinner." Bobby was not in the least interested in Scouting, but I had to get Ben out of my house.

"You really have to see the Yaqui Deer Dancer," he said. "You have to come to it with me," he said. "You have to see the deer dance."

I nudged Ben out the door gently. I hadn't told him I had decided to go to California with the Jack of Diamonds. Jack had decided to make the break with Tombstone—he'd been offered a job heading the public relations department at a California junior college. And he himself had an offer to make me: come with him, and, no strings attached, he'd support me and my son. All I had to do was manifest through prayer and meditation enough material security for him to finally be able to teach Gurd-jieff's method of Work. He'd give me a week to think it over, but he was leaving, whatever my answer.

Of the men I'd met, he was the most persistent, insistent about winning me, but what I really wanted from him was a steady man who could raise my son. Bobby was lonely for a man in his life. I was not the kind of devoted mother he deserved, and I was worried about him. So I struck a deal with Jack. I liked him. I was intrigued by his intelligence and knowledge, he was fun, he was moving to a good job which promised the financial security I currently lacked, and the "deal" had the appeal of being like a business arrangement—I'd do my part, he'd do his. That seemed like a welcome relief from the ambiguity of my previous relations with men. I wanted clarity. I'd had enough of the intermittent current of my own ups and downs. I wanted balance.

In March of 1975, we drove away from the ghosts of Tomb-stone, and the ghosts of the Rockies and the Plains behind them and the past that was behind that, and started out for California at nightfall in the midst of a freak snowstorm. Lightning forked around; in the dull glint of the instrument panel, Jack looked strange to me, impenetrable. I felt as if I were cargo for surviving winter, never mind that the laws of spring should have been coming into sway, that maybe once again I had been trapped by power, by male power, even after forswearing it. Bobby lay dozing in the back, turned toward the window. I patted his leg and pulled my heavy coat over him. Jack said nothing as we drove onto the interstate. The headlights shone into the distance. There, where they frayed at the edge of the darkness, I watched attentively, thinking there was no way to know which way into the night we were headed. It could have been down into the earth as easily as west to the promise of California. I decided I was just reflecting my fear. I leaned my head onto Jack's shoulder and slept.

In the fall of 1978 two important things happened: I admitted to myself I wasn't happy in my marriage to the Jack of Diamonds; and I met Aunt Charmaine.

Several months earlier, in January 1978, after Jack's business ventures brought us to Las Vegas, I contracted pneumonia, a disease I've been susceptible to since childhood. As I began to recover, in the ensuing days and weeks I had a recurring lucid dream about a long, narrow building with a mural of stars, moon, and planets painted on its side. Inside it was actually like a cave occupied by a man and woman. The man wore the cloak of Merlin; the woman was an Indian who needed no cloak—her aura of carnelian and fire was strung like a magnificent fetish necklace with birds and bears. The man and woman were preparing oils and incense. They gave me the candle called High John the Conqueror and explained how to anoint it with oil extracted from the plant of the same name. The woman in the dream was fierce as a crow. Nothing escaped her. As the dream ended she handed me a Seal of Solomon.

I told the dream to Doug, one of our business partners, who with his pregnant wife, Marilyn, shared a big two-story house with us. I drew him a picture as I narrated the dream. Seeing the wall with the stars on it, he said, "I've seen that place. I think it's over on East Charleston."

My husband and his close associates were very protective of me, partly because my health had become delicate, but also because my psychic powers had been of immeasurable value to our business. Jack and Doug had formed a highly profitable commodities business investing in metals on the futures market. A shrewd observer not only of human behavior but of the human obsession with money, Jack had parlayed a small inheritance in the 1960s into a tidy nest egg in the early seventies when the government opened up the gold and silver markets to investors. Jack bought up Mexican fifty-peso pieces, which were pure gold, weighing in at slightly over an ounce apiece. When the price of gold went up sharply, coins originally valued at fifty dollars apiece were suddenly worth four times that, over two hundred dollars a coin. Quietly, all during the seventies, even after the value of gold dropped, Jack had continued to watch the commodities and metals futures markets, and without much fanfare had been living off his income from employment while buying and selling futures with the investment account he'd been accumulating.

After a year and a half of administration and finance, Jack left the college where he worked and formed a small group of Gurdjieff students. The Gurdjieff method, at least the way Jack presented it, always seemed to me artificially structured, rigid, abstract. It was Jack himself, who modeled himself after Gurdjieff the man, who had the impact and effect on me and the other group members. We all wanted to awaken to the reality of what life is; for me, the Work meant trying to manifest absolute prayer in everything I did, day in and day out. That was an enormously difficult project, but one which I felt grateful to be a part of, despite the effort required.

Jack's emphasis was on shocks, big and little, to our egos. He could be confrontational at the evening meetings in which each of the group members would review with the others the times in the day when he or she woke up to the real Self, as opposed to remaining asleep in self with a little "s." We'd discuss—sometimes to death, it struck me—what went wrong and where, replaying incidents and examples so next time we'd be more aware. We'd listen to Jack present important concepts, like the "mask," and for a period of time we'd all concentrate on seeing our various masks, then removing them, then deliberately putting the masks back on, acting on purpose the self with the little "s."

Sometimes, if Jack felt we were getting too staid and comfortable, we'd pull up roots and just transplant the group to New Mexico, Nevada, or California, and in each new place we'd arbitrarily start businesses just to see if we could do anything without attachment to liking it or disliking it with our mere egos.

The events that led up to my marriage in 1977 also led to the ultimate failure of the "deal" Jack and I had kept to—or, I believed, I had kept. Before settling in Las Vegas, we spent the summer of 1977 in Tucson where the group lived comfortably in a large house with a pool on the northwest side of Tucson near the Catalina Mountains.

After two years together, Jack had fallen in love with me, but I had yet to feel the same rush of happiness he felt in my presence. It was true that Jack was the first man, aside from George Allen, who had really seen me as I felt I was. And he was so good at saying the right words, which were, after all the intellectual content was removed, that he'd take care of Bobby and provide for me. Jack often told me he believed I was the reason the universe had manifested the material security which allowed him to leave his salaried job and form a spiritual teaching group. He'd realized his dream of having his own spiritual Work group where real Work could be practiced; in tandem came increased riches for him. I believed, that summer of 1977, because Jack had his dream and was living it, I was now free to awaken within that dream. I thought my awareness of being awake would release me straightway to just conjure up whatever was next for me. I thought what I wanted was as easy as ending our agreement and leaving. In my heart it was even simpler: unless something amazing happened, I wasn't going to feel more for Jack than I already felt.

One Friday in July I told Jack that though I loved him and was grateful to him for all he had done, it was time for me to try something else; this did not seem to be all I wanted. Jack's face drained color, and his lips compressed slightly. Then he seemed to think of something, and the color returned to his face.

"Where will you go if you leave your family?" Jack asked me coolly. I replied that I could stay temporarily with a girlfriend out in the mountains on the other side of Tucson.

"And Bobby. Is he going to sleep on some floor with you? How will you make a living—buy some hotel to start an antique shop?"

His irony hurt me, and confirmed my suspicion that it really was time to make a break.

"Here's what I think, Heather," Jack said in a slightly paternalistic way, which he tried to remove when he realized I'd heard it in his voice. "You are by nature kind and generous with others. Your openness is such a gift to us all! But it's also what you aren't able to protect without help, and I've done that. Haven't I protected you?" I agreed that he had been a wonderful provider and protector.

"All right. Whatever your love is for me, I'm not going to try to measure it against mine. I know you. I know you very well, and you are making a big mistake thinking of going. You do love me, I know it, and it's your naïveté and immaturity which you're refusing to look at that makes you think there's something better for you than our life together."

Jack always could out-argue me. But my feelings didn't change: I wanted my freedom, like I'd always wanted it, even when I'd gotten sidetracked or stayed somewhere too long. I went to our room and packed my things in a suitcase and went to look for Bobby. I called my friend in the mountains; she would leave as soon as we hung up and come get me. I busied myself for half an hour, hoping to avoid a scene, then went with my bag to the kitchen. I couldn't find Bobby, however, and by the time I'd looked through the house, Doug had seen my bag and asked what I was doing. I told him it was time for me to leave the group and Jack.

"Jack says you have to stay here, Heather. He says I'm not to let you leave, for your own safety, if you try to. So please don't make it hard for both of us. I'll take your bag back to the room."

I grabbed the grip before Doug could and headed for the door. Outside, down by the driveway, my friend was stopped, talking to Marilyn. Abruptly, my friend turned her car around and drove off. I ran down the driveway waving after her, but she was gone. Doug had already gone back into the house with my bag, and Marilyn and Ed, another group member, asked me to come inside. I felt as if I were some crazy woman in a Hitchcock movie. But I wasn't crazy! They sat me down inside and Doug said, "Since it's come to this, Heather, Jack wants you to know he is protecting Bobby in his custody. For your own safety and protection, you have to stay here. I'm sorry."

"Sorry!" I screamed at him. "Where is my Bobby, Doug? How dare you take him from me! How dare you!"

"I'm sorry, Heather. Jack loves you very much. Very much. You're under a lot of emotional turmoil that's all part of the

Work of seeing who you are. Jack's been like a father to Bobby, and you know he loves him. What Jack says is it's time for you to face the truth about yourself. If you will, right now, today, you'll know what to do and this crisis will be resolved. Meantime, you can't go out of the house."

I was so incensed, so frightened, so shaky, I just got up and went into my bedroom and locked the door behind me. I had to get out of there. I went into the bathroom and slid out the window near the toilet and started walking around the house and down the driveway. It never occurred to me that anyone would be watching for just such an escape. From behind me I suddenly heard footsteps crunching, turned, and saw Ed. I started to run and he tackled me. By then Doug also was standing over me and the two of them carried me into the house, took all my clothes away, and nailed the bathroom window shut.

A day later Marilyn came into the room like an old dear friend instead of a betrayer. She sat down beside me. "This isn't like you, Heather. Think of Bobby."

"What's that bastard done with Bobby?"

"They're at a motel with some other kids. Look, I'll level with you. Jack wants to marry you. What's wrong with being with a man who's crazy about you? Just say yes and he'll bring Bobby over, we'll fly up to Vegas and get back to normal."

A few weeks later we had moved to Vegas, I'd been married ten days, and Bobby knew nothing of the kidnapping—to him he'd had a weekend of pizza and movies with Jack and some kids. Jack himself was authoritative, composed, dignified— either the guy was a consummate actor or else I was not dealing with my past history and he had been, out of deepest love, protecting me from my own vulnerability.

I couldn't make sense of it. What I saw as the basic fact was this: at any time, at his whim, he could take my son from me. It was all so knotted up with my own childhood, when I'd been terrified of being kidnapped.

I'd been living with Aunt Charlotte. Perhaps I was three years old. It was Halloween and some neighborhood boys had come to the door to trick-or-treat. I had no concept of Halloween, so what I saw was two people in black, with black masks and black caps and cigarettes in their mouths. One said in a gruff voice,

"Trick-or-treat," and Aunt Charlotte had said lightly, "Oh, dear, I don't have any treats left," so the two people in black had rushed by her, snatched me up and had headed for the door. I screamed for my aunt, and the next thing I knew she was calming me down. She made the two masked people take off their masks and show their pale faces, and I could see they were embarrassed. But the incident was further exacerbated by my father, who showed up one day after that to take me to another aunt's house. I loved Aunt Charlotte and I wanted to stay there. My father's impatience quickly turned nasty, and I ran upstairs to get away from him. I didn't like him, and I told him so. But he caught me on the stairs and tugged me off the ground. I clutched desperately to the banister—I still recall the feeling of my father prying my fingers loose from the rail, carrying me over his shoulder, saying "Bye" to Aunt Charlotte, who stood covering her mouth, tears in her eyes, waving to me as I bounced down the walk over my father's shoulder, reaching toward her with both hands.

Against this background, in the fall of 1978 I went to meet the man and woman in the dream I'd had during sickness. I told Jack, who did his business from an office in our ordinary, Las Vegas tract home, that I was going to the university library to pick up some books on astrology. Jack always encouraged my pursuit of esoterica. Having received a perfunctory "okay" plus the admonition to go easy and not stay out too long or overexert myself, I drove down East Charleston looking for the building that had the mural Doug remembered seeing.

It didn't take long to spot it—a narrow building, next to Ray's City of Cars. The building was unmarked, except for the mural of starry skies encrusted with astrological symbols and a Star of David. I parked and went inside.

The man behind the counter had a very high forehead and piercing blue eyes. He said hello, and walked over to a table where some statues were displayed. "Hello," I said. "What is the name of this place?"

"The Bell, Book, and Candle," he said. "I'm Julian." He extended his hand, and I introduced myself.

In front of the door, near the counter, was a table with several large Mexican terracotta santos, or statues of saints. I picked up one of the unglazed, unpainted statues. "Can you tell me who this is? I've seen this one before in dreams, only he was wearing a green cloak, holding a coin with a Roman head on it."

"That's San Cipriano," the man said. "He's the patron saint of healers. That's why you saw the green cloak. Would you like to have him?"

I nodded. "I'd love to, thank you!"

"My pleasure." We chatted about San Cipriano and Saint Jude, who looked somewhat alike, and I mentioned in passing that my mother had had Saint Jude in our house when I was a girl.

"Jude is the patron of actors and the stage. When I danced, many years ago, he was my patron, too. Whereas, San Cipriano isn't about protection so much as Saint Jude. He's not so European, so cultured, yet he's definitely connected with a higher expression. Healers look *to* him rather than seek his protective wing. They invoke him, as magicians."

At the end of his description of the two saints I thanked him. "Well, Heather," Julian said, "I'm happy to have cleared up the mystery for you." He motioned with his head toward the back of the store. "There's someone back there who can tell you more."

I walked past shelves full of apothecary bottles, candles, incense, and oils. It got darker. "Come here, sweetheart," a woman said. She was seated at a small round table. A floor lamp near the table shone on her steel-gray long hair, which was tied up on top of her head. "Sit down." She motioned to me. "Let me see your hand." I sat down at the table and let her have my hand. She was elderly, though I couldn't tell clearly how old at that time, with black, shining eyes and high cheekbones, a tight mouth that she frequently pursed. Her hands were cool and slender. She smiled almost as soon as she gazed into my hand. "We are the same," she said. "We have the same medicine, and we come from the same place." Then I remembered the woman in my dreams who had been like a raven in my Kansas garden.

It was the first of countless meetings with Charmaine, who proceeded to tell me I was the daughter she'd lost in other lifetimes. "It's good to see you again," she said with deep feeling. "Time gets to be so short." She said there was much she had to tell me.

And indeed there was much she had to tell me, especially about the relationship of people to the planet earth, and, following from that, the nature and role of women on earth. Until her death, Aunt Charmaine, which was how I addressed her, told me many things about myself and my fate, things which were hard, at that time, and even to this day, for me to understand.

Aunt Charmaine was a witch. She said the word with bluntness, and added a word of warning: "Whatever you do, don't take a man's words to heart, don't let a man teach you, because no matter how well-meaning, he'll teach you so as to convince you of *his* ways, and his ways can't help being tainted by the patriarchy."

Given Aunt Charmaine's relationship with the men in her life, I often found myself wondering about the discrepancy between what she told me about women and what she herself had done.

Charmaine was both English and Indian, like me. She had been born on the reservation in Broken Bow, Oklahoma, the child of a Cherokee prostitute and an Anglo car salesman. A sickly child with an alcoholic mother, she was rescued by a white aunt and taken off the reservation, was nurtured and grew to love dancing—the true religion, she told me. As a young woman in Texas, she had fallen for a marine sergeant and had borne a child of his out of wedlock. For the rest of her life, this son of hers caused her heartache and trouble, for once grown, the son became a cheat and gambler, stealing from Charmaine to cover gambling debts.

During the Second World War, Charmaine and her young son lived in New York City, where Charmaine danced in a burlesque review. It was in New York that Charmaine met Julian, who was a classical dancer uptown. They both had the same agent and met in his office one morning. Aunt Charmaine gave him a donut—he'd had no breakfast—and they struck up a conversation in which Julian learned where Charmaine was dancing.

Julian would perform, then take a cab downtown to the club where Aunt Charmaine was booked as one of the headline acts: "Charmaine, the Champagne Blonde!" Charmaine and Julian fell in love and got married. Then Julian was in a car accident and his sense of balance was permanently impaired. Without his old equilibrium, he was forced to end his career. The couple moved to Texas, where they bought a large house in Houston and began making theatrical costumes, a business they continued even in Las Vegas, though by then profits from what was a good business were increasingly turned over to the profligate son to whom Charmaine and Julian could never say no.

In Houston Charmaine and a close friend from England founded the Houston Theosophical Society. Charmaine already was following the ways of the religion of the Druids, Wicca—the "religion of Nature," as she sometimes called it, resonated with both her Cherokee and English blood. Charmaine never actually studied Wicca; she was just naturally attuned to its ceremonial expressions and learned them as she grew up. But she was a very eager learner of other systems of thought which appealed to her strong philosophic mind. As she loved the dance of the body, she also loved the complex steps the mind could make to its own intricate music. Charmaine studied particularly the teachings of Marie LaVeau and Madame Blavatsky. She found in them, and in numerous other writings from diverse systems of thought and organized religion, expressions of God's presence in all things. In such studies Charmaine was simply extending her own witch's nature.

The religion of the Druids—Wicca (the word was once pronounced "witcha")—was a remnant of the original Mother-oriented life that predated all recorded civilizations. Wicca was a ceremony-based religion, Charmaine said, because life is a dance and dance is the truest religion. The best thing we women could do was dance wild and free to celebrate our flesh and thank our Mother. It is a greater privilege to be born here a woman, since this is a feminine planet, Charmaine said. However, because men had tried to rule this feminine planet, things had gotten very out of balance, very bloody and constantly in conflict, which seemed to lead nowhere except to the self-aggrandizement of a few over the many.

"The competitive nature of men has gotten way out of hand," Charmaine said, "and it's we women who have allowed it by letting ourselves also become unbalanced. We have one more go-round to make things right.

"You gifted young women—it'll be your duty to the ancestors and those who come after to make things right. The time of balancing is at hand. You know, honey, don't you? This place is only an experiment. Mother will live forever. But Mother will shake us off like a dog shakes off fleas if we don't get it right soon. These beings who live on Mother will not be allowed anymore to violate her. The big 'if' is with the gals your age. Can you make it right before it's too late?''

Charmaine and I had many discussions about men and women. All of them were bounded by intersecting links in an immense circle of one great thought: that the central fact of life is that we live on a feminine planet and our life is the planet's life in miniature; likewise, she herself is a microcosm of the much greater life of the solar system and the stars. We have our roots in the stars, Charmaine said, but our problems here and now are so pressing that longing for starlight is best understood as a desire for perspective. The first order of business is to reinstate the power and proper place of Woman. Because Earth herself is feminine, all human beings partake of an essential femininity, men as well as women. The patriarchal conspiracy, Charmaine believed, had succeeded in brainwashing women into letting men organize and rule civilization over the past several thousand years.

Nevertheless, in both men and women dreams continued even as history clicked forward with its seemingly endless clock of wars, deals, organizations, and institutions, its education that sought to control the possibilities for members of civilization so that the clock and its system might perpetuate itself—which, Charmaine noted with bitterness, it certainly had done.

The hope for mankind, in Charmaine's view, had dwindled rapidly as the inner, dream realm, which even in our time carried the ancient sources of life and rejuvenation, had been devalued and preempted by analytical theoreticians and academics.

"Real life is a dream," Charmaine often said. We talked about dreaming power, which she also had. One afternoon when we were talking about the nature of dreams, I asked her if she could tell me who I am. All my life I have been certain that my dreaming was a talent, but that it did not especially help me know what to do with the dreaming, especially in understanding who I am or what my place in the world is.

Charmaine got reflective. Instead of answering my question directly, she told me about her husband, Julian, who was not in the store at the time. "Sweetheart, don't ever take a man as a teacher, never let a man initiate you into his teaching. Because you're already the goddess, sweetheart. You wanted me to tell you who you are? The goddess. And Her Highness doesn't need any more school!

"I love Julian. Always was attracted to his power, I was even enchanted by it." I thought of Julian, his penetrating intelligence, his strong upright carriage, his physical attractiveness even as an older man, but I could also see he had been a man who was attracted himself to the darker mysteries of power—there was a sadness about him I couldn't define.

"Julian will always have a place in my heart. He's been a true father to his stepson, and we've had wonderful, high old times together. But don't you know," Charmaine said with a wink, "he's still a man, honey, and good is good, and man is man and you and I are women, and as long as men are the kind of men men have to be because of history, take my advice—love them, but don't give one of them your power!"

Her voice had softened and drifted. She seemed a little sad, for all the defiance. As if responding to my silence, she went on, "Truth is, I haven't completely resisted his magic—so I've gotten the wonderful, shimmering side of him, but not without that black side. He's a man, and love them as we do, it's next to impossible to turn them around from that fascination with themselves, with having power—power *over*. I think it's practically a genetic trait by now. And women, we love these damn men despite what Mother Nature shows us about creation. We even follow them deeper into their obsessions with personal power. The trouble with Julian was he unleashed his power and then couldn't control it. Now it's like one of those twisters we used to get in Oklahoma—blue sky, then suddenly all hell breaks loose and if you don't know where to seek shelter, you get devastated.

"You know why I'm telling *you* this. We're the same," she said, squeezing my hand. I leaned closer to her chair and hugged her. "I gave in to him. I love Julian, honey, but giving him my power was the biggest mistake I ever made."

Charmaine pressed both hands to my face, then with each

word patted my cheeks: "Whatever you do, save your seed corn. Hide it if you have to, but don't turn it over to any man!" There was real fire in Charmaine's eyes. She was practically shaking with intensity.

Charmaine's words ran through my mind so often they became an image: I began feeling as if there were a black horse running around in furious circles in a corral. Nobody could ride that horse because it was so fierce. But how had it gotten captured if it was so tumultuous? Without trying to answer the question, the answer came—I had quieted the horse, I was the one who'd convinced it, I had led it into the corral. I had done it out of best intentions, for very simply I had wanted to be one with its beauty and power, its spirit that I admired. It was the most beautiful horse in the world and I'd had to have it. Now, seeing it like this, I felt remorse—I'd harmed its wild, free nature by wanting it. I decided the only thing to do was ride it out of the corral and set it free again far away in a place where it would not suffer for lack of its own kind, nor of any of its needs.

The image captured all too accurately my own situation. But where was the woman who would come to my corral and set me free?

Meanwhile, as the summer of 1979 drew toward a close, Jack's investments in silver—despite our supposed nonattachment to money—had yielded results that matched step for step the Hunt brothers' killing on the silver market. The business gave me a wonderful life-style; but no amount of style could alter my feeling trapped.

On October 5, 1979, there was a full moon. Aunt Charmaine called it "Pan's Moon," the lovers' moon. A woman who wants to know about her true love asks for a dream at this moon, and her true love will be revealed. I prepared my altar early in the day, lighting red and pink candles. I filled vases all around the house with pink roses, white and pink daisies in honor of Pan. I anointed the candles with Charmaine's love and vision oils, burned a mixture of herbs Charmaine had made for me, placed three rosebuds on the altar—pink, flanked by red and white buds—and prayed.

I thanked Mother for the Jack of Diamonds' protection and the security he had provided my son. I was grateful that I had whatever I wished for in a material sense. I said that though I could accept a life with Jack, if it were meant to be, my heart felt empty with him and I needed to know once and for all if I was destined to stay here with him, or was another love meant for me? If it was to be Jack, I prayed to have the emptiness taken from me and replaced by contentment. All night I dreamed I was a hummingbird making love to a giant saguaro in the desert night.

In the winter of 1980, after I had settled into a pattern of resignation, I suddenly had a strong desire to go to Yaqui Easter in Tucson. I had been having vivid dreams about masked dancers. Bennett D'Angelo's invitation to the Yaqui Easter ceremony echoed in my memory. I felt called and supported by Indian women who came to me in dreams. Oddly, they soothed and calmed me, gave me the confidence to propose at one of the weekly group meetings that I should go as an emissary to the Yaqui Easter ceremony. Jack and the group had a policy of randomly selecting people to receive tithes. It was their way, Jack said, of not being attached to money, to be directed instead to the Work on Oneself. Money wasn't the goal; waking up was.

Sometimes the group would also make large donations to people whose houses had burned down, or people on the TV news who had a child needing an operation. There had recently been a story in the newspaper about Indians of the Southwest, and included in it had been brief descriptions of the Yaquis, the Hopis, the Navajos, with side stories on the culture of each and the living conditions of the people.

To my surprise, I convinced everyone, including Jack, that the Yaqui, because of their unique talents, were people who needed an acknowledgment in cash of the good they did the entire planet through their ceremonies. Even more astonishing to me was that Jack himself proposed it would be especially good for Bobby to go with me; not only could he protect me, but it would give him experience about the importance of putting spiritual knowledge to work in the world.

I first heard the name "Anselmo Valencia" the night in February 1980 when I called Directory Assistance for Arizona. I asked the operator for listings for "Yaqui Tribe." But there were no phone numbers. I asked then for any listings with the word "Yaqui," but all I got were a few businesses. "What exactly are you looking for?" the operator asked. I told him I wanted to find out where and when the Easter ceremonies were being held. To my astonishment the operator replied that he lived near Guadalupe in Phoenix, where there was a Yaqui village, and the Easter ceremonies were there. If I liked, he offered, I could even stay with his family.

I thanked him but said I really had to go to Tucson. "All right," he replied, and, as if reluctant, said, "I'm going to give you the number of the Yaqui chief in Tucson. But don't tell anyone I gave it to you."

I called the number, and a man answered. I introduced myself and said I was very interested in knowing where and when the Yaqui Easter ceremonies were, and that I had been told this was the number to call to find out. "Am I speaking with the Yaqui Tribal Chief?" I asked.

"I am Anselmo Valencia. I am the *spiritual* leader of my people," he said. "So if you would like to talk about our ceremonies, you have the right man." There were both warmth and irony in his voice. I asked him for the dates and times and where I should go to see the ceremonies.

He told me the Yaquis had a new, small reservation called Pascua Pueblo, on the southwest side of Tucson. Why didn't I come to the ceremonies at Pascua as his guest? He asked if my family would be coming with me. I replied that it would be just me and my twelve-year-old son, Bobby, and we wished to make a donation to the tribe because I knew the Easter ceremonies and the Yaqui people were special to the entire planet.

I said I'd be honored to be his guest. He then gave me instructions on how to reach the Pascua Reservation and told me to be sure to come to his office there when I got to Tucson. I said I would. "Come as soon as you can, then. You must make an effort to stay for the entire ceremony."

4 ▦ WHY HAVE YOU COME HERE?

"THERE'S THE BLACK LIZARD. AND THERE'S THE BOLT OF LIGHTNING," Bobby said, pointing at a long, black mesa hunkered like a chuck-walla in the hot sun. In the center of it, Anselmo Valencia had said, we would see black lightning. We headed toward it after our brief visit to the graveyard. We turned onto Tetakusim, passed the new fire station, turned again at Vicam, and parked in front of the Yaqui tribal offices. The pink-and-white walls were covered with murals of Yaqui deer dancers and the pasco-las, the Yaqui clowns.

We walked in. A short, pretty, round woman dressed in blue blouse and pants looked up from her work and blushed bash-fully. "You are here to see Mr. Valencia," she said, before I could even introduce myself. We followed her down a hall into another office.

On the walls were memorabilia from children—a plastic panda bear, and paper dolls of Yaqui women and men with the words in Yaqui for "man" and "woman." Next to a drawing of a cat with big eyes was the declaration and pen used by Jimmy Carter to sign the Yaqui Tribe into legal existence. There were national and local recognition plaques: "Anselmo Valencia: Native American of the Year." "Anselmo Valencia: Thank You. Pascua Yaqui Tribe."

The man at the far end of the room rose from his desk to greet me. Dressed in a cowboy shirt and jeans, he could have been a Hollywood mogul, a lord of the Mafia underworld, an Americanized Mideast sheik. Whoever he might have been, when he took my hand in greeting there was no question I was in the presence of someone of special authority.

"Welcome, Heather and Robert. We are glad you have come."

He introduced Tina Molina, his secretary, who blushed again and looked down, and David Ramirez, the tribal chairman, a young, handsome man with short-cropped hair. David Ramirez shook my hand politely and stepped deferentially to his chair in front of Anselmo Valencia's desk.

Anselmo Valencia motioned for us to sit down. I gave him a donation for the culture, for which he thanked me. "You are interested in my people's ceremonies, is that right?"

He related some local Yaqui history, how the Yaqui live in both Arizona and Sonora—"wherever the long-armed cactus grows"—how the Yaqui were the poorest of the poor, treated as less than human by both Anglos in America and Mexicans south of the border, how the Yaqui came to be the only Indian tribe recognized by the Mexican government because after the conquistadors came in 1525, the Yaqui never stopped fighting. They were fierce guerrilla fighters who retreated into the mountains above Rio Yaqui and learned the skills they needed to survive the next four centuries of attack and enslavement. Into this context Anselmo Valencia poured the pure gold of his culture, the Easter ceremonies in which both the ancient deer dance and the more recent Passion of Christ were wed.

As I listened I could almost make out his eyes behind the dark lenses of his sunglasses. I had the sensation that he knew I was feeling his words in a very physical way. Then I thought I was imagining it, that surely he had given the same talk many times before to other visitors. Anselmo Valencia spoke in a somewhat formal way, as if the English he used had been earned one word at a time, then through long usage and practice had taken on the appearance of naturalness.

He spoke softly. If I hadn't paid absolute attention, I'd have been unable to hear him. I was on the edge of my chair, leaning slightly toward his desk. After a while I began to distinguish a kind of lilt to his phrasing. I thought of counting out the feet in lines of poetry. Then I noticed it was my heart beating, rather loudly I thought; perhaps it showed through my blouse. The room had filled with a mild carnelian light. For a second I took my eyes away and glanced toward the western window above his desk, to see if the sun had set, but it was only early afternoon.

Anselmo Valencia did not look like other Native Americans I'd met. He had curly black hair and golden sienna skin. Despite his cowboy shirt and the big, square turquoise beaded belt buckle on his trim waist, he reminded me less of Native Americans than of ancient Egyptians I'd seen in reproductions of funereal murals. Except for his mustache, Anselmo Valencia's profile, right down to the little goatee, was very similar to likenesses of the pharaohs. I couldn't guess his age, although he was no longer young.

Abruptly, he changed the subject, "I would like you to explain to Mr. Ramirez why you have come here."

I stood up. Without the least hesitation I stated that I knew the Yaqui Easter ceremonies were important to the well-being of all people on the planet. I said I had dreamed of the ceremonial dances since I had been a child. I was honored to at last be where I could experience them in person. As I continued on, however, I started to separate from the room. I seemed to go straight into Anselmo Valencia.

I could hear the echo of someone speaking and recalled that it was I. My words were quite faint; they were coming from behind me while the sound of a waterfall grew louder and louder across a tropical glade in front of me. I was slightly winded; I had just run through fields of flowers with this same man who sat before me in the tribal office. He had my hand and we were running with deer. The sunlight shone in such a way that it revealed its smallest interstices, an incredibly delicate and complex web-like structure. Several hummingbirds were drinking from red hibiscus flowers in my hair. We were laughing at the foot of the waterfall, or perhaps our laughter was the sound of the water, which then became the sound and rhythm of my breathing.

My happiness was almost unbearable. Everything was both transparent and solid, doubly real, as had been my dreams as a child. But I had never moved with another person from the temporal world to the transparent one. Given my elation, when I sat down I was surprised at my composure. I thought to myself, Your dream is real. It exists and it's here, in this room.

Anselmo Valencia thanked me. He looked at the tribal chairman, then back at me again. "All you have spoken touches me deeply. You know more about the meaning of our Yaqui culture than many of my people. I would like you to record what you have just said so that it may become a part of our library and our children may know what you have experienced through us." I nodded in assent, but I was bewildered. What did I just say? I had no memory of it.

"I would also like you to visit my mother. I will have my daughters take you to the cemetery."

"Your mother and I have already met," I replied quickly, without thinking. Anselmo Valencia seemed surprised, although his face hardly expressed it. His eyebrow appeared to rise slightly.

"Her grave is the most remarkable one in the cemetery—it has a teapot on it and beautiful calla lilies."

"Yes. Then you certainly have met my mother," Anselmo said, somewhat amused. He got up from behind his desk and told me to come back on Wednesday afternoon for the beginning of the next group of ceremonies, which would culminate in the Running of the Gloria and the deer dance for the twenty-four hours between high noon Saturday and Sunday. "Please come and participate in as much as you can," he said. I thanked him and left.

On the way to the car Bobby tugged at my arm. "That was the man I saw at the Mission, that was him, right down to the shirt and the sunglasses!"

"Yes. I know." What I didn't tell Bobby, or even admit to myself, was that just as dreaming was the gift that held the secret of my destiny, Anselmo Valencia was the secret of the dreams.

On Maundy Thursday, Anselmo Valencia asked how I was enjoying the ceremonies. I was standing by myself at a food booth after the evening procession to the Garden of Gethsemane, when the soldiers take Christ from the Garden. I said I was very honored just to be there as the guest of the people, and was very happy for all the attention paid us, especially by the society of masked dancers, the chappeyekas, who had fed us our meals. He asked then if he might have a talk with me in a little while—there was something he wished to discuss privately and would I please stay close by so that during a break in his duties he and I might talk.

About an hour later he escorted me behind the food booths and across a field of scrub to the tribal office. Inside he gestured for me to sit in the chair in front of his desk. He took his seat, folded his hands in a teepee and began talking.

"I have a favor to ask of you. You and I are complete strangers, Heather, yet we have always known each other. Because of your knowledge of ceremonial magic, I feel directed to confide in you about a problem I have discussed with no one else."

My lifelong sense of myself as a natural student of magical arts had, thanks to Charmaine, begun to be directed into forms of ceremonial magic. But I was certainly not yet a master of my talent. That Anselmo wanted me to *do* something for him amazed me even more than how he knew in the first place I was familiar with ceremonial magic. Reflexively, I took out my tarot deck from my purse and placed the cards on the desk. Anselmo pushed them back toward me. "I don't need those today. What I require of you is very specific.

"We have met many times, in many forms and disguises."

"Mr. Valencia—"

Anselmo Valencia smiled. "Anselmo. Hardly anyone but outsiders calls me 'Mister.' "

"Anselmo, I didn't say this in your office the other day. But I have seen you in dreams, many, many times."

"The dream was real. It has given you an unusual familiarity with me, and because of it, I am going to trust you as I have trusted no one here. Besides, no one here can help me with my problem."

Anselmo Valencia had been sitting dead still. He leaned forward very slightly. "You see how it is for me. Everybody needs something from me. Despite how busy I am, I am alone. For what I must do for my people, if my home is not a sanctuary, I will not be able to do what is required of me by the Creator.

"The woman I live with, Marcianna, is the mother of my youngest son, Eladio—the one I introduced to you in front of the church earlier today. Since his birth I have supported Marcianna and all her other children, as well as my son Eladio. It is sad, but she no longer supports me in my work for the Yaqui culture, even though she is as Yaqui as can be. My other children—" Anselmo interrupted himself, sensing my question. "My grown children from a previous marriage." He smiled slightly. "I am married to my people; my first wife wanted an easier life. At any rate, even my grown children have to fight with Marcianna's children just to remain living there. The result is that my people see that their chief is dishonored in his own house.

"I haven't even touched Marcianna in bed for many years. We hardly talk to each other. Nevertheless, she is a very powerful woman. But because she is afraid of her own power, she has done many things in dreaming she isn't even aware of that have hurt people. Her fear has finally come home to roost in my house, and now it affects me, too—the power she is afraid to use has gone to her children. Naturally, being children, they have no idea what to do with it. The girls are more comfortable with their power, but for the boys, there is greater tension. So they take drugs, they drink during the ceremonies. I do not fault Marcianna, but because she doesn't have hold of her power, she has made it impossible to fulfill my duties. Now this must cease.

"My problem is this," he said, rocking his hands up and down a few times as if to gather momentum. "It would be dishonorable to ask her to leave my house. I have all these children of hers and mine, plus two nieces, to take care of. I have all my Yaqui people to take care of. I am not the master of my own house, and yet I must go on tending the duties of this entire reservation which I fought for for over twenty years.

"Marcianna is the mother of one of my children. Therefore I want her to have a good life. I ask you to create a ceremony that will cause her to leave the reservation—but it must be of her own free will. She must go. It is critical that she go. But I stress—she must want to leave here because something better will appear for her. I want you to see to it that she leaves for a younger man, one who will be pleasing to her. She must have a house to live in and she must take her children away. She must under no circumstance be taken from here to something unhappy. Otherwise, I will still be responsible for her, and I will have to pay the price for driving her away. I cannot afford such a tax on my energies. It is over between us. Only emptiness is between us.

"I ask you to remove her for me."

"It will take me a full moon cycle, Anselmo," I said without hesitation. A ceremony for the moon started to form in my mind as a solution to his problem. He got up, thanked me, saying he was sure I would succeed. As he reached to open the door to let me out, impulsively I hugged him, saying how honored I was. He was startled by my affection and just stood there. But neither did he resist the embrace.

"It is still cuaresma, Heather, Lent. For my people, during cuaresma anything romantic is not appropriate—not even a romantic thought." I sensed immediately, however, that he was drawn to me, despite his gentle sternness. As we walked silently back to the plaza, I was increasingly bewildered by his frankness toward me and how he knew so much about me—not to mention by my own willingness to undertake such a task. I really had never tried anything like it, and I wondered, as he said good night, what had possessed me.

After people had knelt before Christ and kissed his feet the afternoon of Good Friday, I was tired and went over to some empty metal chairs that were in the shadow of the church. Just as I was about to take a seat, some teenage boys sat down in them and folded their arms, then just as suddenly stood bolt upright, at attention.

"No, you boys keep them," somebody behind me said. I turned, but I already knew it was Anselmo Valencia. "You boys need them more than we do. They are old and we are young," he explained, perfectly deadpan, to me.

"Yes," I said. "They have spent many, many years raising their children, working hard, and now they should be able to rest."

The boys' expressions changed to confusion, and they asked

Anselmo, whom they called Achai, if he'd excuse them. He nodded his head and the boys took off quickly.

"What is Achai?" I asked.

"It means 'Elder Father.' It also means 'God.' In Yaqui the two mean the same." He motioned for us to sit down.

"Is Anselmo your Indian name?"

"No. In Yaqui it's 'Tori.' That is my clan." A devilish grin broke over his face. "The Tori clan is named for a small rodent that lives in Rio Yaqui where my people also live. So you could say—as many of my own people do right to my face—that I am the 'Rat.'

"I always get a kick out of going to tribal meetings and pow-wows in other parts of the country. This big chief introduces himself: 'I am the Great Eagle.' This one says, 'I am the Night Wind.' Another says, 'I am called Bear-that-Walks-the-High-Mountain.' They come to me and I say, 'I am the Rat.' "

We both laughed. "What is your Indian name, Heather?"

" 'Onamwashnatena,' " I said. "It means the 'High White Lightning.' "

"That's Plains, isn't it?"

"Cherokee and Potawatomi."

"That's a good name for you. In Yaqui we have also the same words, only they mean something a little different from your Plains name. In our language the words for lightning mean the same as 'the Great Serpent Sticks out His Tongue.' " And Anselmo Valencia startled me by suddenly wagging his tongue slowly, just as a snake does when he is tasting the air.

"You remind me of the Egyptian kings. They wore the snake on their heads."

Anselmo Valencia looked at me without speaking. "I've never been anything but Yaqui," he said with quiet firmness. "This life and all my lives. Nothing but a Yaqui.

"In the religion of my people, as in some others, like the Hindus, human beings return to live over and over. When we die, we return to the sun where all that we have been in this past life is exposed to His merciless rays. Those who cannot withstand the light come back to the planet to try again. A year after we die, if it is our fate to return, we find a new Yaqui mother and

father and our spirit animates their lovemaking and creates a
new child. So we do not have death as the Anglo culture sees it."

Before the first deer dance, Anselmo described what I would
see and some of the meaning layered within the deer dance.

The Enchanted Flower World

For the Yaqui, our beautiful little Grandmother the Earth came
from the stars, where she played in the heavens with our Grandfather the Thunderbird. Grandmother's love and her body made
the perfect beauty of this world, and upon her beautiful, perfect
body we walk. It is she who is our real mother, for before anything was real, Grandmother dreamed it. She dreamed all of us
to share in her dreaming.

The Enchanted Flower World is Grandmother's dreaming garden, the place where all things in creation are at first perfect,
beautiful, and most alive. The deer, our Little Brother, is the
door to the Enchanted Flower World, and when man dances the
deer, when he becomes the Little Brother, the door to that world
opens.

The Deer and the Deer Dance

Long before the conquistadors came to the New World and
spread the Catholic religion like a heavy brown varnish, the
spring deer dance celebrated in joyous thanksgiving the reawak-
ening of life. Superimposed on that celebration is the profound-
est teaching of the Christian church—the resurrection and
rebirth of Christ. The essence of Yaqui Easter is the word Yaqui,
not Easter, although Catholicism has helped cement the culture
into a coherent structure that has nurtured the people in changing times.

The man who dances the deer does so to the accompaniment
of the deer songs. There are as many deer songs as there are
things that exist in nature. The songs name everything in life so
they can exist, and the deer dances them here. In this way, the
world becomes a dream again.

When the original things were created, nothing moved until there was sound. Only when there was sound did life begin to move, dancing to the original, sweet music. In the deer dance, life quickens to the call of the flute. Even in his mother's womb, the deer dancer hears the flute and moves to it. When children are small and hear the rasp, rattle, and drum, they come to the sound and move like the deer dancers throughout time. The deer singers, the musicians, the pascolas, all the ceremonial actors select themselves through their attraction first to the music, following their predilection for one or the other of the several roles that a Yaqui can take. They may also, as did Anselmo Valencia, find themselves doing all the roles. The tribal community are psychically attuned to one another, and very often the people who sing together as deer singers have sung together before in previous lives.

The deer songs have been passed down to the present day from the beginning of time. If you are born to be a deer singer, your ancestors will talk to you about carving an instrument or even give the words of a new song. Sometimes the songs are passed by word of mouth from father to son, brother to brother, uncle to nephew, but sometimes a deer singer is walking in the desert or anywhere else where nature is strong and a new song comes to him because he is part of something unbroken and timeless and therefore can hear when the dead tell him new words.

The training for the cultural participants, whatever their sacred roles, happens in a very natural way. If you are a singer or dancer or musician, your elders will sing or dance or play to demonstrate correct techniques. There is no set age or system of tests which dictates when a child is ready to perform—it is natural. I have seen a four-year-old boy deer dance three sets of songs and dances because he was with the culture and the ancestors were talking through that child. The body itself tells you when you are ready. It hears the timeless voice whispered by countless ancestors since the beginning, and the embodiment of that original utterance of being is what all the dancing and singing and playing serves: to feel the beginning in every cell and fiber of our bodies.

*   *   *

In the most ancient part of the Yaqui Easter, the deer at first dances at the Running of the Gloria, on the Saturday before Easter, when with the help of the smallest children he beats back the storming of the church by the forces of evil, the chappeyekas. But after the first set of deer dances and songs in the plaza, the deer is taken from in front of the church to the deer lodge where he dances the rest of the time.

How the deer dances depends on the song the deer singers sing. If it is the "Song of the Eagle," the deer dancer will spread out his arms and fly. If the deer singers sing the wood lizard, the deer will act as though he is climbing the walls of the lodge.

The deer dancer dances bare-chested except for special yellow, red, and white beads and an abalone cross around his neck, the yellow being the color of the Flower World, red the sacred flowers, and white the spirit. Down from the waist, he wears a black, fringed rebozo, folded as a skirt, and a broad belt of pyramids or chevrons and leather fringe. Tied to the fringe with amazing intricacy are three hundred deer hooves. The deer wears a scarf of some color tied over the belly and making a triangle that points down toward earth. The white cloth of the headdress is folded down from a rectangle into a triangle and tied over the forehead, then pulled down over the eyes and bridge of the nose so that the man dancing the deer will not be distracted by this world but will stay in the Enchanted Flower World.

On top of the white headdress he ties a deer's head which has been carved from wood and covered with the actual skin of a young deer. The young deer's antlers, wrapped with hot pink or red ribbon to attract the hummingbird, crown the headpiece. In the center of the antlers a red rose is fastened. As he moves to the deer songs the deer holds two golden gourd rattles attached to his wrists with thongs.

Each of the three deer singers plays an instrument. The head singer sits in the middle and plays a rasp with a long thin stick, flanked by a second rasp to his left, and the water drum, a low wooden bowl filled with water on which floats a big, halved gourd, on his right.

The drum beats like the deer's heart. The two rasps, of huchaco, a dark red wood from Rio Yaqui, are his breath, one the inhalation, the other the exhalation. The worm cocoons wrapped around the deer dancer's feet buzz and stir like the mantle of life closest to the ground, insects in particular. As he dances to the deer songs, the deer shakes his rattles—he is brushing up against bushes and twigs. Everywhere around him the forest is alive!

The deer and his party of deer singers sit on the west side of the deer lodge, which, at Pascua Pueblo, is made of modern building materials. But the floor where the deer dances has been left alone. The deer dances directly on Mother Earth. The other half of the floor is concrete. In front of the opening of the lodge, on the south side, a fourth man, the tampolero, plays a small drum and a flute at the same time. He leans back against a tall, rough carved piece of wood, and plays for the death dancers, or pascolas. Each set of dances is begun by the tampolero, whose songs, be they of morning or night, wind or river or animals, set the mood for the others. The pascolas dance in the north end of the deer lodge, behind the deer dancer. The pascolas dance three times before the deer begins dancing to the specific song of the deer singers. Their dance counterpoints the deer's.

With his drum on one knee and the flute on top of the drum, the tampolero drums a quick, irregular beat, tapping both ends of the stick back and forth against the drumhead. The tampolero starts off each set of three dances with his drum beat, then his flute. Each set consists of three dances and songs, followed by a rest for the participants, and then a new set of songs and dances and so on for the next twenty-four hours following the Running of the Gloria. For one whole day, the deer is with us and the Enchanted Flower World is open to everyone.

Strong, heroic, poetic—where the deer dances there is life. The pascolas know the darkness; that is the basis of their service to us. By dancing they can perhaps free themselves, and others, from the dark forces that are a part of our world. They know death. They know the earth, and knowing both they are jovial, humorous. Yet they dance apart from the deer, for the deer is completely unself-conscious about himself and his qualities. Therefore he is purely joyous. The pascolas make light of death, they may even joke about it. But they also have the serious task of escorting us between the two worlds. For the Yaqui, death is the gap between the world in which our consciousness is housed in our bodies and the world in which it is in the eternal dream place.

Where the deer dances it is eternal. Where the pascolas dance, there is death, so the two parties of participants are separated. Yet, for people, life and death are only apparent opposites, contrasting with one another, and their contrast creates a dance within the larger framework of eternal life where there is no death. The pascolas would like to be in the Enchanted Flower World, but they can't get there and so they tease and taunt the deer. The deer is too noble to respond to them, however; his dedication of being keeps him centered in his own reality.

The alchemy of the deer dance is in the mingling of the everyday world of human activity everywhere, and the eternal Enchanted Flower World. The dances show us the separate natures of dark and light, of death and life, and in the dance itself we can experience the union of opposites into timeless joy.

At all times of the year except during cuaresma, Lent, the deer dances. But the most powerful deer dance is held at the beginning of spring. Yaqui Easter marks the end of the time of emptiness when things are not fertile. The deer dances then to end the cycle of the dead and his dance renews everything.

Recalling the deer dance, memory makes my body happy. I taste again so many rites of spring, so many Yaqui Easters, Anselmo Valencia in full sun, at the midday, in black and red, his copper skin intense against the colors of his regalia . . . The remembered presence of the sun weighs again on my face and again I am sitting behind Anselmo, in my place once more, the wife's place, behind the chief, as he bends over the rasp. Flanked left and right by the two other deer singers, Anselmo scrapes his rasp with a stick as if he were peeling away the appearance of things, vigorously, unceasing, his arm shaving quickly across the wood; Anselmo in the plaza in front of the Church Cristo Rey after the Running of the Gloria, after the defeat of evil; Anselmo the lead deer singer, the center of the three, three the sacred number, three playing and singing the songs that must be sung for life to continue . . . This was the first time, when I knew everything and knew nothing; when without understanding or needing to I realized a long journey had ended, and I was home where I belonged with the man I had met in dreams. I sat dressed in the yellow of the Flower World, at the center of the beginning of my life.

Saturday morning hundreds of people, including Bobby and me, crowded tightly up and down the plaza in two long lines that formed a causeway stretching from the church to the deer lodge. Little twigs of cottonwood punctuated the sacred path. An old man with a big belly was patrolling the lines, shooing away spectators who strayed into the pathway where the chappeyekas, in their terrifying animal-hide masks, personifying evil, would assault the church, and where after the Gloria had been run, the deer would soon dance.

It was hot as we waited for the sun at last to come to power. A woman from Colorado named Caren chatted with me about her personal life, but it seemed quite natural—such was the mood of expectancy and heat. Caren, too, had been drawn by vivid dreams of Yaqui dances and a desire to share in the meaning of the ceremonies.

One of Anselmo Valencia's sons, Roy, was standing next to his father at the south side of the church. "Who is that standing next to Anselmo?" Caren asked.

I told her it was Anselmo's eldest son, then teased her with the chief's admonition about romantic thoughts during cuaresma, during which the people abstained from making love.

"Well, I know we're not supposed to think about romance," Caren joked as we sat talking near the front of the church and next to the deer-singing blankets, as instructed by Anselmo Valencia. "But Lent is almost over, and I sure think Roy is good-looking. If I could have any man here, I'd want him. Isn't he handsome?"

"Yes, but his father is the most beautiful man I've ever seen."

Caren looked over the tops of her sunglasses. "The chief? My, you're ambitious! Doesn't he already have a woman?"

On a signal from Anselmo, the caballeros, his lieutenants dressed entirely in black, escorted the chappeyekas in two lines out of the walled compound, or guardia, next to the church. The crowd quieted as the chappeyekas tapped their sticks and swords together. Veiled with black over their hats to cover their faces from evil, the caballeros accompanied the twenty-two chappeyekas past the concession stands toward the cross at the east side of the two long lines of spectators. They assembled at that end of the plaza and faced the church. The deer dancer and his party of two pascolas appeared and the deer singers sat down right in front of us.

The deer dancer, a wiry, lithe young man, adjusted his head-dress to cover his eyes, then tied the deer head to his own. He picked up the big rattles and slipped the leather thongs over his wrists, looked east and west, and took the stance of the deer. He ran nervously from his station in front of the deer singers into the center of the plaza where he faced down the chappeyekas at the other end.

Little dust devils whipped up spirals of confetti. Then the caballeros in black and the chappeyekas marched toward the deer and the church, stamping their feet as they moved forward, the chappeyekas striking their swords and sticks—tap-tap, tap-tap-tap, over and over. They seemed so bold and full of themselves, so cocky as they taunted the deer. Would they attack? Some of the more brazen chappeyekas lowered their heads like bulls and raised their wooden swords as if to say, "We will get what is inside your church, we will take it from you!" but instead of storming the church, the procession turned and trooped back up the plaza to regroup for the next foray.

Several times this same, almost military move was executed by the caballeros and chappeyekas, and each time they neared the church the deer dancer stamped and nervously moved out into the plaza to fend them back, lowering his antlers that were festooned with red ribbon and flowers. The pascolas, too, moved out toward the chappeyekas, gesturing with their chins, smacking their shakers at the evil spirits. I noticed Anselmo watching from across the plaza where he stood with the musicians. He struck me as oddly isolated by some consideration. The tension in the crowd increased. I could feel it in me, too.

Just then Anselmo Valencia rushed forward, knelt down on one knee and raised a silver sword, the only metal one in the ceremony. As he made the sign of the cross, a big bell tolled; the chappeyekas stormed the church for the first time, startling the crowd. The deer reflexively took up his rattles, stamped and shook them, *chshoochshooschshoo*, a sound like wind, like violent rain, warning the evil spirits away. My heart beat very fast and the lines of people, the racket and bustle of the ceremonial fight, all started to grow fuzzy and white, as if a cloud had passed in front of my face. Except for Anselmo and the deer, I saw nothing but this hazy, heated white, and I thought I was passing out.

Suddenly Anselmo was in front of me. He threw something in my face—water, I hoped, but it was a handful of confetti. It was so sudden, he was gone when I realized what had happened. He had smiled at me, I had smiled, and a pink castle rosebud had flown right into my startled mouth.

What do you do with such a shock? I didn't know, so I just ate the rose. Something unconfetti-like and hard had tumbled into my blouse. I captured whatever it was with one hand, then discreetly worked it up to the top of my clothing—it was a nautilus shell, pearly and petite, I'd never seen one so small and perfect.

I must have sat there like a woman who either was turning into a tree, or who was a tree emerging into a woman, there was so much green glitter of leaves and flowers on me. Anselmo took his place as the lead deer singer in front of me, on his deer-singing blanket. The first three songs were sung. The ceremony was overpowering in and of itself, but, as I gazed at the shell in my hand, tasting the rosebud still, it seemed to me a personal communion, a reunion, which the nautilus perfectly signified—the inner dream unwinding, unfolding, opening out. I saw that this little shell in my hand was a sort of shell-of-plenty, and the strange, beautiful new world around me was the center where I was supposed to be. That's when I first understood the Enchanted Flower World. I knew I was there, and like that little shell, my world extended in all directions simultaneously, smooth, shining, miraculous. I had never seen anything more beautiful than the Running of the Gloria, and at the center of all that beauty was Anselmo. I felt absolutely complete. I had come home.

Two bare electric bulbs filled the deer lodge with a strangely intimate light. The three pascolas smoked cigarettes. The deer dancer slept on Anselmo's deer-singing blanket. All afternoon and throughout the night, after the deer was installed in the deer lodge, I had watched one set of deer dances after another.

Now the tampolero dozed against the backrest of his instrument. My son leaned sleepily against the center support for the ramada, still wearing his cowboy hat and poncho. Outside the south opening of the lodge a few men were talking low by the coals of the big mesquite fire. To the south there was the Black Lizard Mountain against the predawn sky. I sat against the adobe wall of the deer lodge on a gray folding chair that Eddie the deer morro, who was in charge of keeping order in the deer lodge, had brought from the Cristo Rey Church. In the quiet the chill of the early morning air made me think of the day's shimmering warmth, the first flash of the deer dancer's rattles, the chappeyekas in their unending marches through time. Faces in the whirlwinds, dreams . . .

I pulled my sweater over my knees. Anselmo Valencia took off his Zorro-style hat. In the dull light of the deer lodge, his black hair shone where it curled over his collar. He lifted the black and white poncho over his head, put his hat back on and came over to me.

"Would you like some coffee?"

In the three days I'd been around him, he never twice looked the same. "Yes, please," I said. I watched him round the wall dividing the deer lodge from the cultural kitchen, then I peeked through a hole in the blocks. I could only see him in fragmented glimpses on the other side—the dark eyes of a gypsy, the cheekbones of an Egyptian, the copper, golden skin of the Dark Lord in my medicine dreams. An old crone with a blue-flowered bandanna and flowers all over her dress handed him two cups of coffee. Her eyes brightened and her pinched, fierce mouth softened when Anselmo Valencia reached across to take the two cups from her. It occurred to me she knew I was watching.

He came back around the corner of the wall followed by the deer morro, who carried sugar and spoons for the coffee. When I took the Styrofoam cup he handed me, I also took his little finger which was hiding beneath the bottom—one of those sudden contacts that make you wonder if you really felt it. The mildly electric pulse of his touch stayed in my hand as I held the coffee. He crouched in front of me. After a few sips of coffee, he looked toward me, rather than straight at me, and said, "My people knew you would finally come here. You have felt drawn to this place for many years, without knowing where we were. But you were drawn, just as the hummingbird is drawn to her flowers. She doesn't know where they are exactly, but that doesn't hinder her from finding the bright flowers of her destiny. Among my people there are some ladies with a special purpose to the people. We call them dreaming women. Both here in Pascua and in Rio Yaqui, in Mexico, where my people also live, your coming was known in dreams."

It was hard for me to speak because of my growing excitement. "Have I been here before, Anselmo? I know you and I were together in dreams I had for years when I was a girl, for years of dreams. We were the king and queen of an ancient kingdom before the coming of white people. And some of these women I have seen here, they are like women who also came and taught me things."

Anselmo listened intently. "It is true. The dream of another time and place, when you were with us—that dream was real. The dreams you have had of me are real also. You know how to see, you have the dreaming medicine. You had no choice but to come. All my people have seen you, Heather, because you have the same dreaming medicine. You had to come, just like the hummingbird." He turned more directly to me with a sheepish smile. "You *are* the hummingbird. Did you know it was the hummingbird who brought all the different languages people use? That is why you love to talk," he added, not quite keeping a serious face.

"We must appreciate the magic as it unfolds. Everything has its moment," Anselmo said mysteriously. "And when the moment of magic happens, we should be alive and sure! The Yaqui culture has served the planet for many generations, but nothing stands still, people and cultures included. The needs of the planet change form, although the needs remain constant.

"That is the purpose of the culture—to respond to the needs of the larger being we live on, Mother Earth. Mother Earth wants her children to be happy, so she can be happy. But the Mother, too, has requirements which are dictated by the stars beyond her.

"Without the culture, my people will lose their powers and their place in the world. They will not disappear as people. But they will change into something different, and it won't be Yaqui.

For my people, I must be a thousand percent Yaqui. That responsibility is getting harder and harder to fulfill.

"I have another request to make of you. You are a gifted artist. Would you consider coming this summer to teach art to the children? Such a program would be very valuable to my little Yaqui people."

I said I would love to, provided my family consented.

"Your coming is a very good omen, Heather. For the sake of the young people of the tribe it is good. Sometimes we appreciate what we are only after we see ourselves through the eyes of others. One day you will tell them what you have seen about us. They will see through your eyes who they are. Perhaps this will help the culture to continue."

He paused for a moment. It occurred to me how persuasive he was, how undeniable. Perhaps he was reading my mind at that very moment. If so, he saw that I envisioned myself standing beside him, exactly as we had been so many times in dreams.

"I cannot wait much longer," he repeated in a very precise way, as if having already measured my reaction to what he was about to say. "Alone I cannot finish all that my Creator has set out for me. We Yaquis are sorcerers and dreamers. If I do not have a special kind of help at this critical time in the life of my people, I will not be able to continue and much will be lost. I am asking you to help me."

Anselmo Valencia got up. I looked at him, dumbfounded yet calm. I felt as I had long ago, after the dreams of the Dark Lord would cease for the night. I also had an absolute sense of certainty and rightness.

"I know you care deeply for our children. Come this summer and create an art program for them."

"Anselmo, I can't promise anything, but I will try to be of help. When I get back to Las Vegas I'll ask my family if they'd object to my coming for part of the summer."

"Get some sleep," he said, and walked to the other side of the deer lodge. Though it was nearly dawn, I felt fresh and awake. I roused Bobby, and we drove back to the guest ranch, showered, and lay down for a short nap. Perhaps I slept. I heard flute music. With my eyes open I still heard it, and the tap-tap, tap-tap-tap of the chappeyekas.

*   *   *

Bobby and I drove from the north end of the Tucson Mountains all the way to Black Lizard Mountain and the Pascua village at the south end. The sun was just barely above the mountains to the east. Only a few people besides the ceremonial participants had gathered around the deer lodge. Anselmo Valencia greeted us, his black clothing grown dusty from all the exertion of leading everything. "Good morning! Have you eaten?"

He invited us into the deer lodge for some breakfast, and we all sat together at a picnic table in the cultural kitchen. Everyone was smiling; the cantoras, the women who sang the prayers during ceremonies, sang out "Good morning!" Tortillas, coffee and sweet bread went round. Anselmo ladled out some soup. He took a seat next to me. "This is the same soup my people served in the beginning—guacavaci. Chick peas, garlic, green beans, squash, carrots, onions, ears of corn, and meat."

He grinned at Bobby. "It may be old soup, but it's new soup, too, fresh this morning!"

"Good," I said, turning to Bobby. "We're both beginners, aren't we, Bobby?"

Soon all the tables had filled. The assembly quieted for prayers of thanksgiving delivered in Yaqui by Anselmo, and answered by all the other cultural participants who stood in their black regalia in a circle around our table. After breakfast, Anselmo deer-sang for all the little boys who wanted to deer-dance, and many others danced as well. The formal, rigorous part of the ceremonies over, everyone seemed to feel like dancing.

I stood behind Anselmo Valencia—later I was to learn that it was the place reserved only for his wife—as all the assembly gathered around the deer dancer, the pascolas, and Anselmo. Anselmo prayed for nearly an hour during which he mentioned every person by name, enumerating the trials and hardships each had endured during the year, or even during a lifetime.

After the prayer, he motioned me aside. "There are some people here who want to thank you." Before I could say, "What for?" he escorted me to the entrance of the deer lodge where the deer singers, the deer dancers and pascolas, the musicians all filed by, their hats off, and thanked me. Don Chico, the old harpist, hugged me and called me his sister. His words were so overwhelming, I started to cry. Anselmo handed me one of the pink crepe-paper roses that adorned the deer lodge.

"These represent the Seatica, the Enchanted Flower World. They are blessed after spending the night in the deer lodge." I laughed at this odd image of the roses sleeping together, and took it.

He walked away into the full sun. Outside the deer lodge all the people assembled in two lines, and a little girl in a white formal dress, crowned with a tiara of blue and white, ran the same path as the Gloria of the day before. She carried a statue of the Virgin into the Cristo Rey Church. The deer danced one last time, three songs were sung, and Yaqui Easter concluded with a big Good-bye Circle in which all the dancers and pascolas held their regalia in their arms, ordinary people again, ringed by at least a hundred onlookers. Everyone walked in a counterclock-wise circle, shook hands three times, and dispersed.

I did not want it to end. The ground was flecked with the confetti from the Gloria. I scooped some up and put it in a Kleenex. I walked over to the church and looked at the beautiful Madonna. I went back to the deer lodge. The big paper flowers had all disappeared.

Finally the last person had spoken to Anselmo, and he came over. That was what I wanted most. "Write me immediately. I'd like to know how you felt about this. Write and tell me when you will be coming." As I touched him, as we shook hands, I felt his strength and his otherworldliness, his transparency.

Once I was sleeping in the sun on a mountain in the Rockies when an eagle flew over me and brushed my face with the wind from his wings. It was an exquisite experience—it happened, the wings of an eagle, imagine! Yet it was only the wind of those beautiful wings, and I wondered then, too, did it happen? That's how it was when Anselmo Valencia touched me. Was he the shadow of my dream? Once touched, I did long from then on to stand next to him, to feel, if only for a moment, the wings of that touch.

5 ⧉ BURNING CANDLES

WHEN I BURN A CANDLE AS MY AUNT CHARMAINE TAUGHT, I OPEN ONE of the doors to the dream place. Charmaine liked to say that the practice of magic is nothing more than creating forms for our attention, whether the magic is high or low, white or dark. The catalyst in any case is our intention. Magic practiced for our personal gain, especially at the expense of others, leads us only deeper into the dark. Charmaine could have practiced dark magic, but because she was also a dreaming woman, her obligations, whatever her personal inclinations might have been, channeled her abilities as a magician into forms which served the dream that originated with Mother Earth.

After Yaqui Easter 1980, I went to Aunt Charmaine to enlist her help for Anselmo. She was the only one who could supervise such an undertaking. All I told Jack and the other group members about Anselmo Valencia was how strongly the Yaqui culture had impressed me, and that I had been invited by the people to return in June to teach art to the Yaqui children. I knew if I gave any hint about how Anselmo had affected me, Jack would not want me to go. "Give the Yaquis money," I could almost hear him say, "but don't give them your energy—we're your life."

When I went into the rear of the store, Aunt Charmaine greeted me with a red-and-green hummingbird candle. "Here. Burn this."

I kissed her on the cheek and thanked her, then asked, "What's this candle for, Aunt Charmaine?"

"It's for love."

"For me and Jack?"

"Just burn it, Heather." I told Charmaine about my trip to Yaqui and Anselmo Valencia's request. But little escaped Aunt Charmaine.

"You're in love with this chief, aren't you? Oh, boy! You have a real knack for courting danger, Heather, a real knack. Let me tell you something, sweetheart. This Anselmo has been calling you since you were a girl. I've felt him coming ever since I met you. I've tried to prevent it, but your chief is big, big medicine. I don't like the looks of this one bit. I know all about men with big medicine. They'll eat you up with love until you're just two dead eyes staring at the stars. Meantime they've taken your power and moved on to the next meal."

"I don't care, Aunt Charmaine," I blurted out. I was so full of emotion, and I'd wanted her to be excited for me. "I have to go there, I know it, I have to go, and if he wants to eat me up, I'm still going to go!"

"That's a foolish thing to say! A very foolish thing. Think about what I'm telling you—Anselmo Valencia is a sorcerer. I know this man, and you must not go with him, Heather. Do you hear me? Don't do anything for him. Stop before it's too late."

She put her arms around me. "I can't, Charmaine, I can't say no. I have to go with the chief. It's my destiny, my whole life destiny!"

"I know," Charmaine said ruefully. "You're going to go. I knew it. I had to warn you, Heather. You know, if I'd had someone who could have seen with clearer eyes than I had years ago, I'd still have gone with Julian, and damn anyone who told me otherwise. He was my destiny and I thought 'destiny' was the ultimate destination. You know," Aunt Charmaine said, her hands on my face, "Destiny isn't all there is. Destiny is just the path. I just wanted yours to be smooth. You're my daughter, after all!"

I laughed a little. Charmaine wiped my face with her finger-tips and handed me a Kleenex from the table. She prescribed for my own health the hummingbird candle, because humming-birds are love medicine, with instructions to spend an hour every day in prayer and meditation in front of the candle. The candle would guide me on the path of destiny.

"All right," she said, taking charge. "You need to send this woman away. Let's get started."

"Okay," I sniffed. "Charmaine, don't let anyone have more candle magic than me. I want this man!"

Charmaine's sternness evaporated and she chuckled and shook her head as she went to various jars, collecting incense for the candles. Aunt Charmaine was an acknowledged expert on candle magic and other aspects of Wiccan ceremonial arts. She had published a book on rune stones, and another, *The Magic Candle*, was an esoteric sourcebook on that subject. In her practice, Charmaine didn't focus on the future, as I did. Rather, she believed, she said, that the future was already present in the moment, and the point was to manipulate events in order to affect the future, whether one saw it, as I did, or not. The best way for me to change the future, she felt, was by drawing people to me and seeing to it that they became enchanted with themselves, so that what I desired was what they too desired, and the power of their wishes ultimately would change the future accordingly.

Aunt Charmaine assembled three small red candles and a large white one and told me to begin the night of the full moon and thereafter every night until the dark moon to perform a prayer ceremony while burning all four candles. She anointed each candle with some special oil. I was to light them in a particular order, and extinguish them in reverse order.

"You look carefully at how each candle burns, Heather, and pay attention to what the wax does. If a candle burns all the way down, just replace it. But on the night of the dark moon, stay with the candles until they are completely gone."

The first night, on the full moon, I went out into the backyard. I told my family and group members I was not to be disturbed because I would be divining for the future—which was true; I just wasn't divining the group's future. I lit the candles as Charmaine had instructed and entered a meditative state. I watched the candles melting as I did so; a feeling not unlike that of having a sleeping dream arose in me. Very soon I saw a Yaqui woman with rich curly hair and an extremely sensual face. She was older than I, perhaps in her early forties, striking, dark and voluptuous. It was Marcianna. She was waving to someone from the prow of a small fishing boat. She smiled at me with eyes that told me we were sisters, and therefore she would trust me to help her free herself from terrible anguish. Because I wanted to help her, she would tell me everything I needed to know.

The next day I went for a hike in Calico Canyon. The Mojave was starting to respond to the warm April weather, and there were wildflowers all over. I stopped to look at the beauty around me. Twenty feet away in a small clearing were many bleached bones. I walked over and stooped down to see what they were from: bighorn sheep. I picked up a rib bone. Weighing it in my hand I believed it was a female bighorn, and I took the bone with me. That night, after burning the candles and saying prayers, I slept with the bone on my altar in the bedroom. Marcianna came to me in a dream to tell me she wanted to be buried in the cemetery at Pascua. She must ultimately return to the land of her ancestors, so wherever I sent her, the path back to Yaqui must not be closed to her when it was her time to die. And, most critical, since I was sending her away, I must agree to stand by her parents should they sicken or die during her absence. To this request I readily agreed, as a real sister would.

As the moon waned toward darkness, night after night I lit the candles for Marcianna. I burned the hummingbird candle for myself, and from out of the red and green wax many Yaqui people found their way into my dreams, including Leoway, Anselmo's mother, who joked that I hadn't taken very good care of my previous husbands, but it would be different with Anselmo. I had a destiny with her people and her son, and with her, too. She would always be my comfort and friend.

The Story of Marcianna

The mother of Marcianna was as capricious a Yaqui as ever lived. Doña Mercedes had the dreaming medicine, and when she gave birth to identical twin girls, each inherited the power of her mother. Yaqui twins are formidable. One twin takes its power from the light world, the other from the dark. In Yaqui, it is said that if the dark twin does not die at birth, the mother will take its life herself before the dark power can develop in the world. Upon the death of the dark twin, the living twin is released to realize fully the wholeness of their combined power.

I learned this story many months after my ceremonies were completed. The great stories in Yaqui evolved because invisible forces come through the people the stories tell about, and in the case of Marcianna, some versions of her story had it that doña Mercedes killed the wrong twin at birth. In any case, Marcianna was no ordinary woman. From birth, she inspired jealousy in people. She was born the Saturday of the Gloria in Old Pascua. Anselmo was fourteen at the time, and recalled holding her when she was born. Anselmo married his first wife, Frances, who bore him nine children before she tired of being Anselmo's number-two wife—his first being the tribe itself. Fed up with waiting for him to treat her with the attention she thought she deserved, she divorced him in 1969, and Anselmo moved into the home of his mother, Leoway.

At that time Marcianna was the most beautiful woman anyone had ever seen in Yaqui. Such was her sensual appeal, and her own haughtiness, that she'd take for a lover any man she chose, and when she tired of him she'd discard him like a gum wrapper. In this way, she bore many children, all by different fathers. Anselmo was far too proud to let anyone know that his head was turned by Marcianna's beauty. He was also far too busy with the daunting enterprise of creating a new land base for his Yaqui nation. Instinctively, however, Marcianna understood his admiration, and increasingly she would appear by his side to assist in meeting the needs of the people. Where she was truly capricious about men, she was also a committed helper in Anselmo's efforts on behalf of the people.

They became lovers. The day of Eladio's birth, Marcianna walked through the chaparral, heavy with the child. She came to Leoway's door—her mother, doña Mercedes, had beaten her and thrown her out of the house for making a baby with Anselmo. The two lovers had broken a Yaqui taboo: in Yaqui, spiritual parents must not marry each other, and Marcianna and Anselmo had many times blessed children together, acting as the little ones' spiritual mother and father, baptizing them into the Yaqui way.

Marcianna stood at Leoway's door, calling Anselmo's name. He came out of the house, and the two disappeared. In a little while he returned to his mother's house as if nothing had happened. Even though Marcianna's water had broken and she urgently wanted Anselmo to take her to the hospital, Anselmo refused. Instead, he took her to her brother's house and left her there. He had to get home to continue preparations for the fiesta she had interrupted.

The following day, however, he did go to the hospital to see if the new baby was in fact his. When he saw little Eladio and held him, his heart went out to this child more than he had ever before let it. He could feel the special power of this son, and the child gladdened him because the ancestral powers shone in his eyes. He went to Marcianna and said he would marry her and make a home for her own children, because she had borne this son. But Marcianna surprised him. She was hurt and bitter that Anselmo had abandoned her, and the only way she would marry him now was if he swore he was marrying her for herself and not because she'd given birth to his child. Anselmo refused. Marcianna and her children did live with him and he did provide for them, but he never married her.

On Anselmo Valencia's joys there were always shadows, and despite his joy over his youngest son, tragedy was not a long way off. On San Juan's Day, June 24, 1970, Anselmo's eldest son, Giovanni, who was beloved by the entire tribe and who seemed destined to take the mantle of power from his father and lead the Yaqui people, died in a diving accident beneath a waterfall in Sabino Canyon. Many people believed that the death of their future leader was due to the bad medicine of the union of Anselmo and Marcianna.

As Eladio grew, Anselmo's other children, as well as Marcianna's, noticed how Anselmo doted on the boy. They resented Eladio's special treatment because they saw how Anselmo protected him, whereas he had been strict bringing up the rest of them.

*   *   *

I went to Yaqui early in June 1980, a week after I concluded my moon ceremonies. During the five weeks I taught art to the children, I would have brief talks with Anselmo between four-thirty and five-thirty each day for a few minutes, but, after I'd return to the guest ranch, we'd talk by phone each night.

On June 18 I was at the reservation, walking with some girls in the cemetery, when Josie, Anselmo's niece, started to cry. Her own parents had been killed in a car accident, and Anselmo and Marcianna had adopted and raised her. I asked Josie what was wrong, and she blurted out that her mother, Marcianna, had gone away without telling anyone, and she didn't know where or why.

That night Anselmo called to tell me that the woman he lived with had gone away for good. One by one, over the next few months, all of Marcianna's children, including Eladio, went to California to join her in her new life with her handsome young boyfriend in a house near the sea.

The owner of the Saguaro Vista Guest Ranch graciously made several casitas and the swimming pool available for me and the Yaqui children. I would drive down to Pascua to teach sixty boys and girls art. We'd eat lunch on the reservation, and then we'd pile everyone into vans and my rented Ford Bronco and drive up to the guest ranch, where I'd teach swimming.

I'd see Anselmo when I returned with the kids. Even as we stood chatting in his office or outside the tribal offices after five o'clock, people would come up to him and make requests or ask questions. He was impressed with my work with the children. I assumed he had heard about it from his own children, for his fourteen-year-old, Valerio, known to everyone as Toasty, was my boy Friday. If there was anything I needed, including discipline with the children, Toasty saw to it. But Eladio, also, who was then nine, had told me breathlessly one afternoon, "Heather, I want you to stay here. We really need you here. I'm going to ask my father to build you a house so you can live with us!" The only trouble I had with the children was over Eladio. A gifted child, he'd done a colorful mural on one of the walls of the room; later I found it shredded and defaced, such was the animosity toward him.

My heart was in my throat when Anselmo Valencia pulled up, late, in his white Buick Riviera. I watched him walk over to the trees beneath which I was sitting. He was two hours late—the radiator had overheated and he had to keep stopping to refill it. My heart fluttered so fast that when I replied, "Oh," an invisible bird suddenly leaped from my mouth.

"There's no time to lose," he said. "I have to tell you many things."

It was beautiful and serene beneath the eucalyptus of the guest ranch. It was summer, the air stirred with bees and humming-birds that chased the intoxicating scent of orange and lemon blossoms. The trees overhead whispered behind their new green hands, and I pointed to the old volcanic mountain to the west of us. "Can we go up there?" I asked.

"Yes, that is where we are going: Fire Mountain."

We got into the rented Bronco and drove out into the day which, at this late hour of the morning, had already turned everything solid into vapor. Everything even a little way down the road shimmered skyward in loose sheets of intense heat.

I wondered what he'd thought of the love poem I'd sent him, against my better judgment. I wondered if I'd been in his dreams as he was in mine during the two months since we'd first seen each other. I had again had no trouble securing Jack's approval for my "mission" to Yaqui as a teacher. From my understated report on the Easter ceremonies, everyone in the Gurdjieff group, including my husband, had been impressed that these ceremonies were of real significance to the awakening of the planet. Because Gurdjieff's teachings were nonexclusive, acknowledging that there are many paths leading to the same spiritual conclusion, Jack and his followers were pleased to have some small part in assisting the work of Anselmo Valencia and his people.

Anselmo was silent as we drove. He didn't betray whatever he was thinking. A few miles from the guest ranch he had me turn left, another mile of quiet, and then he said, "Turn here," pointing to the dirt road that ended at the all-faiths religious shrine at the base of Fire Mountain. I parked by a tin-roofed ramada. We went out onto one of the trails heading up into the mountains, Anselmo walking ahead, leading us up the steep path. He seemed oblivious to the heat, climbing briskly up the trail. I was determined to be unaffected myself by the shock waves of the June sun.

We reached a grouping of rocks partway up Fire Mountain and sat down. I noticed once more how finely proportioned he was, his small, quick form poised, despite the weather, as if he could be a mountain lion ready to spring. He was not even sweating as he looked out from under the black hat brim and the deep-sea-green glasses to the city of Tucson, which danced in quavering pulses and spasms all across the valley below us. Then he turned away from it.

"I'm going to tell you everything right now, beforehand. There's a great deal to present you with and I have little time.

"I've been waiting for you a long time, Heather, a very long time. You were supposed to be here sooner. I thought for sure you'd have gone to school at the university. What took you so long?" His smile faded. I wanted to say something, anything, but didn't know what.

"So, for a long time my struggles have been"—he paused a second before saying the word,—"alone. My strength is ebbing. I feel like this mountain did a long time ago. There is a fire within me, Heather, and I will explode if there is not an oasis for me to replenish my spirit. You are that sanctuary my spirit calls for.

"You have many special qualities I require to finish my duties for my people. You have the dreaming medicine—you have come through many lifetimes with the same dreaming magic as the women of my tribe. In this way, you are Yaqui. But because you have not been here, you are not worn down. Your dreaming power has not diminished. For centuries my people have been fighting, fighting the conquistadors, fighting the Mexicans, the Anglos, fighting the new ways that threaten our culture today. But your dreaming power is still untapped. The ancestors have called you here to help—the women have been teaching you in dreams and our elders know you. Your memory of this will awaken as you come with us."

I reached out and put my hand on his dark arm; he looked at it but kept speaking, and I withdrew it, half-regretful.

"My other wives wanted the ordinary world and were jealous of the many women dreamers who support me in my work for the culture. So there has been no peace or harmony in my home. You will bring peace and harmony to my home, you will bring it to my bedroom and to my children, too, because they feel who you are. You have no jealousy, Heather, because you know there is no woman with more power than you have. My daughters have seen you in dreaming, and you will be welcome.

"But I have to warn you that I am married to my people. You are my queen, but I will be married to you second—my people have always come first."

Anselmo Valencia turned his head and regarded the valley. He was at once matter-of-fact and full of emotion. For a moment I had trouble remembering, This is real, this is not a story he is telling me. When Anselmo spoke, I became aware again of the subtle paradox of his phrasing, which managed without drawing attention to itself to be both economical and otherworldly. It was a voice that had both great control and range. He talked at just the volume that made me lean ever so slightly toward him so I could hear what he said. This quality of making listeners come slightly toward him also set the mood for a remarkably dramatic presence, despite the apparent efficiency of speech and gesture. With Anselmo, everything minute became magnified, his magic was so intense and condensed. I had never met anyone before whose body, whose words had the same impact as if my entire being were designed and prepared to truly receive what he was imparting. As he spoke, I knew that what he would tell me was going to change everything radically for me from now on.

And yet I was by no means surprised. I always had known, now that I was there with him, that everything I had been living, all the confusion, the wonder and terror, was a preparation for what would come. Does Anselmo Valencia, the Dark Lord of my many years of dreaming, know how our story is going to end? I asked myself. And then I heard the warning of Aunt Charmaine about letting a man take your power. It's already too late, I thought. He knows my heart, and I know that what he tells me, for better or worse, is what I want to live.

He nodded as if he already knew, although he wanted to appear grateful. His teeth shone in a mysterious little crescent-moon smile. "We have done this together before—I think you remember it, Feather," he said, and he started to laugh. "You know, Heather," he said, emphasizing the "H," "there's no word in Yaqui or Spanish for your name, and many of my people do not speak English. What's your middle name?"

"Helen."

"Elena, then. Heather Feather Pluma Helen Elena—how's that for a good name?" We both laughed. He shook out a Camel cigarette and lit up. The sun slid from one lens of his glasses to the other as he looked toward me. "You are like a child. You forget all the pain and only remember the pleasure. This is the special quality of Pluma." I giggled involuntarily when he spoke of me like that, as if he were making up a story for my entertainment.

"You are amused by what I say," he said a little sharply, "but I have used up many people before you. What's ahead of you with me won't be easy. Anyone who has anything to offer my people, I have not hesitated to use—and I could use you," he said, dead serious, exhaling some smoke, "Pluma. But there would be too high a price to pay for using you up. So I won't. I promise you now I will not do that.

"Your love of our culture is in your soul, in the memory of your soul. If there is any meaning to the word 'love,' then you have a true love for us. Our culture has called you here. It is the lifeblood of my nation, and for many years the threads of our culture have been very tenuous. As the threads of the culture thin, so does the strength of my people. We Yaquis have been a very special ingredient in the composition of the planet. Who knows? In a few generations our culture may be just a memory that the young people will know only from stories their grandparents tell them. In that day in the future the Elders will say, 'In the days when the culture lived,' and it will be very sad, it hurts me to even say this, to think of our beautiful Yaqui ways displayed in museums and on *National Geographic* specials on TV.

"The culture lives—for now. You bring new strength. Wherever you make your altar, you attract the renewing forces of the Mother. So your union with me will bring new life to the people.

You are my renewal, and if I am renewed the culture will be renewed.

"It is funny, Pluma. I have always thought of myself as a deer singer, more than a leader, even though I know I am Achai, the father to my people. To myself I am a deer singer." He grinned like a big wild cat and leaned toward me with a conspiratorial look. "I'm the best damn deer singer!" We both laughed again.

"You used to draw a deer dance, when you were a girl. You used to ask Indians you knew if they recognized this dancer, if they knew what tribe it was. You were already fascinated by our ancient culture." I laughed and clapped my hands. Anselmo's knowledge of my past was amazing, but I was so enthralled I hardly could think to ask how he knew so much about me.

"This word 'culture' is not something you can just study from the outside. No one who is not *in* the culture can say what the culture means. This Yaqui culture of ours is critical to our Mother the Earth. It is Mother Earth we celebrate through living our culture—every living part of her. She is what we sing. The creatures of this desert"—Anselmo pointed with a jut of his chin and a wave of his hand at all the mountain around us—"are special beings. They live nowhere else. They would disappear if we did not sing them into being. But as the culture weakens there are fewer deer, fewer night eagles who carry the mysteries. So there will be fewer mysteries left on earth. We Yaquis have dreamed the mysteries for thousands and thousands of years. We have sung them and danced them since the beginning.

"To my people, if we are not Yaqui, if we are something else, we are not dead, but we are not exactly alive either. That is why my work is so important. My people know it is just for them I work, and to them I am a thousand percent Yaqui.

"But there is also a critical function the Yaqui people serve the entire planet. That is why so often white people come to Yaqui and are drawn there. They see the ceremonies, but they also see something else that is restored to them—like the story of the blind man's sight being restored in the Bible.

"Through the centuries, since the time of the Talking Tree, my people have had to struggle to survive. In the story, how difficult it would be for the people was foreseen. But can you imagine how hard it was for the people? We have in our recent past, from 1525 until the last Yaquis left the slave camps in Yucatan in 1927, four hundred years of experience of a special kind of group mind which in Anglo people has been buried, left unused because of the nature of Anglo history. Imagine fifty Yaqui men, women, and children in a cave in the mountains. Their survival against the foreigners depends on their ability to meditate together, to create something together, but if even one person does not totally and unconditionally believe that what they are creating together is real, the practice will fail and the people will be killed.

"That is the challenge for us. To believe that strongly in ourselves! And that is our tradition from adversity for four hundred years. That is a skill we have developed from our natural talent and our culture which has dreaming in it and the deer songs and deer dances."

I asked Anselmo to tell me about the Talking Tree. "What happened then, Anselmo, that changed things for the Yaqui?"

"The Yaqui are among the original children of Mother Earth. We have always been here," he said, tapping the rock he sat on. "The deer songs have, since the beginning of my people, kept the light worlds alive. These light worlds are the domain of our ancestors who came from the stars, before the beginning of our life with the Mother here. My ancestors call the Milky Way the Trail of Ashes because it was on that journey from the ancient place in the stars that they made countless campfires each night. When they came here they brought fire from their journey in the stars. Because of this star fire, our world here with the Mother is lighter. Have you ever noticed how on a dark night, when there is no moon, the light from one big star gives you something, if you know what to look for? The stars are the source of our faith, and without a connection to that star fire, things will become hopeless here.

"This Yaqui culture," Anselmo said, beginning his story, "is to earth what that one bright star is to the dark sky. It has been alive since the time of the great lizards, and before the time of the Talking Tree."

The Talking Tree

In Rio Yaqui, in Sonora, Mexico, between Torim and Vicam, is a mountain called Omtame, the Angry One, and on this mountain there was a tree that talked. Everyone knew it was talking about something important for the people to understand, but no one knew the language in which it was addressing the people. The circle of dreaming women got together and stood before the Talking Tree, and though they also could not comprehend its words, they understood that the Tree wished to speak to a young girl who was the purest and most innocent of Yaqui children.

The dreaming women worked together to search for the girl the Tree wanted. In dreams they searched their land around the rivers, in all the pueblos and high in the mountains. Finally, on the edge of the forest high in the Baca Tete, they found a young woman who was a healer and a dreamer and who had lived apart from others since the conception of her child.

The young mother refused to reveal how she had got with child, choosing instead to live alone in the forest where she raised her beautiful daughter. The child had thick long dark curly hair and coffee-colored skin that made her big eyes shine with the radiance of pure night skies. The dreaming women saw that the girl was beloved of all the animals. They knew this was the child the Tree wished to talk to. Her name was Itsceli—Girl Who Came from the Stars.

The dreaming women came for her in dreams that night, and the next morning her mother sent Itsceli out alone with her tortillas and cavim, or squashes, and told her she had to go to the council in Torim and tell them she would listen in the Tree.

The dreaming women took the girl to the Tree and Itsceli understood exactly what the Talking Tree was saying. It told her that the people must get ready; change was coming. No longer could the Yaqui eat only the squash and beans and corn and the gifts of the sea; now they must begin to eat the meat of Little Brother, the deer.

The deer was the most beautiful and graceful of all animals. In those days the people were smaller in stature. They were Surem, the Little People. Little Brother loved the people for their admiration of him, and he offered himself as a willing sacrifice in the hour of change. Little Brother would remind them of the time when their land was perfect and everyone had plenty of food and the leisure to dance and sing and play, to weave baskets and make clothing from feathers, shells, and the fibers of plants. The little deer would remind them always of this. But the meat of Little Brother would also prepare them for a change in the future when it would not be possible for the people to openly harvest the bounty from their Mother's fields. To ready themselves for this change, they would have to grow strong and grow taller. If they wanted to keep their beautiful Rio Yaqui, they would have to fight others who wanted to take their paradise garden away.

The Tree said that everyone could make a choice. Those who wished to remain small could go forever into the Enchanted Flower World and they would always stay as they were now—Surem, the small enchanted people, who would help the animals and plants.

Or they could choose to go into the sea, and those who did, the enchanted people of the sea would take. But if they wanted to remain in their paradise garden, they had to eat the meat of Little Brother. That would cause them to grow strong and tall; then they could fight and defend their land. There was a final dance in the full moon after the girl had repeated to the council all the Talking Tree had foretold. The people made their choices, and for the last time together they did a Circle Dance around the Talking Tree, knowing that for their beautiful land which was paradise, life was about to become different.

As they danced the last dance, the flowers grew more beautiful than they had ever grown, and bigger, and they all bloomed at once. Rainbows of bougainvillea petals, orchids, carpets of lavender water hyacinths that burst forth, little star-filled flowers so shy and tiny they were scarcely noticeable before, all filled the people with joy and awe. There were the orange poppies of the desert and a tree covered with necklaces of amethyst, and the one red flower like a rose, the sacred flower that bloomed on the Talking Tree itself—the paradise garden of the people had never been more glorious. Surrounded by such beauty they danced and danced. On the third day of the Circle Dance, on the third day of the full moon in the year of the Talking Tree, the people ended and went their different ways, those who chose the sea, the ones who chose the Enchanted Flower World, the ones who chose to grow big and become new in order to defend their land against what was coming.

The Tree had spoken of how the people had always had leaders in the communities but never one great chief. The Tree spoke of how there would be one great chief who would unite and teach them how to defend against those who would come to take their land.

Historically, during the time of the conquistadors the one great chief did arise, Anubuluctec, and he was the only one among the Yaquis to be the chief of all the clans. It was known among the dreaming women when he was born in Torim who he was and what he would do. And as instructed, the people who stayed behind placed dirt on their babies' tongues so they would love the sacred garden of their Mother Earth and be prepared to die for her. When the conquistadors arrived in Mexico and news of their coming spread, as the Talking Tree had foretold, Anubuluctec, the great leader, designed the V-shaped battle formations for which the Yaquis became famous. Using this V, the Yaquis would close in on the foreigners who had come to take their land. The aggressive Yaqui warriors beat their drums and the sound surrounded the enemy on all sides. It echoed from the mountains on the north to the mountains on the south and caused the soldiers great fear. Just as the drumbeats surrounded them, suddenly the V-shaped maneuver taught by Anubuluctec had caught the conquistadors in a vise.

However, the supply of soldiers seemed endless, they had guns, and their lust for Yaqui land was insatiable. Anubuluctec was killed in battle; the fight against the conquistadors became harder. The coyote warriors, the society of fighters, were forced to hide in the mountains and make only forays instead of battles against the enemy. The people began to flee from the Rio Yaqui valley into the hills, where there were many caves in which they took refuge. As the Mexican nation was formed, and the Mexicans in the nineteenth and twentieth centuries pursued the same aggression toward the Yaquis as their conquistador forebears had, the people would flee the pueblos and hide in the mountain caves that had sheltered generations of Yaqui fighters. The men would make forays down from their strongholds and retake the towns, the government forces would regarrison the pueblo, and on and on the fighting continued. Because no great unifying leader had ever replaced Anubuluctec, the last great chief of the people, the Yaquis had for four centuries been so conditioned to a state of war that cunning and fierceness became Yaqui traits.

When Mexican soldiers were able to capture Yaqui towns or settlements they would kill nursing babies by slamming their skulls against trees. They would take young boys and girls from the ages of three to seven to be sold to Mexican ranchers as servants. Able-bodied women and older boys were taken to slave camps in the Yucatan where there were plantations. All the able-bodied men over the age of thirteen were killed outright.

The trip to the slave camps was harrowing, and if the journey itself didn't take them, the malaria in the swamps killed them. And if the people survived the horrors of the elements and the trek to the Yucatan from Yaquiland, then their lives were spent as slaves. This slavery culminated the four centuries that ended, finally, in 1927 when the president of Mexico released all the Yaquis held in slave camps in the Yucatan and granted the Yaquis a reservation of land with a million acres bordered by sixty miles of coastal waters on the Sea of Cortez, and stretching eastward into the Baca Tete Mountains, extending as far north as the city of Guaymas and south to Obregón. Because of their indomitable spirit, the Yaquis have the only Indian reservation recognized by the Mexican government.

The Talking Tree foretold that the spirit of Anubuluctec would reappear on earth and lead the people out of the long time of destruction and chaos. When it returned, the Yaqui would have grown strong from the times of hardship, and when they were ready, the people would change again in a new way. That time had come, and though he himself did not tell me so, I inferred that Anselmo Valencia was the embodiment of that ancient spirit.

Anselmo stood and stretched, then sat back down. "Since the time of the Talking Tree," he said, "the Yaquis have had no heroes like Anubuluctec."

"Anselmo, aren't you a hero to your people?"

He laughed at the thought. "No, there are times when people

need heroes, but—I am more like a devil to them. My people say all kinds of things about me. I do what is necessary for my people and many do not understand what they see."

Looking at his enigmatic face, I had no doubt that was true. For a moment I wondered what I was about to get into. Was he warning me? I stared hard at him, but it didn't make him move or look directly at me.

"The people are my children, I am their Elder Father. I have children of my own, but my own children and my people are all the same as far as what I have been called by the Creator to do. I treat everyone of them the same—my enemies come to me and ask, and what they ask for I give. Among my children there are no distinctions, no playing favorites. Those who are loyal to me have parents and grandparents who are dreaming women. They are the ones who give life to our culture. But my enemies know that I will serve them equally, and because I do, my own children get angry. My sons and daughters do not understand why I should protect and care for my enemies with the same willingness I serve those who agree with me and care about me."

"Anselmo, the devil is a fallen angel." I mentioned to Anselmo Gurdjieff's book *All and Everything* in which Beelzebub's expulsion from the center of the universe was caused by arrogance, not evil. After thousands of years in earth time, Beelzebub is called back from exile in our solar system, but only after centuries and centuries of conscious labor. It was obvious, I said, that his people revered him. "You may be a devil like Beelzebub. You are struggling to do what only you can know is right. Throughout history the great leaders have always been the targets of jealousy."

Anselmo grinned. "If I'm the subject of jealous gossip, then I know I'm doing well. Jealousy is an excellent fuel for the fire of leadership. If no one is jealous of me, then I am having no effect on the world."

"I love you, Anselmo." I couldn't believe my ears—the words seemed to say themselves. I flushed, yet I was unable to stop. "I've always loved you."

He turned and for the first time I actually felt him looking directly into my eyes. "You know, in Yaqui there is no word for 'love.' The way Anglos use the word 'love' is quite foolish. It is a weak word, used much too freely by your society. Don't ever expect to hear that word from me."

"How do you say 'I love you' then in Yaqui?"

"I have just told you—there is no word for 'love.' "

"Well, what does a man tell a woman if she is to be his *wife?*"

"Enchi ne watta. It means something different. It means 'I want you.' And I do want you, Pluma. More than I want any other woman. But don't expect me to say 'I-love-you!' To me it is just meaningless.

"You are the one I prayed for, and you are the one the Creator has brought to me. You are my wife now. As my wife you will stand beside me and be the queen of my people. Because I am Achai, the Elder Father, you will be Illimala, the Little Mother to my people. They will honor and respect you, and I will honor and protect you.

"Do you know what it means, to be a queen?"

I said that it meant a woman owns her power and commands her environment.

"That is true. But in addition, among my people, the leaders are the ones who give the most. That is how it will always be for us—whatever anyone asks of us, we must give. The queen is always the giver."

"And who gives to the queen?" I joked, but Anselmo was serious.

"The queen has to be strong enough to give to herself, as well as to others. She must be the river and have no end. As my queen, you will have great freedom. You will have more freedom than any other Yaqui woman, but you will also need that freedom.

"And you have the right to ask things from me because you will stand beside me as the Little Mother of my people. Now you know what I require of you. It is your right to tell me what you require from me. Go ahead."

"All I want from you, Anselmo, is protection for me and my son."

"You have that already," he said. "You have had that all along, even before you came here. And I will always be near to protect you."

"And you will always have my love," I teased. Anselmo replied that it was all right if I wanted to insist on it. We were both in high spirits. I couldn't get over my bewilderment, and I wanted to ask more about how he knew so much about me, but he cut me off.

"Everything is known to those who are part of the tribal mind, Pluma. My people know you—they know I 'want you,' " he teased.

"For many reasons I want you with me. The little children of my people show me I have chosen well by the way they shine when they are with you. The way they smile and laugh—"

"Anselmo, I just don't know a better way to say what I feel about the children than to tell you I love them."

Anselmo said that the feelings a mother has for her children are the strongest feelings known to man. "The grown people of the society you come from, Pluma, when they tell their 'love' it is just a way to get people to like them. They speak from their desire or from their fear of being alone. But for a true man or woman, this so-called love is really nothing compared to what our Creator asks of us.

"My ancestors came here from the stars—and yours did, also. That is the scope of what is involved here, not just some personal feelings. When our people look up to the night sky, they will point to a star and say, 'That is my grandmother.' They have names for patterns in the stars, too. The deer is there. The coyote. The raven. The Big and Little Dippers we call great ollas and from these immense vessels we drink. From the stars we know who our ancestors are, and when we remember who the ancestors are, then we know ourselves."

Anselmo lit a cigarette. The smoke blew hard toward the city in the distance. He motioned with his hand toward the sky. "Your ancestors also came from the stars. I know when you were a child they talked to you and that many times you spoke with your ancient grandmother."

As a child I had often talked to the evening star, Venus. "Yes," Anselmo continued, and you used to sit in a tree and sing to her. You would sing to many stars."

I had in fact done just that, though I would not have known what to say about it then. And I had also often felt the presence of another person near at hand, though I could never find who it was when I turned around to look.

A wave of emotion swept through me. I felt I needed to be restrained because I was with Anselmo, but I was so happy and relieved, as if from the center of the eternal ocean where waves are pulled by the moon and stars and the holy forces of life itself, I was witnessing the wave that was the exact age of my life arriving, washing over me in Anselmo's voice, in the heat, in the desert. Its existence was true, and what I was in the dreaming place was at last seen also in the world, the new world which was the old world of the Yaqui. How small time is, I felt, and how the often agonizingly drawn-out hard times in my life were after all only personal, merely subjective. And all those years and years were nothing to the stars, nothing to the Yaqui, nothing to Anselmo.

Anselmo was looking at me with great kindness, smoking his cigarette, pausing to let me have the time. "Did you realize that your voice is enchanted?"

I said I did not. "So innocent!" he said, shaking his head. "Lucky for me! This will be a source of power for you as you wake up to it. It will help you bring the dreaming place closer to this place. You will be able to go into it the way some people enter another room. It is part of your art. Your love of art makes you understand the naturalness of all this. It is good to be an artist. My people are themselves artists of the natural. In the Anglo world, as in mine, the artists are with the earth and therefore they are with the culture, though for the Anglo artists they are grieving like lost orphans. They suffer for all Anglos who do not know where they belong since they have destroyed their birthright. That is why they fall in love, to use that word you like so much, with Indian ways.

"The future life of the planet is with people sensitive to Mother Earth and to the need for culture. Native culture is spiritual unity with all living beings. The Anglo way is more a life-style than culture. Culture is the result of the tribal or group mind. So maybe the Anglos' culture is TV, football, loud music. The Anglo success in the material world comes at great cost—it makes the Anglo children orphans, cut off, isolated from one another.

"As bad as the Anglo life-style has made life for many people, our Yaqui culture still lives. Of course my little Yaqui people want this for themselves now, too. It is very seductive to them, and very addictive, as bad as drugs. They do not see what it has done to the Anglo people. They do not see how it has destroyed the gift of the tribal mind.

"Perhaps the artists of the world will bring it to the attention of people everywhere. You know, there *is* a network of light. I cannot tell you how many Anglo people have come to see our ceremonies and who return later hungry for me to feed them more of the force they experience at Yaqui Easter. But I cannot help them. There is already too much to do for my own people. I belong to them.

"If you come with me, you must never forget this. My people come first. I am married first to them."

He told about the various members of his family, his grown children. His mother, Leoway, still spoke to him every night when he walked in the cementerio on Pascua, she still came to him in dreams. He spoke about an extraordinary dreaming woman who midwifed him, doña Carlotta, who was nearly one hundred. Both women, and many others, had known about me, and I would meet all of them, when it was time, and then there would be a healing for him because of it, and therefore for the people.

"Women are the real power in Yaqui. In your family in Las Vegas, you, too, are the real source of power, even though you may think it is your husband there who is the center of things. I tell you now, Heather, it is your own will that brought you to me. They have no choice in the face of your will, and you have chosen to come to Yaquiland.

"Women are the real power." He started to laugh. "I remember the last time my mother spanked me. Not just I, but all my people considered my mother a saint, but she wouldn't stand for anything that she thought was wrong. I had been spanking one of my own children, and Granny totally disapproved. I was fifty-two, but she grabbed me by the wrist and started to whip me to show me what it was like. Boy, she could pack a wallop! I was laughing so hard I had to go outside into the arroyo. I didn't want to get her any angrier!"

I told Anselmo that I had seen his mother many times in my dreams and of course she was the first Yaqui I'd met at Yaqui, when the teapot shone light on me. She was already like a mother and a friend to me. Anselmo asked after my own parents. "I haven't seen them in years, Anselmo, and to be honest, I hope I never see them again." I went on to explain the bad blood between my father and me, specifically the sexual abuse I'd suffered as a child at his hands.

"He was not your real father, Pluma."

"Of course he was," I retorted, immediately regretting my defensive tone and the intrusion of my father.

"No, you do not understand me—Achai, the Creator, is your real father. This man was not your real father, he only called himself your father. He is not welcome here. But your mother is. We must always honor the mother—no matter what."

As far as I was concerned, I replied, my mother was more guilty than my father was, because, being a woman, I expected her to protect me, her child. But Anselmo was adamant. "We must always honor the mother. And therefore we will welcome her."

"Anselmo, you just don't understand how it was."

"I think it is you, Heather, who does not understand. There is no blame. We break the blaming circle by honoring our mother. If there are problems, they are really problems between men and their Creator. Human men must protect those they are charged with protecting. Your father failed to do this; therefore he is not welcome among my people. But your mother I will welcome if she ever comes.

"As a woman, you have a greater capacity for understanding the impact of your feelings. You know more than a man does. But because of that your responsibility to Mother Earth is greater than a man's."

Anselmo looked at me cryptically. "The word 'sin' is very interesting. The word 'sin' wasn't here before the Anglos. My people didn't have sins, Heather. The Anglo people's sins are sins my people do not do. Sins of passion are nothing compared to the sins of the Anglos. This is not true of me. I am separate—I have sinned every way there is to sin, the way the Anglos sin and the way my people sin. That's why I take on everything.

"The sins of passion are nothing to our Creator. If you kill a man because you find him making love to the woman you want, this is nothing to the Creator. If you kill a man because he steals your horse, this is nothing to the Creator. But if you use your gift of power to take things away from others for the sport of it, and to make others less important than you, this is a grave sin. And that's what Anglos are good at—the sins of greed and power.

"The sins of the tribal people on the planet are simple sins. The more complex cultures sin more complexly. Before the Anglos came with their 'sin,' there was a Yaqui concept that certain people were dangerous, but that was more like characterizing plants. One flower might be sweet, another could poison. But that is not sin. There are important uses for poison.

"And in Yaqui, everything has a use and is put to use."

I had not seen how far the sun had traveled. Our shadows were now in front of us like spires on the shadow rocks. Looking at them, Anselmo said it was only fair he warn me about the darkness in him. He had been a drunk, a junkie, a real sewer rat, who, he assured me, had done everything bad there is to do. "None of my people has ever sunk any lower than I have, Heather. That's why I can be fair and give good counsel—there is no place I have not been, low or high.

"I have to warn you that you do not really know the darkness in me or how much of it there has been, and still is, within me. We are now being very 'loving' "—he turned from looking at our shadows to see my reaction to the word—"but I am utterly ruthless and as I told you, I will use anyone who is offered to me—and I will not think twice about it. You don't waste time trying to give back to something that has given to you. You take and eat it hungrily and if there's nothing left but a carcass, let the wind dry it and carry it away. It should be none of your concern.

"I could use you because you are so open and innocent. But I know if I do, I will not be finished here and I've been long here working. I don't want to have to do this anymore. If I use you up I will have to come back. So I will not use you, not because you are so wonderful to me but because I do not want to come back."

I said I understood how he meant that, and how important it was to love the work the Creator set for us to do. I asked him if he'd ever heard of Gurdjieff. Anselmo didn't think much of

Gurdjieff, not just because he'd never heard of him, he said with a twinkle in his eye. He said he didn't even need to know about Gurdjieff. What he could tell was that the people I was with in Las Vegas had only used me for my power—especially my husband, Jack. I related to him what Jack often told me and the other group members—that if we ever left the Work of remembering ourselves, we would be lost for good.

"No," Anselmo said. "This is totally wrong. *You* are the Work. Those people are nothing new." He moved his hands together as if turning tortillas. "They were the grist from the corn to make your masa with. Now they are dust.

"It will be very hard for you if you come here, Pluma. Please remember what I tell you—it will be unimaginably hard. Now you have people to wait on you, anything you can think of, you have only to want it and you can buy it. Your son can have a sports car, you can send him to the finest school. If you want to travel, you don't have to worry about your wallet. You have time to dream, time to create and time to be with Nature because you don't have to worry about how things happen in your world. If you come with me, I'm asking you to give up a great deal.

"I have all these children in my home, and no time. I have all these children and no money to build a new house just for you. In our world we will always have what we need, but we can't just run out to the shopping center and buy what we want. People will always be asking and we will have to find ways to get what *they* ask for.

"You are used to the easy life, and your health is delicate." I had mentioned nothing of my previous health to Anselmo, and I was startled, annoyed that he'd brought it up. I didn't want him to think I was frail, especially because I was feeling so vibrant. I had never felt more alive than when I was with the Yaqui children, even though my days went from 5:00 A.M. to midnight. He seemed to notice my vanity about it. A devilish bravado was in his look. "I can cure your health," he said with an air of boasting. "But it will always be delicate. Where I live, there's so much dust, you'll clean the house and when you finish, you'll look back and there'll be dust everywhere, following you.

"Consider this seriously. Take a year to think about it. I don't want you to come before that, because you have to realize what you're giving up to choose this."

He lit a cigarette and took several drags. As he looked out at the city, where the shadows of Fire Mountain were headed, he seemed to drift in thought. "I have told you all this at the beginning so you will not forget that this is not a story. I have told you because Anglo people cannot live without pretending their lives are some kind of story. If you come with me, you will have to leave the story of your old life. Your dreams were calling you here, to leave that story. People like to believe in endings. There is no ending here. If you give up everything and come with me, you will have to give up thinking like a character in a book. There is no happy ending in Yaqui. In Yaqui there is no sad ending. There is only *more*, because where I live the door opens between worlds, as you have felt many times without knowing why. Time is different for us because, for us who have been here since the beginning, the beginning never ends. The beginning is only hidden from those who are not part of the dreaming power, and everything is already known in the tribal mind. Everything.

"I do not like to repeat myself. With outsiders, the Yoris, when I talk to them about Yaqui, I will tell the same thing three times so that they may hear it, because the Yori mind is comforted by repetition. But with medicine people, it is not necessary. Nevertheless, I repeat my warning to you. You must think seriously about what you will have to give up to come with me.

"I am also asking you to please come with me."

He started to get up, then stopped. "Oh. One more thing. When I get up in the morning? I want you to make the bed first thing. Then cook my breakfast—two eggs over easy. One tortilla."

He stood up and stretched and while his arms were out to the sides I put my arms around him. He seemed startled by my embrace, and pleased. I let go. He was smiling, and then I followed him down the rocks and back onto the path toward the car. On the way he said, only half-joking, that I must follow behind him, now that I was his wife. I said, "We aren't married yet. I'm supposed to think for a year before I am your wife."

I said I had no doubts about what I wanted to do. And I knew what coming to Yaqui meant. Anselmo turned and stopped. "Yes, I know your decision. And I repeat for the final time, you do not know what it means. But I am glad your heart wants me. Very glad!" And then he continued walking ahead.

"So you have to walk behind me. That is how it is done in Yaqui!"

I thought he was teasing, so I teased back that I would not, I didn't like being behind a man, and I walked faster and came alongside him.

"Okay. You can walk beside me—but you cannot walk in front of me."

"Why not?" I asked, putting my arm around his waist.

"If you walk behind me, then you are protected. But if you walk in front of me, then you're saying you want to get away from me. At least if you walk beside me I can see who's making eyes at you!"

I have always loved the stars. As a girl I talked to them—they were the garden where my dream life grew to abundance. Whereas many young children talk to themselves or to an imaginary friend, I talked into the dark with happiness and confidence. As I grew into womanhood, I studied the stars, both their astronomical significance and the more ancient teachings of astrology. My mother, actually, was the one who got me interested in studying stars. For her it was amusement; her astrology magazines had the same smell as comic books and lay under the shelf of the sofa table along with the women's magazines and the picture magazines. But for me the stars were a matter of survival—without an intimate connection to them, even before I could put it into words, I knew that lacking their participation in my life, I would be doomed, cut off from the light I hungered for.

By the time I met Charmaine, I had long been studying astrological charts; Charmaine greatly valued the knowledge contained in the movements of the heavens. I had extracted from Anselmo during the Easter ceremonies his birth date and birth hour, and from this information Charmaine had cast his chart. Before I left to start teaching the Yaqui children in June, Aunt

Charmaine had warned me yet again about Anselmo Valencia. She warned me that the man was my destiny—and then she stopped, and I could sense the word "but" waiting in her throat. *"But,"* she feared, "if you make love to him before September, things will not go well. You can't avoid this man, Heather, but whatever else you do, let sex wait until September. Then your love will never diminish. Things will be good for you, *if* you wait until September."

It was only June, and we made love until sundown. It was June, and the orange trees were blooming. Their fragrance carried through the cooler vent and blew over our bodies with the damp, cool air. Afterward, we held hands, absolutely curled into one another.

We talked and made love, and the two acts became interchangeable. Whatever he said had the equivalent weight of lovemaking, and whenever he was within me, we were together in the dream place I had not known with him since my dreams in Missouri. He was the dream of the Dark Lord, and when we made love, I was in the exact location of the dream.

I told him about the fears of my aunt Charmaine. Anselmo listened, then said he had great respect for students of the stars, for his own people had long used the stars for guidance, as I would see, he hoped, when I came to live with him when it was time. As to the timing of our lovemaking, if I had not joined him he would have known that it was going to be a mistake for me to come and he would not have allowed it. "It is true that I could enchant you and use you till you were all gone. I have done it before many times.

"My people have a symbol, the Yaqui handshake over two crossed lances. If you don't know what it means, it looks like a sign of brotherhood. That's what a handshake means, right, to Anglo people? But to us it is a sign of cunning. You use brotherhood to survive. You put it in front of the weapons, and even if the weapons are broken or taken away, you always have the weapon of your cunning.

"When my people in the past have encountered a Yori with a special talent, we have invited this person to our camp and befriended them so we could study what it was they offered, and once we assimilated it, we'd kill them. If we couldn't really

understand what they had to offer, we'd let them stay and become enchanted prisoners. We'd use them till they dropped or
else see what the babies were like that they made with our
people. In this way sometimes new traits could be introduced
into the tribe."

He touched my face. "I want you for many reasons. Now I
have told you what we are like, and I am the most ruthless of all.
But you, too, have the same gift, though you are not ruthless.
You are sweet and open, but you also know enchantment. Look
what you've done to me! I am your slave of love.

"Your little old man."

"I'm not afraid of you, Anselmo. Long ago you enchanted
me, and I suppose you could use me up. I want to help you.
But more than anything I want to be with you. Thank God I
found you."

"You're welcome," he said and we rolled together, laughing.

When it was time for him to return to his home—his "brood"
were waiting for him, and he was a man of form and order and
dinner must not be late—I got into his old Buick and drove with
him to the end of the dirt road along the guest ranch. He drove
slowly, now and then casting a sly glance at my bare arms and
legs. "You won't be able to wear shorts and that top when you
come with me. Dresses only, please. My daughters wear pants
and it drives me crazy."

I was sitting far across the seat, next to the door. I wasn't sure
where the boundary between the private man and the public
man was, so I sat there.

"It's all right," he smiled. "Now we can be like this," and he
put his hand on my bare leg as soon as I settled in next to him,
the car traveling about two miles an hour, we were so reluctant
to let go.

6 ⊞ CROCODILE MOON

EVERYTHING I EXPERIENCED WAS PERMEATED WITH ANSELMO VALENCIA.
Before I left Yaqui to return to Las Vegas, one of the little boys
had pointed out the window of the room where we were working on an art project. The wind had brought a big dust devil. It
whirled in front of the window, tipping as if it were looking into
the building for something. The children grew quiet and became
unusually restrained. I heard "Achai" whispered among them.
They thought Anselmo Valencia was using one of his shapes to
come check on them.

Back in Las Vegas after my teaching ended in mid-July, I was
never far from news of Anselmo. Walking a dry wash in the
nearby desert, at dawn I found a pair of black sunglasses with
the same green lenses Anselmo wore, waiting for me on an
exposed root on the arroyo bank. I'd seen Anselmo at midnight,
after the Gurdjieff group meetings were over and the others
were in bed. I'd stand in the backyard and there above me would
be Anselmo in the moon, his face cameoed by the chiaroscuro of
all the seas and light pools of the moon. And emanating from his
face in three concentric rings of cloud and shimmer were the
faces of ancient Indian women. It looked almost as if the moon

had been scrimshawed with his likeness, dropped into the waters of the sky, and had such an impact that ripples of the ancient, timeless faces made their way in waves toward the edges of earth's horizon.

Doug and Marilyn, Jack, Bobby, and I were going to dinner at Pamplemousse, a French restaurant on Sahara Road. We were celebrating a decision to purchase a ranch in Carson City. We paused at a T intersection where the street stopped and we had to turn. Dead ahead I saw Anselmo Valencia in his black hat and sunglasses leaning against a tall cypress tree, smoking nonchalantly. He looked right into our car as it was waiting to make the turn.

"Who the hell is that?" Doug asked. He and Jack decided to make some detours through the adjacent neighborhood, in case someone was observing our car.

"I know who that is. I can feel who it is." Marilyn, who was very pregnant, flexed her fingers over her middle. "I can feel it in the baby. That's that chief Heather met in Tucson." Turning to me she said in my ear, as if she suddenly realized an indiscretion, "I feel him around you all the time, Heather."

At dinner conversation continued about whether it had been the Yaqui chief or just a man smoking, or whether someone was trying to set us up for a robbery. I said innocently that it wouldn't surprise me if it had been the chief. Who could say, I wondered aloud. He was, after all, a sorcerer . . .

The night before Anselmo was supposed to call me I was under the spell of the moon. Anselmo was more than a memory, more than a dream—he'd become an atmosphere I breathed. In the waning moon that night I saw something disturbing: Anselmo Valencia's face slowly transmuted, before my eyes, from his human face into the face of a reptile so prehistoric and cold the only thing I could compare it to was a crocodile's face. A shiver ran through me. Though it was very warm that night, a chill tightened all the way from my scalp to the pit of my stomach.

Anselmo reached me by phone the next day at Aunt Charmaine's shop, at an hour we'd agreed he would call. I asked him immediately if he'd been in Las Vegas recently. He said we would talk about it when he came the next day, because he needed to see me again, before I made my decision to come to Yaqui. He seemed excited and eager. I told him to meet me in the lobby of the Union Plaza Hotel. I offered to pick him up at the airport, but he said no, he didn't want to draw attention. He'd be there at the hotel.

When I got to the Union Plaza, Anselmo was waiting. I restrained myself till we got to the room he'd reserved; then we made love. I couldn't stop crying and I couldn't stop seeing his face wax and wane between the two different faces I'd seen in the moon. I told him how he had appeared to me so many times.

"Even my family sees you. The other night you were smoking in some cypress trees."

"Of course," Anselmo said matter-of-factly.

"You made quite an impression," I said, drying my cheeks. "People couldn't stop talking about 'that Yaqui chief' all during dinner!"

Anselmo nodded as if only vaguely interested. "I have to use what is most Yaqui to keep an eye on you." Then his mood changed. He turned on his side and looked at me, something he seldom did. "I don't want to lose you even when I know you are only an hour away by plane. Even that hour is too long a gap between us. So I use all that Nature has given me to spy on you!"

I touched his face. I told him I wanted to come to Yaqui when the planet Saturn was in a critical position to help turn my life toward the service of the Yaqui people. I said I hadn't listened the first time Aunt Charmaine advised me about favorable and unfavorable influences regarding love. This time he had to grant me some leeway. I proposed August 29 as the day I would leave Las Vegas for good. If this date was not acceptable to him, I wouldn't come at all—I just had to be either with Jack or with him. I couldn't have two husbands.

"Take it or leave it, Anselmo. That's the best I can offer."

Anselmo smiled gently and put his arms around me. "I take your offer, Pluma. Come August 29." He said that though it would be too soon for his children after Marcianna's departure, it could not be soon enough for him. I felt relieved and also very sad. I don't know if Anselmo realized my tears were for the Jack of Diamonds who had shared so much with me and had tried to

honor and love me, as imperfect as his expression had sometimes been.

Anselmo interrupted the wave of emotion that was pressing
down on my happiness. "Tell me what you want me to do with
the house so I can get it ready for when you come. Do you want
new paint?"

"I want to be the only woman in your life when I get there. I
want a new bed, one no one else has slept in but us. If there are
any of Marcianna's things left, they can't be in the house. I can't
think of anything else now. I'll see when I come. Just make sure
the place is clean."

Before Anselmo went back to Tucson, we drove over to a
goldsmith and had wedding rings designed. My ring was a gold
doe's head with three rubies in a rose tree next to the deer.
Anselmo's was a buck lying down in a rose garden with two
rubies. We worked out the design of these two rings with a
jeweler, and then Anselmo wanted to add a third band: an en-
gagement ring. He let me make the rendering. It was a simple
band, designed like an eye with a marquis-cut emerald that reminded me of the eye of the goddess Isis. It was to fit beneath
the ring of the doe.

If we held hands, Anselmo said, our rings would together
mean that the maso, vaso, and sewa (deer, grass, and flowers)
of the Enchanted Flower World were in our hands. "When you
come, I'm going to personally tutor you in Yaqui." I told him
Yaqui was a beautiful language; just the sound of it made me
happy.

"It sounds even better," he quipped, "when you know what
it means! Who was the Englishman who tutored the girl with the
funny accent?"

"Henry Higgins."

"I will be better than Henry Higgins. You can say you are
learning Yaqui from God himself!"

Anselmo went back to Tucson before sunset, again refusing
my offer to drive him to McCarran Airport. That night Jack took
me dancing at a nightclub; on the weekend he thought it would
be good for us to get away to San Diego. Jack's unsuspecting
attention made me feel guilty and sad, but I didn't want to think
about that. Every night I wrote to Anselmo. If I couldn't get to a

mailbox, I'd have the maid mail my letters. I even wrote to Anselmo when Jack took me to California. Anselmo's invective against the Anglo word "love" replayed in my mind many times. I was hungry for Anselmo—not for Jack. No matter how often I felt bad about being sneaky in order to achieve what I wanted— to be with my dream man, Anselmo Valencia—I could not also unremember the acts of possessiveness Jack had played out in the name of his obsessive "love" for me. But in the end it wasn't some sort of tally-sheet decision to stay or go. I had tried to please my mother and grandmother by marrying Allen Hunter; I had been too foolish to really see Chief George Allen. I had made myself sick, literally to death, because of the struggle to have to choose between the world of middle-class values and the world of dreaming. As always, the opportunities presented me were tests: choose the safe or the magical. And now it was again time to decide. There never was a question in my heart, and while my thinking mind certainly spun webs of confusion, I was going to trust that Anselmo and I would both want, love, and empower one another to do what was required for the service of his people, as well as to fulfill our personal destinies.

I stood out in the backyard and prayed to the Mother for a sign, to confirm whether what was in my heart was right, or if not, to indicate that I must stay with Jack and find a way to live with my present, restricted situation. Two days later, in the last week of August, I got my sign. I seldom kept up with the investments, futures markets, real estate, but I knew Doug and Jack were shrewdly accruing lots of money. There was occasionally concern voiced that silver ingots kept in the safe could make us a target for theft.

Jack abruptly decided he wanted the house secured electronically, with infrared alarm systems installed and telephone lines inspected. He hired someone from Los Angeles—but bringing the man to Las Vegas was like a covert government operation. Jack sent an acquaintance to escort the man from LAX, hired a private plane, paid the man enough money so he'd agree to being escorted and blindfolded once aboard and keep the blindfold on even when the private plane landed in Las Vegas, where it was met by one of Jack's cars which in turn took the man to our house. Only once inside was he allowed to take off his blindfold.

He seemed nonplussed but nevertheless cheerful about the inconvenience, and armed with his equipment, and the alfalfa-sprout-and-avocado sandwich I made him, he quickly went about his business. He declared the house clean of any surveillance bugs, efficiently installed the security system, took his handsome remuneration in cash, was blindfolded, and left.

It was obvious to me what the sign meant. If I wanted to get out of there, I had to *leave*. I knew I had no choice with Jack but to be clandestine and self-possessed. I had no doubt that if my husband thought I was romantically drawn to Anselmo Valencia, Bobby and I would be bound for the Bahamas or the South Pacific, for a "vacation" in a paradise emprisonment. So, that afternoon, I made a dentist's appointment for two days later, August 29. The night before we were to leave, I told Bobby I had waited till the last minute to tell him this, but I wanted to go live with Anselmo Valencia in Yaquiland. I also emphasized that I would not go if he wanted to stay in Las Vegas where he had a good life. I repeated Anselmo's warning to me—that he would be giving up material comfort and good schools. I wanted the decision to stay or leave to be his.

"Mom, let's go to Yaqui. I love the smile on your face. That's more important than anything else. Your eyes get shiny when you talk about it." He said he would miss the Jack of Diamonds, but he would miss my happiness more, and besides, the Jack of Diamonds was always playing his mind games with him. If Yaqui was what I wanted to be happy, that's what Bobby wanted, too.

At eleven the next morning, I parked my car in the long-term airport parking lot, bought two one-way tickets to Tucson, and with just one small bag we left Las Vegas.

Anselmo and his daughter Andrea met us at the airport. My welcoming was brief and muted because of family concerns—that same day Anselmo's son Roy had been in a car accident, so we all went straight from the airport to St. Mary's Hospital. Roy's broken jaw meant his mouth had to be wired, he had a mild concussion and a lot of aches and pains, but there were no internal injuries. While Anselmo was in Roy's room visiting, Andrea said simply, "Are you going to stay with my father?" I told her yes, I was. "Good," she said. "That will be good for him."

Andrea took Bobby with her, back to the reservation. Anselmo and I went to a bank, where Anselmo made a show of emptying his wallet of all his money except five dollars that he put in his pocket, and we opened a joint account in the names of Anselmo Valencia and Heather Valencia. We then drove to the motor vehicle department where I got an Arizona driver's license in the name Heather Valencia. All the legal and financial things he could think of we did then and there. And then we went to the reservation where Tina Molina had already drafted a letter to Jack, in excellent bureaucratese, stating that as of August 29, 1980, the Jack of Diamonds was hereby held blameless for any actions of Heather Valencia, including all debts incurred, and that from the above date, Anselmo Valencia was responsible for her and her son, Robert. Then Anselmo signed it, told Tina to get Jack's address from me, went into his office, came back out and said, "Let's go to your friend at the Saguaro Vista."

I admired his efficiency. "That's all there is to it," I observed, overwhelmed with both happiness and regret at how I'd left Jack, who'd by now realized Bobby and I were gone.

Anselmo looked at me. He knew what I was feeling. "There is no sadness," he chided gently, "in doing what has to be done. It is over with you and those people in Las Vegas. They got plenty of use from you, believe me, and you owe them nothing. You have come here free. Now let's go to your friend's."

I called the Saguaro Vista Guest Ranch and arranged to stay there. We were going to spend our nights at the guest ranch and drive to Yaqui each day for work, until the day in September when he would formally present me to the people of his tribe. Bobby stayed with Andrea in Pascua so that Anselmo and I could have a little honeymoon. We went back to the guest ranch. Mary, the owner, had left us cold cuts and mineral water in the refrigerator and a big bowl of grapes, pears, and nectarines on the table, but we went directly into the bedroom.

When we came back out it was dark. We ate hungrily and brought some pieces of fruit out by the pool. Anselmo told me he didn't trust water, but when I teased him and jumped into the water, he followed. We swam and dove, and Anselmo grabbed my arm and pulled me to him. We laughed, we kissed, swam some more and rolled out onto the side of the pool and lay looking up at the stars, holding each other's hands.

I can't remember, now, where we walked, where daylight met starlight, when sleep separated us from lovemaking. We weren't really on earth, somehow. I remember Anselmo told me many stories in bed, at the pool, or strolling. He told me about all the women in his life. He talked about the Second World War and dancing at the USO in Cleveland, Ohio. I told him my mother was from Cleveland, and he guessed he'd met her, then, because he had danced with every girl at the Cleveland USO. I had my hair in a long braid, put up on my head, and a lacy white dress with a high ruffled collar. Anselmo liked it that I looked so English. He told me about a girl he'd met in Italy during the final days of the War. They'd been lovers, and the young woman had gotten pregnant. That had been hard, since her parents were devout Catholics, and heartbreaking—she died in childbirth. He said he believed I was the reincarnation of that Italian girl who was so beautiful and young, that she'd come back to him, her sorrow transformed.

Anselmo told me his plans for his people in Mexico, how one day he hoped we would go to live there the kind of life he had always dreamed of—a small adobe house which he would build. A garden in the fertile jungle valley where water hyacinth and bamboo proliferate, the bella sombra trees . . . our sanctuary in the place called Torim in Rio Yaqui, Sonora, where his ancestors had always been. He would make masks and carve the instruments of the deer dance out of huchaco wood, I would paint and draw the jungle, its creatures, and the Yaqui legends. He would write the history of his people so that the young would always remember the trail markers on the pathway from the stars. He told me that Torim was the source of his dream call.

"Anselmo, when I was a girl we were together all the time inside a mountain, before the Aztecs ruled. I stopped having that dream, but now I'd like to really go there with you."

Anselmo said that we could go there this minute. He took me to the pool and had us both get in. Yaquis meditate by emptying their thoughts into a bowl of water. We could use the pool as a

big bowl. Anselmo recited certain syllables of a prayer in Yaqui
about the Seatica, the Enchanted World. We were under brighter
stars with no city lights, the desert plush with long grasses.
Deep and majestic the night birds called. The largest owls I've
ever seen hooted in the long-boughed trees above the river the
pool had become. We passed through the midnight air to a hill
north of Torim in the time before the Mexican garrisons, before
the desert came and the wild, lush jungle disappeared. We could
see small campfires scattered on the floor of that fertile Rio Yaqui
valley. He took me to the hole in the earth where you enter the
Dark Flower World and ask for your power. "We must go in
person together someday," Anselmo said in a whisper. I didn't
know where I was when he said it to me.

I was very full of this experience when the dawn broke. It was
as if I had become clear light and spread throughout time from
the dream place in Torim to the pool at the Saguaro Vista. Together, Anselmo and I extended in all directions. His memories
were mine, his eyes were mine, just as I was at his disposal. I
had the uncanny awareness that together we overlapped each
other's mind, and that the key to this mutual access was the
mixing of Anselmo's greater knowledge and my receptivity and
unquestioning trust.

Then Monday came. We arrived at his house on Vahcom
Street. I couldn't help smiling, as I remembered George Allen's
prediction: Anselmo's house was made of adobe blocks. Then
my smile disappeared. I stood at the threshold looking in,
shocked. The living room carpet was a checkerboard of black
and red. The ceiling was orange, the walls turquoise, red, and
green. I felt both horror and amazement. Anselmo was very
patient, however. He took me through the entire house, the rest
of which he and his children had already painted white for me.
He was not interested in hiding anything. The wallboard had
been broken through in many places so you could see from one
room to the next. In some places the exterior wall had also been
gouged away. One wall bore a graffito with Anselmo's name.
The furniture was worn through, except for the bed, which as
I'd requested, was brand-new, the plastic still on the mattress.

I spent the next few weeks putting the house together. Everyone but me loved the brightly colored living room walls, so I
lived with them, too. But I did prevail over the carpet and had it
replaced—not as easy a task as it appeared: Anselmo had glued
the checkerboard carpet with a mysterious, perhaps roofing,
adhesive that took hours to remove. With our limited funds I
bought bedding, towels, dishes, stocked the kitchen with food.
One of the first things I did was install a new altar in our bedroom, a four-foot-long one that I charged with all manner of
crystals, feathers, statues, shells, photos that became objects to
focus on during prayers.

Though we weren't going to sleep in the house, we did make
meals there. My first night eating supper in the house, Bombi,
Anselmo's fourteen-year-old niece, made "spaghetti soup," my
first initiation into the meals Anselmo was used to eating. The
soup was water, a can of condensed tomato soup, salt, pepper,
garlic, onions, and burned spaghetti noodles. Everyone else
seemed to like it, but it was so thin and starchy I couldn't help
making a face, which I instantly regretted. I didn't want to hurt
Bombi's feelings, but it was too late. Anselmo, looking down at
the table as he spoke, said coolly, "In this house, we never
criticize the cooks. We are grateful for what we have. Everyone
here has seen times when food has been scarce. So we don't
waste what's put before us."

There, at the old dinner table, as many of Anselmo's children
and grandchildren assembled for my first night with part of his
family, I saw the romance exit like the cool breezes after summer
rain. Over the years, most of his family lived with us—for all
kinds of reasons, from marital problems to financial ones.
Anselmo took care of them. He didn't always like it, but he did
it. Often he warned me to stay out of the way of his children's
problems and let them work things out themselves, which was
not always easily done in a small house with as many as seventeen occupants at a time. Which was the very unglamorous side
of the dream: real people with real problems. I wondered if I was
up to it, me, a relative stranger after all, yet not. Me, an Anglo,
yet not. An Indian, yet not. Anselmo's true love . . . I had to
believe that part of the dream was unassailable. In any case,

there within his family, I had taken my dream, which was also his dream, I fervently believed, and was about to see if it could take root in the dirt house George Allen had foreseen.

At the table were Connie, who was thirty, and her children, Chana and Jesse; Andrea, who was twenty-one; Roy, twenty-two; Moi, twenty-three; Anselmo's granddaughter Becky, who was seven; my son, Bobby; Anselmo's young son, Valerio, whom everyone called Toasty, fourteen; and two nieces who had lived with Anselmo since their parents died, Josie, twelve, and Bombi, fourteen. Anselmo's youngest son, Eladio, was in California with Marcianna. Margie, Becky's mother, wasn't there that evening either. Still, this was a houseful.

The boys came back to the Saguaro Vista to stay with us that Monday night, and after that, we alternated girls and boys until Yaqui Recognition Day, September 18, the day commemorating the proclamation of the Yaqui people's recognition by the U.S. government as a legal tribe, something Anselmo had worked for tirelessly for twenty years. Recognition Day coincided with the dedication of the Cristo Rey Church bell tower, for which Anselmo and I had donated the bricks. It was also the fiesta day celebrating the annual autumn harvest. To these celebrations was added my presentation to the people as Anselmo's wife. Until I was formally presented, Anselmo would not allow us to "live" on Yaqui, although we worked as hard and as late in the evening as if we did live there already.

"Put on your second-most beautiful dress," Anselmo said. "Not as beautiful as for Sabada Gloria and the Creator, but beautiful for the people." I took my green gauze dress from the closet at the Saguaro Vista and put it on. I put red, orange, and fuchsia silk hibiscus in my hair and the special necklace made by Victor Coochwytewa, the Hopi corn man and chief, and Gilbert Vasquez, the Mayan medicine man and artist. It was a harvest necklace made of spiny oyster shells and fossilized walrus tusks with a big golden stalk of corn suspended from the center. For thousands of years such necklaces connected with the harvest and bounty had been worn by women to honor the earth.

Anselmo put on his red silk shirt, black pants, and the Swiss loafers I'd personally bought him when I saw the worn-out black plastic shoes he'd hobbled himself with. Gilbert Vasquez had also made for Anselmo a Yaqui handshake bolo tie, the right hand of which was modeled after Anselmo's. When Yaquis shake hands, they do not clasp as Yoris do. They extend their right hand and touch palms together. Anselmo put on his hat and the red horse-hair hatband, regarded himself a moment, and then we took our luggage and put it into the Buick. For the last time we drove from the guest ranch to Pascua.

At the ceremonies, I sat in front of the Cristo Rey Church next to Anselmo, who introduced me to the local and state dignitaries, and to Senator Dennis DeConcini and Representative Morris Udall, both of whom had helped Anselmo obtain legal recognition of the Yaquis as a tribe. To both Yaqui and Anglo dignitaries, as well as any of his own people who came to shake hands, Anselmo introduced me as his wife.

For the past two weeks the men of the dance committee and the tribal council had feverishly been mixing mortar and laying up the blocks and scaffolds to complete the bell tower next to the church. Now that it was done and hung with the old bell, we dug a hole in front of it and put a time capsule into the ground. Each tribal council member placed something into it. Anselmo and I put in a deer head and regalia. Brimming with its mementos both nostalgic and symbolic, the capsule was sealed, dirt was thrown into the hole, and the speeches were made.

At the end of it all, Anselmo took the microphone. "If anyone here wonders who the lady in green is, this is Heather Valencia, my wife." There was applause and cheers of "All right!" Anselmo grinned. Friends and well-wishers shook his hand.

Anselmo brought a folding chair and we walked down to the deer lodge for deer dances and pascola dances. Anselmo led the deer singing. It was the first time I'd heard him sing since Easter. Despite the heat in the lodge, and my nervousness, I immediately felt calm. The smell of the tortillas cooking, smoke from the mesquite fires, bright haze of the late afternoon, kids running and laughing: within the deer lodge, this sanctuary, this workroom of the spirit, I knew then I had married it all, that it was for the better, and that a great enterprise was upon me involving more than just my own personal happiness. I took a deep breath and let it out.

*   *   *

In the Yaqui story of Creation, Earth was a little mother in darkness. Our Grandfather Sun talked with her. She asked him how she looked, for she could only *feel*. She told him to put light on her so she could see how she looked.

Grandfather said, "No." He knew if she could see herself in all her luxuriant splendor, she would become vain and difficult, impossible to satisfy. But she cajoled and badgered him until he agreed to her wish. So the first light came to Earth on the first morning to illuminate her magnificence. And Little Earth Mother said, "It's too bright! Take it away! It's too bright."

That is a very Yaqui story.

The word "Yaqui" is not what the people call themselves. "Yoeme" is their word for who they are. "Yaqui" itself means a certain kind of stubbornness.

If you make a decision in Yaqui, you walk with it. You might wake up one morning and say, "This child of mine does not fit well with the other children. The others are good; this one is bad. This one I will send to its aunt's house." And the child disappears from the mother. That is Yaqui.

You never know what the rattlesnake will do. Will there be no venom in his bite? Will he let you pass by undisturbed? Ninety-nine days in a row, respectful of him, you peacefully go your way. And then one day he strikes you because he has had enough of seeing you. Maybe he never strikes. That is Yaqui.

In Yaqui, many times, many times they will just watch you. They will be watching who you are, what you are. If you are arrogant and act with bravado, they will just watch, perhaps with quiet disdain, but nothing will happen besides your bravado. But one day like a pebble in the boot your arrogance becomes too bothersome. They have seen how you are. Or you may have come to Yaqui lighthearted and humble—you will also be watched, perhaps with idle curiosity, perhaps with disdain that you are so unprepared for battle. Because of your weakness, whatever it may be, it may be they will kill you; or then again, maybe not.

Caprice is at the heart of what is Yaqui. And Anselmo Valencia, who is the Elder Father and like a god to his people, is like the lightning that strikes at whim. For sorcery is ever in the moment; there is no prescription for alchemy except the perfect chemistry of the moment. Anselmo's Yaqui capriciousness rendered him perfectly suited for the sorcery of the moment. With it each day he created the world anew.

The evening of my presentation there was a dance on the basketball court. Anselmo loved to dance, and people cleared away for our first dance together, a slow waltz. After that we did a polka, and then Anselmo and his daughter Margie danced the cumbia. Then he and I danced to some wild Papago chicken scratch music.

Between dances I caught my breath. From across the basketball court an enormous Indian man from a northern tribe drunkenly wove toward me. He came to a rickety, reeling halt and stood hovering in front of me. Then, as if to take me as his partner in the dance, he reached his arms toward my shoulders and in one movement pulled my blouse down, exposing my breasts. Anselmo stood impassively next to me. He didn't lift a finger. Within seconds members of the chappeyeka society threw the big man to the ground, wrestled his hands behind his back, then lifted him onto his feet. They escorted him off the dance ground and into the darkness of the parking lot.

I was so stunned with the swiftness of it all that all I could think of was a joke. "Well, Tori, at least nobody saw my knees." But I wondered to myself about the incident—was I there alone? Why hadn't Anselmo himself acted? "Let's dance," was all he said. I set the considerations aside and Anselmo and I danced in spite of everything, or because of it.

I went into the kitchen to make Anselmo his eggs as he liked them, over easy. I was standing at the stove watching the yolks firm, when I felt something behind me. My heart leaped. I turned—it was Anselmo, expressionless. He had ghost-walked up behind me. I grabbed and held him, I was so startled. He remained expressionless, just stood there woodenly.

When we had lived at the guest ranch he would hold my hand, he would be loving, passionate, romantic. Suddenly he was stiff: "Yaquis don't touch each other in public, Heather," he said.

"Anselmo," I said, "this is not public, this is my kitchen."

"I don't want the children to see you do that. They won't understand."

"Well, then they need to understand. You need to teach your children it is appropriate to express affection."

"It's not Yaqui. I told you—there won't be any touching in public." And then he walked out the door and went to work at his office. I thought of my tendency to get in over my head. I stopped before I worked myself into a worry. Everything was new, Yaqui was where I had all my life been headed, and my husband was the man with whom I had come to live this destiny.

The next morning I walked from the shower to our bedroom with the bath towel wrapped around me and began dressing in front of Anselmo.

"Don't ever do that again," he said coldly.

"Do what?"

"You just wore a towel in the hall!"

"So what? This is my home."

"Yaqui women never show their bodies," he said sternly.

"Anselmo, this is a gigantic towel."

"I want you to never be seen by these children unless you are wearing a skirt that is at least two inches below your knees. I want you always to be seen dressed by the people of this household."

I said okay, but it was very disturbing to me. I tried a different tack. I sat down by him on the bed and put my arm around his neck and kissed him. "You liked seeing me at the Saguaro Vista."

Again he made no response but became stiff and indifferent. He wouldn't even look to acknowledge me. "I told you," he said, now bending down to put his shoes on. "Life as a Yaqui is hard."

"I'll never be Yaqui, Anselmo. I don't believe in this. I don't believe this is really Yaqui. I think the Catholics taught your women to be like this. What did women wear before the Catholics came?" Little shell necklaces that came down to here, Anselmo said, starting to smile as he pointed below where a woman's breasts would be, and short grass skirts.

"There!" I said, "that answers it. In the old religion women were natural. Why is this such a big deal?"

"Because today is today, and this is the glue that holds the culture together now and it's very important that you represent what is traditional Yaqui. I want it that way, and I want you to be the most Yaqui woman of all. If you have trouble, act happy. No gossiping. No complaining. You are here to express joy, even in ordinary household chores. So you do the cooking, cleaning, laundry better than has ever been done, as a model for the people to see."

"Anselmo, if you have a mule, a racehorse and a winged horse, they all do different things, but it's a terrible violation of the winged horse to have it yoked and harnessed for plowing a field, and I, my dear, am a winged horse and I am not going to plow fields!"

Anselmo laughed. "Okay. Just make my breakfast. My daughters can cook the rest. Do my laundry—*please* do my laundry. And please sit on my bed and look beautiful."

Anselmo invited his grown children to come over to the house for dinner one night after my presentation to the people. Seventeen of us crammed around the table. To this assembly Anselmo announced, "This is Heather. She is my wife. Anyone who doesn't like it, that's too bad." I assumed this was meant as a joke, but nobody laughed. With that said, in front of his children he turned to me and said, "You have the right to have a new house, if this one doesn't suit you."

It was obvious there was going to be no time or resources for Anselmo to make a new house for me, even if I'd asked for one. So I just said, "This house will do fine, Anselmo. But I would like to have my own bathroom. That's all that's missing."

"All right. We'll have a new bathroom. Anyone have any questions?"

Nobody did, and that was that.

Anselmo got up every day at sunrise and was at the tribal office by eight. During the days at first I busied myself with running the house. I wasn't used to keeping house myself— Anselmo had been right. I didn't realize how hard it would be to give up material comforts and luxuries. But added to how little money we had was now the lack of privacy. By afternoon most days I had to get out of the house. Anselmo's daughters all watched TV, and I couldn't stand to be in the house when the soap operas went on.

To escape, I began to get involved in tribal activities—there was no shortage of needs to meet. I spent a good deal of time visiting sick people in the local hospitals. Early on I tried to help raise money, since it was expensive to hold the fiestas that went on nearly every weekend to mourn the recently dead and celebrate the anniversaries of those who had died a year earlier. Anselmo always administered rites of the dead, and we took to ceremonies flowers, food, candles, offerings of money for the family of the deceased. Week after week, the fiestas and ceremonies for the dead and the reborn required such preparations, and my part of it, like many other Yaquis', was to help allay the costs of doing what was at the heart of the culture: to give our services willingly to the people. Anselmo tried to make sure the cultural participants who performed roles and sang as part of the deer dances were reimbursed for travel and other expenses they incurred in their efforts to fulfill cultural obligations.

To raise funds I organized Psychic Fairs which were held in the tribal chambers. I enlisted friends and volunteers from on and off the reservation to conduct tarot, palm, and aura readings, along with numerological, astrological, and handwriting analyses for anyone willing to pay an admission. Sometimes I would take private readings for pay in order to help Anselmo, with his small salary as a tribal official, meet cultural obligations that had to be paid for. It was going to be a never-ending cycle, raising and spending money, raising and spending, on and on. It became as familiar as the dust that covered everything, as Anselmo had said, just when things looked tidy . . .

I began to feel increasingly isolated. I started to take long walks out in the desert. Sometimes I wondered what kind of an adventure I had gotten myself into, and my thoughts would return to the warnings of Aunt Charmaine about how Indian men would take everything I offered and not look back once it was used up.

*   *   *

Everything that happened to me in Yaqui, all that I witnessed and over time came to understand, was presented to me in a hurry, my first year. In fact, Anselmo had said it himself—on Fire Mountain he did actually tell me everything. And he was right about stories, which have a beginning, middle, and end. I should have known—I was about to say, I should have known that a culture for whom the dead live can have no story with a beginning, middle, and end. But what is truer is that for me the door to my freedom opened much sooner than I could have imagined, but because I was so in love with Anselmo, so attracted to him as a master of magic and as a soulmate, I wasn't paying attention when the door stood wide before me to my own freedom. Even early on, within my first weeks, the door was opening, opening. I noticed increasingly that the hinges strained and creaked with the load.

"No yakking with the ladies. You are the queen now. If you feel unhappy, you must not show it. My people must see joyousness and beauty, the way you do. That is why you must wear traditional clothing—skirts and blouses, no pants. The people will see how they can be when they embrace the culture, when they are strong with it as you are."

When Anselmo talked like this to me, it reminded me of Gurdjieff Work. I was glad I had had an introduction to it, for I did want to live present in the moment, awake within the dream of life. Like Gurdjieff, Anselmo was causing me to confront myself through the friction he created with his dos and don'ts. Once I made a mental list of some of them. Not that he had such a list; far from it. But he expected a great deal from me, and sometimes, almost from the beginning on, the magic seemed far, the petty all too near.

Do not talk gossip to other women.
Do not speak badly of anyone.
Do not tell anyone you have problems—problems are what others will bring to you; you are the queen. Always be happy.
Never let your knees show. No pants or shorts. Never wear white. Red and pink are best for fiestas. Black for wakes and funerals. Mirrors deflect dark spirits. (I had a dress from India with little mirrors all over it, and this was an especially good

black dress to wear at wakes of ones who had died violent deaths. Anselmo said it would deflect their anguish away from me, as well as their questions from the other side, since my light was very bright in the other world and the dead would be attracted to me.)

Sing to snakes. Talk to them until they talk back, then send them away from where there are people.

Don't talk to other men unless accompanied by one of his daughters. No hugging or touching other men. No teaching other men; women, okay.

Don't look a Yaqui directly in the eye.

Despite my desire, as Anselmo had said, to be the Work, the pettiness, I realized, was part of me. And yet I did not feel despairing of the dream and the magic. It was just much harder than I'd seen it would be. But I did as Anselmo asked. I followed his requests. And grew lonely. I had no friends to talk to, except Anselmo, and he was gone all day. I got in the habit of visiting Leoway's grave and talking to her. I began to understand why my husband liked to come to be with the dead. Who else could he tell his troubles to, as the chief?

But as soon as he came home, we would eat—usually Andrea or Bombi would cook meals—and then walk together to the cemetery, where he would tell me stories of the old days or of his people and their legends.

"Heather, is this for you?" Andrea said, handing me a special-delivery letter that was addressed to me in care of the Yaqui Tribe, Tucson. "It came to my house. The postman was looking for you, but I signed for it. I didn't think you'd want anyone to track you down." I thanked her, and set it aside. I knew whom it was from, and I waited until Anselmo came home to read the Jack of Diamonds' letter. He'd had several weeks to react to my departure. Anselmo's business letter had alerted him to where I was. I tried to hide my agitation as I read it, then handed it to Anselmo for his reaction.

If he'd meant to upset me, Jack had succeeded. The letter was full of Jack's fury at me for having left him, the group, and the Work. He'd had an ominous dream, he wrote, in which I was sinking into the earth. My face reminded him of John Lennon's album with Yoko Ono's picture on the cover. As I sank, Jack said, Anselmo Valencia was walking over me, pressing me down into the dirt. Jack volunteered his dire interpretation of this dream: Anselmo was using up my flesh and bones to sustain his own life, and as long as I fulfilled his needs he would take care of me, but as soon as I asserted my own needs, Anselmo would misuse me, he'd have to trample me.

I was infuriated by Jack's transparent ploy to manipulate me by invoking dreaming. He knew, as did I, of a particular card reading I had done on behalf of the group members in 1977, the upshot of which was that a proposed outing to a northern Nevada lake should be abandoned—I saw in the reading an injury to a child on the trip. Jack had been outraged. He charged that I was using my skill as a diviner to scare and gain power over certain adult members of the group. I vehemently denied that. If reading cards was something for my pleasure and benefit, I said, I'd long ago have given it up for an easier form of self-indulgence. The group went on the trip. Not a child, but one of the adults was badly injured water skiing. My original resentment at the accusation came back and flushed my cheeks.

But there was more in the letter than Jack's bitterness toward me. Of greater concern to both me and Anselmo were veiled threats about Bobby. If I didn't come to my senses and return to my spiritual family and friends in Las Vegas, Jack seemed to promise, not only would I lose my chance to wake up; because I had left him and the group in the manner that I had, the magic that had attended and protected me would desert me, and, Jack warned, he foresaw serious, perhaps even fatal, injury coming Bobby's way.

"What should I do, Anselmo? I think Jack wants to hurt Bobby to get even with me."

"Give me the letter, Heather. Nothing is going to happen to Bobby. He is protected here. We're going to go visit Granny."

We took the letter to the cemetery. For a long time Anselmo said prayers in Yaqui. Then he scooped out a hole in Leoway's grave, inserted the letter, covered it, and we walked away.

A week or so later, at bedtime, I noticed Bobby was acting subdued. I asked him if anything was the matter. At first he pretended he was just tired, but then as an afterthought he added that it was probably just from playing football that afternoon. One of the big Yaqui kids had really pounded him with a tackle. I tucked him in and kissed him good night.

Bobby was very slow in getting up the next morning and coming to breakfast. Anselmo's daughter Mui was helping with breakfast and said she'd go see what was keeping him. "Heather, you better come here." We went into Bobby's and Toasty's room. Bobby was standing in his pajama bottoms. I turned him around—there was a melon-sized swelling on his backbone.

I was shocked. At first I was disappointed that Anselmo had not protected Bobby. But that was only a superficial, even vain reaction. Anselmo did not operate like a cartoon magician. And neither did the Jack of Diamonds, whose effectiveness I had underestimated. What surprised me most was that Jack was that destructive.

"Anselmo, why would Jack do this, and to Bobby?"

Anselmo paused a few seconds before answering. "He realized it was *you* who tricked him. He thought he was controlling you. You left quickly and quietly, like a coyote, and he didn't appreciate seeing he was the rabbit. A pretty big rabbit, I'd say."

Bobby and I cracked up at the image of Jack as a large rabbit. Anselmo grinned at his own joke.

"Anselmo," I asked, "do you think it was just an accident?" Anselmo shrugged. But I answered myself. "No. No it wasn't. I know Jack's hand was in this."

Anselmo said Bobby was going to be all right. He assured me he would deflect any negative magic threatening Bobby.

"Bobby, why didn't you tell me you got hurt?"

Bobby shrugged, just the way Anselmo would have, an understated, minimal expression that seemed magnified because it was so subtle. "Because I was playing football." Bobby knew I hated football. It had ruined his father's, Al's, shoulder when, among his many football injuries, he'd been tackled hard.

"I was standing out back when some guys called me over because Eddie Soto was running all over their team and they wanted me to help turn the tide." Eddie Soto was four or five years older than Bobby, well-muscled from weight training, and a ferocious athlete.

"I didn't even have sneakers. I was in my hiking boots, but I forgot. So I went over and Eddie was all pumped up and crazy, nobody could stop him. When we got the ball, they tossed it to me and here comes Eddie, BAM! God, he just creamed me from the side, my foot got caught in the dirt on something and I went down all twisted. Man, he just popped me."

"You're okay," Anselmo said to him. "Let's go over to St. Mary's and get you fixed up."

"You know who I mean, Anselmo? That big kid Eddie?"

Anselmo laughed and nodded. Though he didn't lift a hand, at that moment it became clear to me how close he and Bobby were—it was as if he *had* rested his hand gently on Bobby's neck. The three of us got into Anselmo's white Buick and Anselmo drove to the hospital, where they drained the fluid, but X-rays showed a vertebra was completely destroyed.

I had to know. One day when I was visiting Leoway's grave— because the loneliness didn't abate, and I still occasionally talked to her in desperation for friendship—I dug into the dirt to find the letter. I wanted to see some evidence that Anselmo could do what I had believed he could do. The letter was gone. I fished all around for it, and then I started laughing. I remembered a dream I'd had not long before about Leoway's grave. Leoway often came to me and did silly things. In the dream her grave was going up and down and music was coming from it as if it were a calliope in the center of a merry-go-round. Leoway knew how to diffuse that which was too serious. You can never laugh too much, she told me. Otherwise you will be overcome with how hard it is, you will forget your place and lose your way.

I told Anselmo I was going to have my lawyer in Las Vegas take care of filing divorce papers from my legal marriage with Jack, even though I *felt* divorced from Jack the moment I left him, even though I *felt* married to Anselmo now that I had acted on my wish to be with him. Within a month the Jack of Diamonds had signed the necessary documents and I was of- ficially free, so to speak. I didn't want trouble from my past, and it was clear to me that Anselmo expected me to be on an equal footing with him. And that meant sidestepping any traps, self-made or otherwise, that could have dragged me away from the present moment, with all its hardships and all its freedom.

In bed Anselmo asked if I'd have been attracted to him if he had been a lowlife bum, because that was what he'd been, he said. "This great chief Anselmo Valencia Tori who dazzles you with his charm and good looks, I was once nothing but a bum. So would you have wanted me?"

"No!" I hooted. "Never! I love you because this is who you are. I want a magician, nothing else!" He grinned with all his teeth showing and bit my neck.

7 ▣ DAY OF THE SKULL

THERE ARE CERTAIN DAYS WHEN THE WALL BETWEEN WORLDS BECOMES so porous that the living and the dead can pass through without being subject to the laws of space or time. In the autumn are two such days: the first weekend in October marks the celebration of the Day of the Skull, and November 2 celebrates the Day of the Dead. At no other time of the year is the power of the tribal consciousness more effective than on the Day of the Skull.

Just as at Easter when the deer dance occurs at an intersection between the ancient Yaqui religion and the newer Catholic one, the Day of the Skull marks a special spot on the map of Yaqui life. Anselmo and I drove a few hours south of Pascua to join in the pilgrimage to the Church of San Francisco in Magdelena, Sonora, to honor San Francisco. Yaqui ritual is the source of both the people's unity and their identity. But it is also a special focus for many powerful Yaqui magicians. On the Day of the Skull not only do pilgrims come to pay homage to the Catholic saints; the greatest deer singers from the coast and mountains, the forest and farmlands, the million acres that constitute the Yaqui lands of Mexico, journey to Magdelena to test their powers, and, in

certain cases, to *take* power from those they vanquish. For the
Day of the Skull is also a battle of magicians.

Magdelena is a pretty colonial town built on a square around
a small cathedral-like church. It dates from the 1600s and repre-
sents the Spanish-Mexican style of that era at its sweetest and
best. The other buildings around the square are all high-walled
white adobe with adjoining arched porticoes. The shops are under the boughs of the big trees and beneath the long deep
porches of the buildings, and at this festival time there are also
booths that sell all kinds of crafts and foods on the sidewalks and
under the ramadas.

We parked Anselmo's pickup truck on the square and strolled
among clothing vendors, vendors of sundries, dishes, and furniture. There were vendors of fine-made leather goods, pottery
ranging from little birds to chimeneas that looked like enormous
Aladdin lamps. I watched the tacero cut fresh meat for tacos.
The air was permeated with the smell of mesquite smoke. At
many booths women flipped tortillas on oil-drum stoves. Up
and down the alleys formed by their booths, the merchants of
woven goods and blankets haggled or stood about enticing tourists and pilgrims to "come to me, you need many of these beautiful blankets." There were herb stands with remedios for serious
diseases like diabetes, as well as for common ailments like colds,
toothaches, headaches. One man with a big boa loosely coiled
around his neck and shoulders sold ground rattlesnake meat, a
cure for arthritis.

The blanket vendors did a brisk business; Anselmo and I pur-
chased a number of brightly colored, tightly woven cotton blankets for Christmas presents for his family. The man selling them
to us finished the sale and got back on his battery-powered
bullhorn, screeching his very lowest prices, "the more you buy
the cheaper they are." We went to a stand selling straw hats,
and Anselmo tried on and then bought a new hat—the straw hat
and a bright bandanna are signature Yaqui apparel, along with,
of course, the tire-soled huaraches everyone wears who doesn't
want sneakers or running shoes. We passed by the vendors of
ladies' blouses, and the jewelry stands, both of which were popular with Yaqui women, who buy the peasant blouses and em-

broider them with colorful flowers. A hallmark of Yaqui women is the solid-gold crescent earrings bought from the jewelry vendors. Many come to Magdelena just to buy them, for depending on their size, they signify wealth and status.

The most amazing things for sale, though, were the dark brown, monk-like habits woven of light cotton. I asked Anselmo about these saints' garments. He told me the Yaquis come to Magdelena often to make a manda, or promise, and they will place the garment on the one for whom they are making the manda. If a child has been ill, or a friend or relative, the sponsor of the manda can make offerings to the saint on behalf of the one wearing the garment. This person must wear the garb of the saint until the wearing and washing of it deteriorate the cloth; at that point the saint will have thoroughly intervened on their behalf and they will be healed.

Happy music pumped and surged up and down the square where the full, delicious sun waltzed easily. At the cantinas people sat at tin card tables and watched the carnival, drinking a Tecate or the syrupy Pepsis and Frescas that are everywhere during these festivals.

In front of the church is a large round fountain. For the festival it had been filled with fresh water, its scrubbed tiles gleaming. Well-groomed roses lined the green lawn. As we walked toward the river beneath the big shade trees, we first heard, then watched it surge and curve with gentle sensuality here, with pristine piety there. Under the abundant willows along the Magdelena River south of the plaza many of my husband's people had camped. They had come from Rio Yaqui on the train, courtesy of the Mexican government, which offered free transportation to the festival, to make their annual pilgrimage to see the wooden effigy of San Francisco de Xavier.

Old Mexican widows in black attended the saint, bringing fresh-cut flowers each day, removing the glass candles when they had burned down. These old women scraped the wax from the saint's alcove each day. By the next day's end, the wax would accumulate again in big multicolored landscapes built up of drops and tears of blue, green, yellow, red, and white. Like the beautiful residue of candle wax, the Catholic proceedings are layered upon an ancient religion practiced for thousands of years when the people would come to this spot to honor the return of the dead. Anselmo told me that his people honor San Francisco for one overriding reason: he had appeared to the people there, in Magdelena, on the Day of the Skull when the dead cross over from the Summerland where they live and exert their timeless influence on the living. On just such a Day of the Skull over three hundred years ago, San Francisco de Xavier appeared in dreams to the people, and the Yaquis took it as a sign to revere him.

The church was built over a place sacred to the people, a place where the wall between worlds had a kind of gate in it and communication with the ancestors was easy. Though the town is Mexican, the festival days are more Yaqui than Mexican. To the Yaquis, the Mexicans are Indians whose ancestors did not resist the invaders. Therefore, to the Yaquis, the Mexicans are weak; this mixture of Indian and Spanish blood, Anselmo believed, was also a dangerous one, making for a streak of cruelty in the ensuing generations.

Anselmo's niece Julia from Lencho in Rio Yaqui brought her little son Julio to Anselmo, intercepting us as we headed toward the church. Julia asked him to place the habit of the saint on the boy, for he was a twin, born, as twins often are, sickly. Julio's twin brother had recently died, and so his mother was anxious about the well-being of her remaining son. Julio screamed and squirmed when Anselmo put the scratchy garment over his small head—Julia and I could barely hold him down. For the next three years on the Day of the Skull Anselmo would offer prayers and candles to the saint on behalf of this child.

We filed along through the sanctuary of the church to leave offerings and candles, Anselmo ahead of me. The effigy of San Francisco de Xavier was painted, and where the pilgrims had touched his beard and feet over and over, the paint had worn off, revealing the dark-brown grain stained by the hands of millions of worshipers. On his brown frock were dozens of milagros—little silver and gold effigies of legs, arms, torsos, heads, along with small color snapshots of beloved sick ones. I wondered to myself what the ladies who cleaned San Francisco did with these charms, after the fiesta.

Anselmo kissed the saint's feet and crossed himself, then lifted the saint by his wooden head and laid him back down. Twice more Anselmo lifted the statue about six inches from its bier. I merely touched San Francisco's feet, crossed myself and was about to move along, when Anselmo whispered that I must also raise the saint by his head.

"My people are watching to see what will happen. They must find out whether your sins are too heavy to raise the saint. Go ahead, lift him. If you don't people will think you're a witch. It will be all right," he said, urging me with a jut of his chin toward the saint. Politely I cut back in line and, with some apprehension, hoisted San Francisco. To my relief I could see daylight under his head. We walked out quietly.

We entered the vending zone occupied by the purveyors of saints. From these vendors a person could buy a doll of San Francisco in any size, from a glass cube with a tiny doll in it to a glass sarcophagus the size of a coffee table with a life-sized mannequin within. This aspect of the fiesta seemed to me too far from the ancient Yaqui culture. When I laughingly asked Anselmo how he thought our living room would look with a big saint in it, he wasn't amused. He reminded me that now the culture must incorporate whatever helps keep the ancient ceremonies alive.

"Anselmo, I thought you disliked the priests and their religion."

"What I do not like is the rifts so many of the priests created among my people. But unity is unity, Heather. Don't be surprised because I love this one saint. My prayers and offerings to San Francisco are real."

We walked nearly to the river, where a wonderful, small merry-go-round was rising and falling like the fate of the world. How sweetly it cycled around, up and down, and how happy the children were, throwing back their heads, some looking prim and serious, others scared, dumbfounded as the ponies and music sauntered along. And how happy the parents who were revived by the joy of their children! Now that I was the queen of his people, I supposed it would be inappropriate for me to take a ride . . . I stood there, close to Anselmo, longing.

We walked away from the carousel toward one of the river

camps. We were going to pay a visit to the musician Alcario. The river was very beautiful in the afternoon sun. The water gleamed and divided into rivulets that made eye-shaped islands. Anselmo ran and splashed with me into the shallows of the water, under the thick and handsome foliage, a hundred kinds of birds swooping and swinging from bank to bank, bough to bough. We doused each other, playing like that, then returned to the plaza side of the Magdelena River, emerging onto the bank near a hand-hewn, stone swimming hole, bounded on the town side by a heavy earthen berm. I put my arms out like a tightrope walker and walked the narrow dirt path. From the corner of my vision sunlight flashed on the churning and boy-infested swimming hole below us. There was something odd in the water. I stopped, I looked down. My arms came down to my sides. A man was floating facedown in the water, his black hair and water-soaked shirt bobbing violently from the waves generated by the kids in their cutoff jeans. He turned like a pinwheel, at first grotesquely fast from the roiling of the boys beating the water in their play.

The kids pulled to one side of the swimming hole, lost in some game of keep-away, and as they drew away, the man slowed, slowed, turning counterclockwise. As he completed a revolution, his upside-down body reminded me of Leonardo da Vinci's man inscribed in a circle, arms and legs softly reaching out.

I knew he was dead, yet I couldn't comprehend the strangeness of seeing the children playing, so in my mind I fixed it that he must have been part of their game of hold-your-breath. You're overreacting, I told myself. They are all playing water games. In a moment the kids are going to come over and tap his shoulder, or else he is waiting for the right moment to launch his submarine sneak attack when he will dart underwater and grab an armful of boys' legs, pulling them under into his water-monster lair . . . Before my eyes the young man's face and torso turned over instead, facing skyward. His dark curls washed softly across his forehead like water weeds. Then he was floating totally faceup, his arms out to the side, like any young man in his twenties, enjoying, on a beautiful day in autumn, water and warm sun. He was well-formed; beneath his khaki boxer shorts his brown legs glistened with beads of water.

Back came the young Yaqui boys, splashing and shouting, and the handsome young man, buffeted with the kids' waves, turned over to face the bottom again.

"Anselmo—that man—"

"He is dead," Anselmo said.

"Why doesn't somebody take his body out of the river? Someone should—"

"Heather, my people will do nothing with the body. It is the body of a Mexican." And Anselmo walked down the berm and toward the plaza, leaving me to choose to go with him or stay in my own circle of sunlight and disbelief.

Anselmo seldom left my side. He was both proud of me and concerned that some of his enemies might try to kidnap me. When he told me that, I laughed apprehensively. Who would want to kidnap me? I had an uncertain feeling again—was I being set up for his uses, without my consent? I didn't like his ruthlessness. If I, like the young Mexican, should float into one of the Magdelena River's God's eyes, would he walk away? Anselmo! He could talk about the brotherhood of light across the planet, regardless of races, and an hour later be mean and spiteful as an angry rattler. But then that was Yaqui, that was Anselmo, and that was me, stunned by the beauty of death's impeccable jeweled movement, hungry for both magic and the magic of reality.

The anxiety I had felt even before the trip took its toll. Exhausted, I asked Anselmo if we could sit down. He took me over to a chair next to an herbalist's booth, then disappeared among the neighboring stalls. There was a rustling and shifting of boxes behind the curandera's counter. I stood up and peered over it. A dark Indian woman with remarkably wild, curly hair stood facing me. I gasped, then laughed. Seeing she'd startled me, the woman smiled apologetically and said hello in Spanish, her face filled with perfect white teeth and huge, fiery brown eyes. Though she was not young anymore, her figure full from bearing children, still she had an irrepressible vitality.

"I am Olga Ruiz," she said. "I am Elena," I replied in tentative

Spanish. She grabbed my hand and pulled me into an embrace, then commenced chattering, going about her business, talking away in Spanish and Yaqui, I stumbling like a dancer with a limp to keep up with her words, lapsing into English when Spanish and Yaqui failed me. But Olga Ruiz seemed to understand everything she needed to know about me, and, after she had opened a few plastic bags and done some rearranging, she came out with another folding chair and sat with me.

Anselmo returned just then. "Buenas dias, Anselmo," Olga said warmly.

"I've got some clothes for you," Anselmo told her, and he went to the truck, which was parked nearby at the edge of the plaza. As he walked across the plaza in his jeans and jeans jacket, with his new straw hat, stopping here and there to talk to people, Olga leaned toward me.

"Your husband is a dark tiger. You are a bear, and you are to the dark tiger a beautiful semululukit." She repeated it slowly a few times, "semululukit," but it was not her words that I comprehended—rather, I quickly received a "feeling," a sort of impression that registered in me as the image of a bear which was also a something-else.

Olga Ruiz talked to me with a knowing look in her eye. "You are good at disguises, Elena," Olga Ruiz said, her eyes burning, "but you still need protection for the journey." She had taken my hands and was holding them. I had felt warmth but hadn't realized what it was from.

As soon as Anselmo walked over with a paper sack in his arm, replying to someone over his shoulder, I felt nervous again. He sat on his haunches and translated directly what Olga said, and what I said. Olga grinned widely and we both laughed at the same time, letting Anselmo continue as if we were at the UN.

Olga was a Mayo Indian, "Like my stepfather, Saturnino," Anselmo said. Actually, the Mayo were Yaqui, too, but took their name from the place where they lived, the Rio Mayo, which was south of Rio Yaqui. Olga spent the four seasons in different parts of Mexico, gathering the herbs for the medicines she sold. Clearly, that day in Magdelena, she had the best selection and the most interesting assemblage of cures in the plaza.

"Olga," I asked her, "do you have any hummingbird medicine?" She looked at Anselmo a moment, and went behind her stall. Olga emerged from around the side with a small, pressed, brilliant hummingbird cadaver partially wrapped with red ribbon and sealed in Saran Wrap. "Semululukit," she said, indicating the hummingbird. I clapped my hands. My aunt Charmaine had asked many times to keep an eye out for this special love medicine. I had never seen one before. Olga gestured with her chin toward the little bird as she talked rapidly.

"Nobody knows more about love medicine than Olga," Anselmo said. He described to me, as Olga punctuated what he said with occasional interjections, the correct way to use the hummingbird medicine. You put the bird in a little cradle with pink roses and nautilus shells and lavender, talk to the bird: "You are so beautiful, you are the one who is loved from the deepest part of the heart. Go to the one I want and be for me in their heart and let them know how I feel." Every day you do that. "Go into the heart I love, and let them feel what I am feeling, bring back from their heart." If the one you love feels as you do, then you keep that little bird and if anything goes wrong you talk to the little bird and tell it to come alive again in the heart of your love so it may be good between lovers.

I embraced Olga Ruiz. She pressed something into my hand— just as Quashnay had done years ago in Kansas—a necklace of fish and rattlesnake bones, dyed red, with red and black beads between the bones. There was also a small peach pit, intricately carved into the shape of a monkey. If I wore the necklace as a bracelet tonight, Olga said, no dark magician could steal my power. Also, Anselmo added, I was to be sure to brew the contents of a cellophane package of herbs into a tea and drink it first thing tomorrow

I thought it was to prevent getting dysentery. "No," Anselmo laughed, "it's not for that. Just drink it tomorrow and it will help.

"Come on, Pluma. The sun is going down. There is much to do before the ceremony tonight, many people to talk to. Let's go get some supper." I hugged Olga good-bye, and she patted me on the shoulder. I turned and waved. I wasn't sure if Olga's smile was a rueful one, but the anxiety started to build again, and I wondered what was in store for me.

*   *   *

Just as dark was falling we seated ourselves at a red-Formica-and-chrome table against the far end of El Tecolote restaurant, a huge place with a big arched portico over the entrance and an indoor aviary at the northeast end. Anselmo ordered bistek ranchero for both of us because Tecolote had the best steak in town.

During dinner Anselmo told me in a quiet, offhand way, between bites of food, and without looking at me, that tonight he would perform deer singing against Prieto Saturnino, a man from the mountains who had come to Magdelena specifically to challenge him.

"Who is he, Anselmo?"

"He's a magician." Anselmo wiped up the last of his beans with a piece of tortilla. He leaned back in his chair and rubbed his face. "This battle tonight has been a long time coming. We meet in Magdelena because this is neutral turf, and both of us may call equally upon the ancestors to aid us."

"Is this Saturnino someone who's dangerous, or is this part of the festivities?"

"This is serious business, Pluma. Prieto Saturnino has conquered the Dark Flower World through his trickery. When we sing tonight it will be like magician's high-stakes poker—winner take all."

"What decides who wins and loses, Selmo?"

"That is up to the spectators to an extent, what they feel, and the subtle exchanges between the singers and the onlookers—both seen and unseen."

"So who will win?" I asked, concerned that this was sounding ominous.

He flashed his biggest crocodile grin, said, "Who do you think, Pluma?" and pulled out his after-dinner cigarette and lit it.

After supper I had a disjointed awareness of myself walking around double. I thought it was the heaviness of the food, or exposure to the sun all day, the long drive, my nervousness the first time here as Anselmo's wife, meeting people who deferred to me because now I was another part of Anselmo's strange magic. Perhaps their deference loosened a second self from where she was moored inside of me.

"You!" someone yelled, "Yes, you. I know you!" I turned

around, thinking I was talking to myself in English, but there was another person behind us, a short Yaqui woman with a moon face and long braid around her head. The whites of her eyes were enormous; they shone all the way around the irises. I stood there dumbstruck. Her presence was like something prehistoric, as if she had emerged from a crack in the sidewalk or dropped down on wings from the jungle top.

"Oh!" the woman laughed, "you look just like a little doll!" and she laid her palm on my chest. "A little doll." She giggled, turned around, and walked down the street, still chortling to herself.

"Who was *that?*" I asked Anselmo.

"My cousin Lola from Eloy." Eloy, a cotton-growing area north of Tucson, was where Anselmo had spent part of his childhood. There is still a Yaqui settlement there.

"That's one intense lady," I remarked.

"Lola likes you. She thinks you're a little doll."

"So I heard," I said, reassured by his confident tone, although my heart was still beating fast. But if Lola liked me, then why did I have this sudden foreboding? I was certain Lola practiced dark magic. I realized once more that even if Anselmo was right beside me, the practitioners of magic are not stopped by the limits of the physical world. My supper did a little flip, like a doll tossed in the air. The impression wouldn't leave me: Lola with bits of fabric of the clothes I had on, making a dolly likeness of me, placing it on her altar, and, like that, there I found myself voodooed in Magdelena. Maybe all this was *her* dream-weaving.

We made the rounds of the many pickups parked, as was ours, right on the plaza, and paid respects to those recently arrived since our last circuit. We headed toward the church. As we walked, Anselmo instructed me. "Sit as close to me tonight as you can. If anything happens, you must take care of it immediately." What did he think might happen? I asked him.

"Just watch carefully, Pluma, especially my regalia and jewelry. Anything of mine that might break, watch it like a hawk and don't let anything get away."

Night had filled the little river valley. By nine o'clock the plaza where we waited seemed the only lighted place in the world. Elsewhere around Magdelena the earth was totally black. When all of the participants in the deer sing were assembled, I took my position as Anselmo instructed, sitting slightly behind and to his left. I regarded the dark singer from the Baca Tete Mountains near Vicam, Prieto Saturnino, who had challenged Anselmo. Prieto Saturnino wore a purple scarf covered with an intricate pattern of rhinestones. Around his neck bobbed the traditional, Maltese-style Yaqui cross of huchaco wood, one of which Anselmo also wore, except that his was the culmination of a magnificent and intricate necklace of black heishi and red beads. Like Anselmo, Prieto Saturnino even in the dark had on sunglasses.

Though I understood Prieto Saturnino to be the same age as Anselmo, he appeared old, his flat face and high cheekbones, the narrow-slit mouth, his dark severity, his mystery, so different in complexion from Anselmo's. Prieto Saturnino drew all my attention, so that when the first deer song started with the rasp, I was startled by the sound of his voice. I had naturally assumed deer singing was done by everyone else in imitation of Anselmo's high, light vigor. Prieto Saturnino and his singers took their heavy voices slow and deep, into something very disturbing. The labored, deliberate rhythms of the party of Prieto Saturnino exerted a hypnotic effect that drew my spirit toward him, into him. I couldn't will my eyes away from him. I watched as he also enfolded his own singers so that I could see only him, so that I was made to understand that *his* was the power. That understanding came in a very visual form: I saw his body in the hub of an irregular, carnelian wheel of light whose glowing edges looked like distant forest fires, as if viewed from miles away, like long fuses taking their time to burn down. His light absorbed the light of those around him and grew. I couldn't stop looking at him, so it was hard to gauge at what rate his aura was expanding, but I thought it was growing bigger and bigger, his entourage mere extensions of himself. Then it occurred to me, the extent to which I, too, had become involved with him.

The man who deer-danced for Prieto Saturnino was skinny to the point of emaciation. He was frightening in his unhealth and brought to mind the deer after the famine, except there he was dancing at the edges of Prieto Saturnino's blood-red power. I had the anguished feeling that I was being drawn into a vortex with no bottom, dragged out of the present into the abyss where all of human history began again. I felt myself teetering as I was drawn into the current he created, lamenting over what it would be like to have to gain back inch by inch all the lost eras and millennia of human living that I had endured . . .

After the third song, Anselmo and his entourage responded with the high, vigorous dexterity I had come to love about his expression. I felt lucky and grateful when he and his singers, Juan Kitito and Albert Garcia, and the chief of Potam Pueblo, Silvario, who deer-danced, snapped the hold Prieto Saturnino had on my attention.

Back and forth it went, however, with each side performing three songs, three separate rounds. Every time Prieto Saturnino sang, I experienced the same pull from him, but because Anselmo had also sung, I had something like a lever to resist him with—the memory of my husband's voice vibrating inside me. Just sitting there, being mindful of my vigil for Anselmo, was exhausting work. Every time Prieto Saturnino sang, I got an intense ringing in my left ear.

Between the second and third sets, right after Anselmo sang, there was a little pause. I looked up. It was so dark in the plaza that the sky and the town were one thing. The only light on the face of the earth seemed to come from the participants themselves. When Prieto Saturnino started up again, the air smelled like ozone right before a storm. The ringing in my ear was almost too loud to bear. Suddenly the side of my head erupted with a CRACK! as if I'd been hit with a bolt of lightning. Reflexively I darted left and right, sweeping up Anselmo's burst heishi necklace. Instantaneously I watched the flight of the red beads which glowed like incandescent coals. I reached and swept and somehow collected all the beads. I squeezed them tightly in my hands. I had no idea how I'd managed to do it.

After Anselmo sang, I beside him still clenching down hard on the necklace, the dark one, Prieto Saturnino, burst into a fit of coughing that wouldn't subside. One of his retinue brought a bottle which he tipped—I assumed it was some sort of herbal remedy—and tipped a second time. He sputtered and coughed some more and then withdrew from sight, not one word to Anselmo.

*   *   *

Prieto Saturnino left as quickly as a dark wind, his retinue
scattered behind him like a handful of dry leaves. Anselmo
looked impassively at me as I gave him the heishi beads in a
small pouch. "I'm exhausted, Anselmo. I'm going back to the
truck to lie down." I was half hoping that he would walk me
across the plaza, but he just said that was okay, he'd be there
later. He was going to stay deer singing.

As I crossed the small distance to the truck, I was not only
tired but apprehensive. I thought about the battle, to divert myself from feeling a growing physical malaise—what would happen to Prieto Saturnino, who was he, what did Anselmo get
from his victory—all the while I crawled into the camper, rearranging our clothing, sweeping off the foam pad, where I lay
down in my clothes. Restless, I sat up again, drank some water
from a plastic jug. I lay down again.

Then high and sweet the voices of Anselmo's deer singers
followed the drum and flute of the tampolero. I felt feverish,
flooded by the noise of cars passing by, the scuffing of feet
walking by the truck, doors slamming, voices from both sides of
the camper. The truck seemed to be slowly yawing back and
forth as if it were a sloop, or a coffin, pitched now toward shore,
now farther out to sea . . . Far away I heard the drum and the
flute and singing . . .

I must have dozed and then awakened. I was vaguely aware
of the eyes of watchers outside. I could see through the walls of
the fiberglass shell. Benina, a woman from Marana village, was
telling her daughter, "She is in the Other Place." The child
wanted to know what Tia Elena was doing in there and the
mother in a barely audible voice—which I nevertheless heard as
if it had been spoken into a microphone connected directly to my
ears—told the girl, "She is in there talking with the ancestors,
they are using her, they are talking to her, she is in the Other
Place that takes her on the Trail of Ashes."

So that is what is happening, I said to myself, and I looked
around where I was and saw the woman was right. I realized I'd
been seeing a tide of ancient faces for some while, but they
hadn't registered because my attention was fixed on the time of
Magdelena. I had a fleeting memory of Anselmo's words about

passing between worlds and the eternal time of the Other Place, but I couldn't use it. I felt as I had at the battle of the magicians when Prieto Saturnino was pulling me down into the dark abyss of history, but then that was only fear, because on the other hand these people who came around me, whom I knew immediately were the dead, were very warm and welcoming. I felt, as soon as I noticed them, that I was aware of myself, as if certain unused muscles suddenly were awakening, and if I focused on this feeling, the feeling deepened and got layered and then wasn't me anymore, but layer after layer of Yaqui men and women—an accumulation of generations.

It is easy to go between worlds, I thought, once I sensed their benevolence. I remembered Bobby and Anselmo just then, and felt torn. I gravitated toward the ancestors, but I wanted to be part of the present with the man I loved and with my son. I tried to call Benina. I thought I was saying to her, "If you know this about me, then wake me up, I don't want to be here anymore! Please come get me, somebody help me!" But the words traveled only as far as the edge of my mind.

I had two selves that I was aware of; one of me, like a sponge, was carried easily and relentlessly among the dead, assimilating their tribal essence in spirit form, while the living part of me slept hopelessly heavy, like an iron effigy of myself. The dead were omnipresent, and so light they floated to the surface of the faces of the living and made us seem heavy crude vessels in which they brimmed like fine oil to the crown of consciousness. I simultaneously felt a crowd had gathered around the truck, and they were watching me sleep. Ringed round them were the dead who knew everything.

I saw that there was no difference between the living and the dead, I couldn't tell them apart except by memory of the actual place I wanted to be in. Memory of work to do with Anselmo, people to care for, held me the more strongly to a particular world. Otherwise, I saw how little it meant to be in one place or the other. I really wanted to be with the living and the trouble was I couldn't get back to them, I kept traveling farther into the timeless place. The ancestors, who didn't ask anything of me, were happy to have me with them. But of course, I said to myself, I never left to begin with. I was still the daughter, mother, sister, wife they'd always known. I couldn't figure out where I belonged. My body had expanded and diffused so greatly, if I stayed much longer with the ancestors I would never return to my husband, my son, and all these people with whom I lived. I was so hot the truck seemed to be glowing. I could see the faces of the people illuminated by the incandescence of my body.

Someone was holding up my head. Water trickled down my chin. I swallowed: real water! It was Anselmo who was caring for me! I was so relieved. "Anselmo!" I pleaded, "please stop this now! I don't want to do this anymore, please wake me up, Anselmo, please wake me up!" But nothing came out of my mouth. He was laying me back down, while I was practically screaming at him not to leave me there alone, please! He closed the door of the camper and I heard him walk away.

I felt equally divided between the echo of Anselmo's footsteps and the faces of women and men by campfires, looking at me, making spirit eye contact. The words that arrived in my understanding came from the women; I passed through generations and generations of them. Their beautiful serene faces comforted me and instructed me not to have fear, despite my anxiety that Anselmo was using me for some dark purpose.

I was amazed to see Anselmo sitting up in the camper, putting his clothes on beneath the blanket. I sat up with him, holding the sheet around me. It was morning. "Anselmo," I said, "I have to get a bath, a shower, anything! If I don't I'm going to be really sick."

Anselmo looked at me closely and saw that it was true. He put on his shoes and said to wait there, he'd be right back. He climbed out the back and closed the camper door. I smelled camp stoves and fires with breakfast cooking, but I wasn't hungry. I was so tired from last night I wanted to lie down again, but worried how that would look for Anselmo, if his wife were to appear weak or to withdraw from participating in the culture. I reached through the sliding window into the cab, opened the suitcase on the front seat and began to dress. Seeing this piece of luggage from my life in Las Vegas, I thought of places I had gone with this brown Samsonite case, with Jack, I wondered how

Marilyn's new baby Dylan was, I saw Jack's face looking sadly at me across the room, late at night, just a year ago in October . . .

Anselmo opened the door again; I must come with him. I got out my magenta dress, and took a little shower kit with me. The shower was across the plaza in what had once been a good hotel. I turned on the water full force. The shower head dribbled and spit, and finally got up to a halfhearted spurt, just strong enough to make some impression on my skin. I had to duck down to get my head under it, but the water instantly refreshed me and I started to feel much better.

Anselmo had posted several guards from the society of warriors, the coyote society, around the door to the bathroom. I could see the backs of several Yaqui men outside through gaping cracks in the wall of the old building. I was a real curiosity to the Mexicans, apparently. Several men flocked about the door and pressed their faces to the breach in the building, trying to get a glimpse of the blond wife of the Indian chief. The Yaqui men came over and took their stances with their backs to the room I was in, and the Mexicans melted away.

Anselmo and I ate breakfast at El Tecolote. After we had finished, he brought out the cellophane packet of herbs from Olga Ruiz. "You need to drink this, Pluma." He mixed the contents into the leftover tea water, stirred it, and in a few moments poured me a cup. I drank it, we paid the bill, and after a few perfunctory conversations with some of his people, got into the truck and headed toward Rio Yaqui. Within ten minutes I was sound asleep.

8 🔲 COMING BACK TO PARADISE

WE DROVE THROUGH EMPALME. A LITTLE WHILE LATER ANSELMO POINTED through the windshield at an old volcano. "See if you can find the mouth of the serpent." A round line of sharp, needle-like rocks jutted together just like snake fangs. "That's Boca Abierta," he said, the Open Mouth.

"In the time when the big lizards walked the earth, my people say, this same huge serpent came and was eating all the Yaquis. Fire came from his mouth. A young boy saved our people. He placed himself below the serpent's head and shot a poison dart into the roof of the great serpent's mouth and punctured the serpent's brain. That's where his head fell. All over these mountains you can find other pieces of his body from the day when the boy killed him and saved the people."

At that time, Anselmo continued, during the days of the waterfly society—the waterfly is the dragonfly—the waterfly dancers made a big ceremony to honor the slaying of the great serpent, and they said that boy conquered the serpent world with his little arrow and the waterfly people would always serve him. The waterfly society, Anselmo explained, was a society of dreamers. The Surem used to ride back and forth between the worlds on the wings of the waterfly. But the society disappeared when the conquistadors arrived.

Anselmo was in an expansive mood—we were not far from Rio Yaqui, and he confessed that whenever he returned there he felt he was coming back to paradise. Today his happiness was making him talk. I loved his stories, but I wanted to ask him about what had happened to me in Magdelena. "Anselmo, last night when you came in to give me water, why didn't you wake me? I tried to ask you to wake me up, but you didn't."

"I did wake you. I gave you water and I saw that you were choosing to be in the Other Place."

I told him I had been scared I'd never see him or Bobby again. At the same time I'd been drawn toward the serene beauty of the dead, especially the women. I wanted him to explain what had happened in the truck and where I'd gone.

The highway had become narrower and less maintained. We passed the school at Cardinas. "You came to the place of the ancestors, Pluma, and they knew you and touched you. My people have seen this about you. You are like a door that swings both ways, and where you are, the ancestors and the living come together."

"But I was afraid I'd never get back to see you."

"That was what you had to prove to yourself. If you had chosen to go with the ancestors, you would have been endlessly happy. It is not easy for us, Pluma, to do what is asked of us here. Give yourself credit for your courage. Now the people know the degree of your commitment to the culture. And now your own mind and the tribal mind can be one mind."

I sat there in the cab, the beautiful land an affirmation of what Anselmo said. A serene knowledge I'd already known, but hadn't looked at because I was so fixated on Anselmo, surfaced. Coming to Yaqui wasn't just about fulfilling a love for the Dark Lord of my dreams. There was something more, between me and the people. Anselmo had brought me to Magdelena not knowing beforehand that I would meet the dead in the truck. Last night in the truck he had looked in on me, at that moment seen what was happening, and had simply trusted my intuitive nature to know what to do. And I also had to trust myself. He wasn't going to step in and do anything, because what had happened in the truck was bigger than either of us. It was between the people and me, and it wasn't Anselmo's place to intervene. I was there, as was he, for the people.

Anselmo drove toward the sunset with total disregard for speed limits. The white truck hurtled over patches of dirt where the blacktop had eroded, traveling upwards of eighty miles per hour. Anselmo looked as casual and relaxed as if he were driving down a quiet lane, one arm out the window, the other on the wheel. To the west the sun had erupted and the molten sky flowed into the Sea of Cortez behind the dark and impenetrable silhouette of the Baca Tete Mountains.

Anselmo slowed the truck and turned west onto a dirt road. I knew immediately we were on the road to Torim, for there was something significantly different about how it made me feel—the dirt was like pink flour, so light and fine that the truck raised plumes of dust the same color as the sky, as if the road had been milled from countless sunsets. On either side of us were the traces of where the roadway had been abandoned. The earth was so soft that the wheels of cars had dug ruts deeper and deeper into the ground until it was necessary to create a new road next to the old one. In places the new road intersected its former selves, presenting new eyes like mine with a dizzying choice, given that Anselmo was still rocketing the old truck along. Ironically, despite the need to be constantly reinventing the dirt road, to this day the people of Torim Pueblo do not wish their road to the main highway to be paved.

Here and there, irrigation canals ran under the roadway through concrete culverts. There were cattails and mesquite and the pitaya cactuses, which look like the saguaros, being long-armed and tall, except that the pitayas have many arms growing from the same point in the trunk. I began to notice big shade trees surrounding cornfields, men and women pedaling bicycles in the twilight. A few men rode rawboned little horses. Harvest was upon the land. We passed a green-and-orange crop plane parked next to an airsock and stacks of fifty-five-gallon drums. Big farm trucks were rolling past us, headed back toward the highway, their work done for the day.

In the dying light we drove through a swamp. I could just

make out the water cypresses and distinguish them from the cottonwoods, which were not as plentiful. We rumbled across an iron bridge. The night birds had begun to call. We passed a high-walled adobe building with a string of sparsely spaced bare bulbs. "That's TiTi's," Anselmo said, as we passed the local store. Some kids were sitting on the wall in front drinking sodas, watching us. Some men worked on a water pump by the light of a few cans with rag wicks.

We turned parallel to the dry stream bed of the Rio Yaqui, once a major river, Anselmo told me, until the Mexican government dammed it upstream. Now it ran only in the rainy season. We bumped along past several mud and bamboo houses owned by relatives of Anselmo and his nephew, Manuel Valencia, whose house we were approaching. I could make out, to the north on a small hill, the ruins of the old Mexican army head-quarters, the cuartel, and on an adjacent hilltop the ruins of an old church, a few crosses silhouetted against the charcoal-smudged sky.

We pulled into the compound of Manuel Valencia. Manuel's was the last house between the river and the plazas where the ceremonies took place—the best site, befitting his position as jefe, or chief, of the Torim Yaquis. Manuel Valencia was just getting into his pickup truck when we drove in. Seeing us, he stopped his truck and hopped out, calling in Yaqui for one of his sons to open the truck gate farther down, beyond the house. Anselmo got out, as did I, and another of Manuel's sons hopped into our pickup and drove it off.

Manuel Valencia had the classic Yaqui build—slight, wiry, about five foot seven, with the litheness of a deer. Like Anselmo, Manuel had short, curly black hair, but had no mustache on his warm, open face. Anselmo had told me that his nephew was thirty-five.

"Lios em chonia wyla"—God be with you, sister—Manuel said to me, touching the brim of his hat with one hand, while with his right hand he touched his palm to mine, as if we were impressing our handprints on each other, in the traditional Yaqui greeting.

I said, "Ketcha ma leia"—And with you, too.

The air was heavy with smoke from the burning cornfields. It hurt my eyes and lungs, and I was worn out from the drive, the newness of everything I was seeing, the exhausting night in Magdelena. Manuel told Anselmo he was just on his way back to the fields where his wife, Macaria, was still helping with the food for the harvesting, which would continue into the night. He'd come back to the house for some supplies. We should come to the camp; Macaria wanted to meet me.

Anselmo told him we'd be there in a minute. Manuel's son, Mago, could guide us there, Manuel offered. Anselmo led me over to two women who were waiting for us. A big red pig walked through the front yard; Manuel shooed him, then returned to his truck and took off for the fields somewhere out in the darkness.

Both Manuel's elder cousin Chonita and his beautiful Mayo daughter-in-law Hilda greeted me by the front door. From the edges of the house I could hear the giggling, muffled voices of children. Hilda shooshed the invisible children, no doubt amazed by the Elder Father Anselmo Valencia's young blond wife. Chonita, who was tiny and reminded me of a bird, said in a lilting way, "Elena! You are just as pretty as you were in my dreams. We've all seen you, just like this!" I knew many of the individual words from Anselmo's Yaqui tutorials, but it was because Chonita had put both her hands around my right hand that I almost instantaneously understood the exact content of her words.

But no sooner had we exchanged greetings with Chonita and Hilda than Anselmo motioned for me to come. Mago was ready to take us to the harvest camp where the corn was being cut. "You will come to know Chonita well," Anselmo said, as we piled into the front seat.

"I've already met her, Tori, just like I did you when I first saw you in dreams."

Mago drove us through the tangled jungle paths, the headlights jerking and poking as we negotiated the crude road to the camp. The night sky was as full and complete as I have ever seen it, no moon, only stars above, the looming shadows of big trees, and, off in the distance, the red and orange glow of fires where the fields were being burned off.

There was dust all over the hood of the truck, and it came

mingling into the cab through the vents, though the windows were rolled up. "Before the Spaniards dammed the Rio Yaqui," Anselmo explained, "the land was fertile and green everywhere, not just in Torim. Now only this pueblo remains green. All the other villages have seen their land become dry and cracked."

We reached a small hill and stopped at the crest. In front of us was a large ramada filled with smoke. I could make out only shadows moving around by the light of a few open kerosene-filled cans with rag wicks. The entire ramada looked like a cave from long ago. I walked between Mago and Anselmo. Inside the ramada men sitting in the dirt were eating from paper plates, talking quietly, drinking coffee. It was incredibly hot and I couldn't even see the other side of the ramada, there was so much smoke stinging my eyes. Outside the wind whipped the dust into the ramada, and some of the men tucked their heads down till it passed.

Macaria, the only other woman there, looked up, wiping her hands on her apron, and crossed through the smoke like a figure emerging from another world. She had been working for eighteen hours, cooking all day for the field hands, bearing corn from the fields to the trucks, nursing her three-year-old, Gaby, when he was hungry, breathing the heat and the dust and cook-fire smoke—she had been on that schedule for the past two weeks. Macaria came directly to me and hugged me as if I were a relative she hadn't seen for years.

The men greeted Anselmo with great respect, nodding their heads and touching his open hand with their open hands. He passed among them saying this and that to each man, then stood with his nephew, Manuel. Macaria was holding my hand all this time, occasionally touching my hair, my cheek, looking so glad to see me.

Because Macaria was the wife of the chief of the Torim people, she was expected to be the one who gave the most. Macaria, whom I had seen often in dreams and whom I had heard of often in Pascua from Anselmo, gave unstintingly and without complaint. She and I were nearly the same age—in our mid-thirties—the same height and build and, like dark and light sisters, had our hair up in the same way. Macaria's face showed none of the fierceness Yaquis are known for. She was softness, fullness. Her little son held onto her skirt and stood behind her, peeking at me.

Having made the requisite visit to his people, and seeing how tired I was, Anselmo said good night. Macaria squeezed my hands and let me go. I doubted I'd be the mother to the people Macaria was. She made her way back across the ramada to continue cooking. I looked over my shoulder to wave, but she had vanished in the heavy smoke.

At dawn the next morning I got up from the back of the camper where we had slept the night parked in Manuel Valencia's compound. In the fresh light I crossed behind the main house, went first into the outhouse, then into the bathhouse nearby and took a bucket bath. Anselmo carried a few pails of hot water for me, mixing it in with the cool well water so I could wash. Anselmo looked relaxed and jovial in Torim. His romantic nature resurfaced, and with an abandon he would not allow himself in front of his people in Pascua Pueblo. He called me "Pluma" often.

We made our way from the bathhouse to the ramada where Manuel's family had set up a long table for our meal. We sat on old, handmade chairs—not one chair matched another. I sat on a bench, which was more comfortable to me. Manuel's youngest children took washcloths and fanned away the flies.

Hardly anyone ate eggs in Rio Yaqui, but Anselmo loved fried eggs over easy, so that was what Hilda, Manuel's daughter-in-law, cooked for us. Normally, Manuel's family, like everyone else in Torim, breakfasted on potatoes and beans, with tortillas, perhaps a little meat, and some thick coffee. I am not a coffee drinker, but the Yaqui-style coffee, very much like sweet espresso, was irresistible.

Word of Anselmo's visit to Torim had already spread, and several of the old men of the tribe joined us for breakfast at Manuel's. They immediately started talking politics with my husband, telling about how the Vicam Yaqui opposition had tied up Tio Lucario and whipped him. Tio Lucario was the spiritual leader of that area, and the opposition leaders wanted to get more money from the Mexicans by leasing some of the Yaqui lands to them. The traditionalists were vehemently opposed to even the idea of letting the Mexicans on their land. So the elders at the table talked passionately, then waited for Anselmo's advice about what to do. Anselmo ordered them to retaliate in the old way, the only way it could be done. Later, as I found out, punishment was meted out on the opposition Yaquis—a punishment, carried out by some of the gentlest of Anselmo's relatives, for which those who opposed Achai's wishes paid an extremely high price. Yaquis in serenity are serene—but then they can cut your legs from under you with the greatest efficiency and not blink twice.

Anselmo's point was unmistakable—better not cross the leaders of the people. There was no leasing of Yaqui lands to any Mexicans that year.

Every day that we were in Rio Yaqui, one of the pueblos would hold a junta because Anselmo was back. Typically, these big meetings were convened under a long ramada. If the junta was small, I sat down next to him; if it was a big meeting, I'd sit at one end with the other women. These meetings often consumed upwards of two hours, beginning with Anselmo and me sitting near the ramada in our truck. At Vicam Pueblo a number of men came to speak to Anselmo in our truck practically the moment we parked. Anselmo listened for an hour and a half as people related problems through the open door of the truck. Anselmo rested his feet on the running board, facing each man. When Amador, the chief of Vicam Pueblo, came, we all went under the thin, palm-covered roof, and the men, by rank, filed in and assumed their places on the benches.

The juntas were highly democratic. Anselmo was the Elder Father of all the Yaqui, but on the other hand, he was only one voice, one vote. The jefe of the village remained the headman, and Anselmo showed each local leader respect. Indeed, Anselmo never displayed the least air of superiority. On many occasions, he would insist certain things be done for the benefit of the pueblos, but he would not act on anything without the consent of the chief of each village.

Upon assembly, the junta began with a long, formal prayer by the jefe, to which Anselmo would rise and respond with another prayer. Then the chief of the pueblo would announce what the meeting would cover, and the discussion continued until every-one had spoken. Almost always the pueblo juntas concerned problems with the Mexican banks and the difficulties of running the various Yaqui agricultural and fishing cooperatives. In Rio Yaqui there is never enough money to buy equipment, trucks, shrimping gear, ranching implements. How would they get money to finance these needs if there was no money to borrow except from the Mexican government and the Mexican banks?

Throughout the meeting at Vicam, I sat in the place of honor reserved for the wife of the leader of all the Yaquis. Bernarda, the head dreaming woman of Vicam and wife of Amador, the jefe, sat next to me.

Bernarda touched my hair. "Tutuli chonim. Sawalii chonim"—Pretty hair, yellow hair. Then she touched my earrings and said, "Tutuli rapim." We touched each other's clothes and talked back and forth, very, very quietly so as not to disturb the meeting, "Tutuli sewam, si tutuli sewam"—pointing at the flowers on her skirt, pretty flowers, very pretty flowers, and Bernarda laughed and put her arm around my shoulders.

Did I have children? Yes, one, Bobby. Bernarda asked me to tell her all about Bobby, and, in the same way Olga Ruiz, Cho-nita, and I had been able to communicate, I told Bernarda about my son. The woman near my right complimented me on how pretty I was, how lovely my clothes, where did I get this blouse, who has made it for me, what pretty earrings! They spoke in whispers so barely audible they sounded like the voices of dreams, and, in fact, that was just what they said—over and over the women of the pueblos would repeat it: "We have seen you in dreams. We are so glad you are here!"

In Vicam, in Amador and Bernarda's bed, I confessed to Anselmo that I didn't think I'd be able to remember everyone's name in each of the eight Rio Yaqui pueblos. I always have prided myself on my ability to remember details about people—names, phone numbers, names of children—but I was over-whelmed in Rio Yaqui. People had eighteen kids, or sixteen kids, dozens of grandchildren. I told Anselmo I was at such a disadvantage; everyone knew my name, but I was unable to respond in kind.

*   *   *

"I guess now such things aren't as important," I said, answering myself. I moved as close to Anselmo as I could.

In Rio Yaqui Anselmo *was*, as Olga Ruiz had teased me, a dark tiger, a passionate, frequent lover. At Casas Blancas we slept in a large communal room with many cots and people. Anselmo made love to me despite all the people sleeping there. I could feel them listening in the dark.

After supper back in Torim, several days later, Anselmo showed me around Manuel's compound. The house and cooking ramada, along with the bathhouse and the parking area for Manuel's trucks, were all on one level. But behind them was a sheer drop-off of about fifteen feet down to a barnyard with pigpens and horses, goat corrals and a garden. And behind this terrace was another drop-off, this one of at least another twenty feet, where big trees grew beyond the cane fence that enclosed the entire compound and where the Rio Yaqui itself had passed by in its final exit into the Sea of Cortez twenty miles to the west of Torim.

On a hill just north of the village were the ruins of a stately castle-like building, the cuartel from the days of the Mexican occupation of Torim. It had been the headquarters of the army during the many decades of guerrilla war which drove so many Yaqui men, women, and children into the mountain caves. The roof had been torn off by the people during one of the numerous raids the Yaqui warriors had made during the 1920s, and no matter how often it was reroofed, the roof continued to collapse until everyone gave up trying to restore it.

"That's your new home, Pluma. My people want us to live there. It's our wedding present," Anselmo said, leading us toward the hill. We crossed the plaza and stopped in front of the bella sombra tree in the center. With its amazing intricate branches and roots, the tree gave the appearance of something from biblical times, with a naturally formed bestiary: deer, frogs, lizards, birds, and men and women in various positions of lovemaking—a kama sutra of animals and people.

On one side of us, as we walked on, the Rio Yaqui turned in a lazy U; across the plaza were several compounds of the people's homes. We took the path up to the cuartel, passed the ceremonial guardia at the base of the hill, walked by the graveyard where the oldest, most ancient ancestors of the Yaqui are buried, and entered the building, with its long high rooms and arched windows. I climbed into one of the windows and stood up with plenty of headroom to spare. From the casement I surveyed a panorama of mountains and mesquite forests in all directions.

"Anselmo, I've seen this place before. That must be why I keep looking up at it from down below. I used to see this same scenery when I was a girl back in Hannibal." I told Anselmo that when I was eleven or twelve my bedroom was on the second floor of our house. When I looked out my window I could see the roof of the old Cruikshank mansion, which was on the next hill across from us. In the summer that I began having the dream about the Dark Lord and the underground kingdom, before I would wake, I would be the woman Zyla at a window looking out at a temple carved from the green mountain.

This temple led inside the mountain; when I awakened in Hannibal, from my pillow I would see the roof of the abandoned mansion jutting as if out of the jungle in my dream—as if indicating the dream was almost there. Then, to nurture the link between my dream and the world, I would take a mirror and tip it in the window. My grandmother had given me an antique grooming set which consisted of a gold brush and mirror, the backs of which contained two small doves flying up opposite sides of a heart. Inside the heart was an ornate rose whose tendrils veined into the heart. Upon waking each morning, after the dream of my life with the Dark Lord, I'd take up the gold mirror and tip it in the window sill, focused just on the Cruikshank mansion and all its attendant greenery, excluding the telephone and utility wires and all extraneous neighboring buildings. There in my golden mirror resided the truth I had begun to feel. Seeing that the Cruikshank mansion was the temple of the underworld kingdom of my dreams, I witnessed the overlapping of the ancient time and the world of the 1950s, and I sensed, however rudimentarily, that I lived in both.

Now the child who dreamed the woman *was* the woman remembering the child, looking out across the jungle toward the sea. "And then," Anselmo continued, "you remember the wars that went on all during the time we were together in that place." He took my hand and jumped me down, and escorted me to the opposite window from which I could see the village.

"Even from up here you can see bullet holes on the walls of many of the houses where the soldiers lined my people up and then shot them." It was getting too dark below for me to see distinctly from that distance, but I knew Anselmo had memorized every incidence of bloodshed. The Yaquis never gave up, never surrendered; they would retreat and then return to attack the Mexicans. Now this cuartel was theirs, and I knew from my husband's quiet, as he sat on the floor below me in the bright dark, that all this history was still alive in him.

I took out the two sleeping bags we'd brought and spread them on the dirt floor.

"This is what you are here for, Pluma," he said in an expansive tone. "You model joyousness for the people. You will make all of us see that no matter how hard it is, in our hearts this life is the hummingbird dancing in midair. This is all you really have to do!" He indicated for me to be next to him. I was going to be flip and say, This and a half million other things, but I stopped myself. What was the point? He was absolutely right. There was only my self in the way of my life.

I loved to hold Anselmo's hands and look at them. They were large for his build, and darker from work in the sun than the rest of his skin. Sometimes it surprised me what a contrast our skin was. He sensed what I was seeing. "The dark world. The light world," he said. "Nothing between." He pulled me down.

That night, the women told me later, many people saw shooting stars falling over the hill where we made love. The rumor was that there was treasure buried beneath the place where the bodies of Achai and Elena had lain together. More than one man, so I heard tell, lent a hand digging an enormous hole into the earth below where our lovemaking had marked the magic X beneath the chart of blue and silver stars.

The morning we were to leave Torim to go back to Tucson, before breakfast, Anselmo insisted we go to the burial ground. When you walk into the jungle-like vegetation to go to the cementerio, you see that Torim was once very big and had many buildings, the goat paths neatly set at square angles, even an aqueduct system—all of it laid out long ago. The Yaquis refused to share their secrets with anyone, so they just let the jungle take back their capital.

This cementerio at Torim is very special to the people. Because the ground is so soft, graves have sunk ten feet in places, headstones have been heaved onto the wrong grave, and other graves are mounded up like pregnant women lying side by side. Graves that start out separate end up sliding together so that the remains of anyone in particular might now lie within the remains of another. The dead do not resist each other.

A thick mist was rising from the warm ground into the cool morning air. Anselmo, standing near one of the sunken graves, looked down into the mist that had collected in it. I walked over and looked, too. He seemed thoughtful in a way I seldom saw him in Pascua where he was always in a rush to take care of business. "This is my tia Ramona's grave," he said in a very soft voice. I put my arm around him. In the lavender silt below us, a cat's cradle of tree roots inside Tia Ramona's grave formed something like a grate over a deep well, and from somewhere inside the dark vault where the Yaqui ancestors' bones had been heaved by earth and river, the steam rose as if a campfire had been lit.

"Tia Ramona is cooking breakfast," Anselmo said in perfect deadpan. We sat down. Anselmo lit a cigarette. It was very quiet and peaceful. A few dogs barked in the village. Someone ground the gears of a truck as it shifted, lumbering dully in the distance.

"My tia Ramona was a very famous freedom fighter," Anselmo began.

Ramona

Ramona was renowned for her fierceness. She lived with her family in Torim during the occupation by the Mexican soldiers, and because all of the Yaqui men had either been enslaved and sent far south to the Yucatan labor camps, or else had taken refuge in the mountain caves, the soldiers acted with swinish brazenness toward the women who remained. As smart as she was, Ramona was also beautiful, with very long dark hair that curled at the ends, the mark of Anselmo's Tori clan. While she was petite, she had a sort of uncorrupted allure that made her irresistible to the soldiers. She would go into Vicam to entice the Mexican soldiers who were smitten with her enchanting beauty. Ramona acted out the part of the young woman only faintly aware of her charms, whose sensuality nevertheless could not disguise itself. Cleverly she overdressed, as if to hide some secret burning passion that only the right and most worthy man might unleash.

Thus the Mexican soldiers would come by her mother's house and sing songs to her. "We want to see the beautiful Ramona," they would serenade from outside the wall which enclosed the family home. But neither Ramona nor her mother would respond to these preliminaries. It was often the officers who had the boldness to actually petition for a personal interview. "Come back at such and such an hour alone," her old mother would say, "and we will see if you are worthy of my Ramona."

The young officer would come to the gate of the wall and call out. Ramona would keep the suitor waiting a sufficiently long, anguishing time, and then the young man would hear the door of the house softly open. "Yes?" Ramona would say from her side of the wall. "May I implore you to join me for a stroll?" the young man would say.

In this wall around her house were several holes, apparently randomly made and at various heights. "Why should I see you?" Ramona would tease. "It may be you are horribly deformed and ugly."

"No, far from it, if I may say so. In fact, so I am told by members of your gentle sex, quite the opposite is true!"

"Well, seeing is believing," Ramona would reply. "If you are so handsome, show your face to me through this window," and she would place a cut rose in the lowest hole in the wall so that the young man would have to get down on his hands and knees to show himself. The young soldier would then eagerly respond; they would see each other, he smiling hopefully just before Ramona pulled the trigger of the shotgun, blowing his head off at point-blank range.

*   *   *

I was to go across the street from our house in Pascua and call
on doña Cheva the day before the Day of the Dead. I walked
over to her pink adobe at the corner of Benem and Tetakusim
streets. There was a big black caldron in the center of her backyard, visible from the street, as if to announce that here lives a
witch, and, as I walked to the door, sure enough, there was the
regulation calico cat and then doña Cheva, wearing her white
apron and a blue bandanna around her hair. She looked at me
hard, with her piercing little eyes, jutting her chin a few times
like an old mare who knows she's the boss.

Doña Cheva was the crone I'd seen through the chink in the
cultural kitchen wall during Easter, and she brooked no nonsense where her beloved Anselmo was concerned. I felt I was
being tested. I was.

Doña Cheva made it clear—in English and in Yaqui for good
measure—that it was my duty as the wife of Anselmo, and because the ancestors had called me to Yaqui, to cook for the
dead tomorrow at my house. Inwardly I groaned. I was to buy
all the ingredients for the guacavaci and in the morning she
would come to my house and together we would prepare the
food for the ancestors. Anselmo was to move the caldron from
her yard to ours across the street. She listed on her fingers.
"Six heads of cabbage. Twelve ears of corn. One big yellow
onion. Four garlic. Bag of green beans. Bag of chick peas.
Three bunches carrots, big bunches. Six pounds soup bones.
And salt. And pepper."

Anselmo's daughter Margie had warned me that Cheva was a
miser and always cooked too little. "Whatever Cheva tells you,
double it. And when you put in twice what she told you she's
going to shake her head and think you can't count and wonder
what Pa saw in you, a woman who can't count!" Margie
laughed, then added sympathetically, "They never tell you you
are okay."

The next morning, Cheva knocked at our door before we had
finished breakfast. She was ready to cook! I fed her some sweet
rolls and coffee first while Anselmo went out back and made a
fire for the kettle. Doña Cheva wasn't about to be distracted by
politeness. She left her coffee cup half full and proceeded out to
the kitchen. I took it that I was to follow her, and I came along.

"No time to lose. This soup takes all day. We can't make the ancestors wait just because we've been drinking coffee."

She went right for the drawer with the knives and opened the refrigerator to take out the fixings. She indicated for me to quarter each cabbage, halve the ears of corn, but not skin the carrots. She cut the onion in quarters, and then we put everything in the caldron outside. Cheva filled it with water from the garden hose and poured in the salt. She was so slight and small and cute, she reminded me of the Morton's Salt Girl with her blue bandanna on.

Anselmo brought over the four-foot-long spoon from Tio Serrapio in Torim, a wedding gift. Cheva grunted her approval upon being presented with it to mix the pot. She even smiled. "I haven't cooked with a cutawesaiee like this for fifty years. My father used to carve them from logs."

Margie had come outside to watch and whispered to me to be sure Cheva didn't walk off with the spoon.

After the soup was started we prepared wayaa, the Dead Pudding made from black ragweed seeds. As Cheva showed me, looking up now and then to see that I was really paying attention, the ingredients in the big wooden bowl had begun to turn into a grayish gruel. Cheva grunted questioningly—did I see how to do it?—and kept stirring until the gruel was the consistency of Cream of Wheat. This food, Cheva said, tapping the spoon on the edge of the bowl, was the single most important food for the dead.

Cheva said with a curt little smile that it was a good omen—she hadn't seen this Dead Pudding for years. Amador and Bernarda had sent the seeds to us—Amador had been harvesting when he came across the patch of ragweed and so he'd combined it and bagged the seeds for Anselmo.

Since October 1, the Day of the Skull that year, the dead had been walking among us, and at the end of this day, November 2, they would return through the wall between worlds and go back to the Summerland. We would feed them and pay tribute with our prayers and food. All around Pascua people were cooking, but it seemed to me that everyone in the village came over to our house. By ten that morning, Anselmo had set up lots of oil drums for others to cook on. The mesquite smoke was so heavy

and thick I could barely breathe. The scene was eerie, appropriate to Halloween and the new look of our house. I'd spent the
week having the house repainted magician-robe purple, and
Anselmo had had an ingenious idea for a fence. He sank eight-
foot sections of clay sewer pipe into a trench and set the pipe on
end, one next to another. Don Luis painted each pipe black and
I painted a mural of a green dragon across the front of the entire
fence.

Anselmo was engrossed in the activities. Some young girls
cooked fat, flat enchiladas and sauce while Anselmo steamed
chunks of calavasa, green pumpkin, with lumps of brown sugar.
One of the girls worked on meat tacos helped by Tina Molina,
and Andrea flip-flopped tortillas in her hands, then heated them
on the oil drums.

I was already tired. I would have liked to lie down, but that
was not possible. I kept hearing people right next to my head, it
seemed, speaking loudly in Yaqui, but if I turned to smile and
say hello, nobody would be there. I was still under the eye of
doña Cheva. I asked if that about wrapped up our work.

"No!" she said, looking at me as if I were a barbarian. "We
cannot leave here. We have soup to stir. Until it is done. If we
leave now the ancestors will think it is finished. They will believe we have no respect for them if we give them meat that is
not properly cooked." She turned back to stirring. I couldn't
imagine how the meat, after all these hours, could not be cooked.

"The ancestors are waiting to taste what we have done. This
food is not for us, Elena. It is for them. It is for the ancestors. It
must be perfect."

Anselmo's grandchildren Chana, Becky, and Jesse were running in and out of the house. They came up to me and asked for
something to eat. Cheva shooed them away, guarding her pot
from all intruders and marauders. I didn't know what to do,
although I was glad to have a break and went to find them some
hot dogs and ice cream bars. Margie came over and gave me a
taco and a plate of food. I walked over to Anselmo and asked
surreptitiously if it was all right to eat. "Of course," he chuckled.
"The cooks have to eat."

Finally Cheva told me to take a nap—the smoke had really
started to hurt my lungs and I was coughing heavily. When I

slept, the dead visited me, all manner of ages of Yaqui people, asking for this or that, where's the bathroom? was I the one who had cooked their food? what a nice job I'd done fixing up the house, where did I get these pretty dresses? . . .

I awoke as exhausted as I had been before the nap. There seemed to be no escape from the burden of work, whether the work manifested itself through my body or through my dreaming. It was all work and smoke and noise and all these people I had no way of avoiding.

About an hour before sunset Anselmo and I hopped into the pickup truck and drove over to the cemetery on the Papago Reservation where his two children Giovanni and Chenta were buried. I had made two baskets of silk flowers, and Anselmo brought a couple of cans of water, rakes, and shovels. The Papago graveyard is behind the Mission San Xavier where Bobby had first seen Anselmo sitting in midair. Anselmo's children were buried there because they had died before Pascua had had its own graveyard.

Anselmo and I began to pick the tumbleweeds from the dirt of the graves. We threw water on the packed soil to loosen it and the cleanup went easier. After we weeded and raked, Anselmo freshened the dirt on the mounds of the graves, and then we arranged the silk flowers and lit candles. We stood together at the foot of the graves and Anselmo said long prayers.

I was crumbling the dried heads of bunches of flowers, scattering the debris away from the graves of the children, when I noticed some tendrils of smoke had wound loosely up my ankle. I dispersed them with a wave of my hand. Anselmo was still saying prayers. I watched the ground where the smoke was. It promptly returned to my feet and began curling up my leg again. I swished it away and walked over to the source of the smoke. It came up from the ground in a single vine-like stream about the diameter of a large hose. And then, nearly hidden in some tumbleweeds I saw a weathered, unpainted cross about three feet from where the smoke started.

"Tori," I said softly, but he didn't hear me, so I went over and stood next to him, "Anselmo, the man in that grave over there is asking me to honor him."

Anselmo opened his eyes and regarded the smoke on the

ground, then gestured with his chin. "Honor it if you want to. That's the man I don't call Father. I will not honor his grave." He turned away and continued his prayers for his children. When I looked back toward the grave of Rosario Moses, the man Anselmo wouldn't call his father, the smoke had vanished.

Even early in our marriage, Anselmo joked that my curiosity coupled with my personal power created mischief, sometimes outright danger. He liked to say that while I knew a great deal about the complexities of power and medicine, as simple a thing as curiosity seemed to get the better of me. "Do you think I'm arrogant, Selmo?" I asked him once, and he'd made an amused face without answering.

I left Anselmo's side, not intending to "honor" but merely examine the grave of Rosario Moses. I knew little of him, except that he had abandoned Leoway and her children. For Anselmo's part, there was no love lost. At the unkempt grave of Rosario Moses, the smoke became more urgent. It seemed to ask me in a beseeching, moaning way to help it. I turned back to see what Anselmo's reaction might be, but Anselmo wasn't even watching me. If there was moaning, I was the only one hearing it, and the voice of the smoke said in a quavering, weepy way that if only I would honor the father of the great Yaqui chief, his son Anselmo Valencia Tori, I could have a gift of a choni. I was keenly aware that bargains presented between the dead and living are nothing to trifle with. I turned away from the grave. We gathered all the tools and boxes and went quietly back to the truck.

Before the next cultural obligations, Anselmo and I stood in the yard watching the sun set. The sky rouged, draining quickly toward deeper shades. Anselmo stepped on his cigarette. "Your father came to me again, after I told you, and said if I would honor his grave, he would give me all his dark powers. He told me he would give me a choni. I told him I didn't care what he offered me, he had dishonored you and your mother and I would never honor his grave. What did he mean by a choni, Selmo?"

Anselmo said that in Yaqui a choni is a long black braid of somebody's hair with red ribbon in it, the hair of a man or woman with power, and if you own a choni, you can send it to do work for you. Chonis are used by people who do dark work.

"Marcianna inspired envy in others and therefore was prey to them. Before you came to me, one time someone sent a choni for her. Someone who imagined some injury she'd caused them was trying to get rid of her. But she had a lot of personal power. Marcianna was hanging out clothes when she started coughing. She couldn't stop. Something was stuck in her throat, she could feel it with her finger. Then she started pulling out a lot of long black hair that seemed to have no end. She couldn't even lie down to sleep because if she did, she'd start to choke on all the black hair in her throat. Whoever was after her wasn't very good at it. Usually a choni just kills the one it is sent to—like that." Anselmo snapped his fingers.

Anselmo was in a receptive mood, apparently. He went on to describe how to catch a choni. Anselmo had a long rope of braided horsehair he used in the Easter ceremonies. To cure Marcianna, he had her lie down to sleep in a ring of chaparral. He put that thin horsehair rope all around her in a big circle. When the choni came for Marcianna, it got trapped by the horsehair rope and when it saw that it couldn't get out, it let out a horrible, whistling scream. Anselmo was able to see it and then catch it. Then he burned it, and the whole time it was on fire it screamed terribly.

"If you want to keep a choni, Pluma, you can have one yourself. You tie it up in a silk scarf and use it when the right occasion calls."

However, I don't think Anselmo used chonis, himself. At least I never saw any evidence of it, although you never know with Anselmo; he is truly impenetrable. For a while after this incident, if I went to Leoway's grave at sunset I would hear a high-pitched whistling. It only happened when I went without Anselmo, and only at Leoway's grave. I asked Anselmo what it was. "There's a choni out there, Heather. If you want it, take a red silk scarf and put it on my hat on Granny's grave, and the choni will come into it and you can have it and use it."

I didn't do it. I felt that the sender was his father and I refused to be drawn into his sphere, although I did think about the voice of the smoke and I did want to know more about Anselmo's father. But Anselmo refused to talk about the man he would not call his father.

*   *   *

We took a folding table in the truck over to the Yaqui cemetery, along with six boxes of candles, some utensils, and all of
the food we'd been cooking. Anselmo asked me to place candles
all around the Mount Calvario he'd built with his own hands. As
I climbed it, planting candles and lighting them, I mused that
Anselmo Valencia, Tori the Rat, was like a geologic force to his
people, capable of making a mountain out of a rathill. I decorated the rocks all around the 360 degrees of the top with candles
and then paused. The November twilight was still lingering,
glowing like cooling lava. The moon had waned almost to in-
visibility. It hung above the western ranges of mountains on the
Papago reservation, the Coyote Mountains. It was very quiet
except for the sounds of people moving and car doors now and
then opening and closing, sounds it was easy to lose in the face
of the majesty of the sky and the earth, both of which were about
to become one darkness.

I came down from the little mountain and helped Anselmo
make fires and set out food on the tables. Then we walked out
beyond the cemetery and randomly set candles in the chaparral
to honor all those who had died in the wilderness.

At each grave in the cemetery, the maestro, the traditional
priest in the services for the dead, prayed and the cantoras
keened the Latin prayers for the dead. I could never hear that
wail without being drawn to join them, which I did. Hearing it,
I always felt that I was listening to the grief of every mortal
creature, as if the keening began in the animal cells of my body,
which were trying to break the hold of the mineral cells of my
body, just as the human part of me sought release. Wailing with
the cantoras, I felt the unbroken chain of beings within me extending backwards into the oldest life forms and forward toward
the stars. I was completely at home, surrounded eternally by life
itself. The dance of life itself was expressed with astounding
variety. I sang the griefs of all those appearing and receding
forms—including my own and those I cherished and loved.

Awhile later I told Anselmo that when I died I wanted to be
laid next to him. And, I said, my heart full of the dead, I would
not want to live after he died, but we would die together.

After all the dead were given food, after each grave was sung, we, too, ate from the food of the dead that was left over. I thought it was beautifully fitting: only after the dead eat do the living have their turn. So we are caretakers here, the custodians and stewards of those who have gone before, whose lives we continue, only our names and appearances changing, and so Mother Earth is fed by our personal living, as we are fed by the ancestors. The distinction between the dead and living was very slight. We differ from one another about as much as the left hand differs from the right, as those who cook the food differ from those who are served as honored, beloved guests.

After the singing and feeding, the maestro and the cantoras left, and Anselmo's son-in-law Joe Rivera, Anselmo, and I cleaned up the trash, put the fires out and loaded up the trucks. I took little doña Cheva home. Wrapped in her big black rebozo, she nodded off and her head drooped forward. When I pulled up in front of her house she was fast asleep. For a moment I felt I should carry her into bed as if she were my little girl, absolutely tuckered out.

9 ▣ THE DARK LORD

ANSELMO WAS A DIFFICULT TEACHER, ALTHOUGH HE NEVER WAS UNGENER-ous in his explanations of things I didn't understand. His life was organized around duty to his people. They and his strivings on their behalf were his clock, and by this clock he lived his days and often his nights. If someone from Rio Yaqui called from the Nogales, Sonora, train station at 11:00 P.M., then Anselmo was the one they called and the one who went. If someone's family member had been possessed, then, whatever the hour, they came to Achai for help. Grieving widows and families came to have Anselmo put rosaries on the dead. Perhaps we could ease the pain of a son thrown in the county jail, or see into the future and find a lost child . . . So if there was teaching, then it was because I asked him at a time when he could tell me. Or wanted to tell me. For Anselmo *expected* me to do what the Little Mother of the Yaqui is supposed to do, and sometimes I didn't know the extent of that requirement. But most of the time I did not ask much about the culture. What I couldn't pick up from dreaming became apparent as I lived it.

No, most of my questions were actually about Anselmo him-self. Over the first months of my life with him, I'd glean anecdotes from him late at night in bed, after we turned off "M*A*S*H," his favorite television show, which was rerun each night after the ten o'clock news. I heard many stories of Anselmo from the elder ladies, the dreaming women who were his unbreachable circle of support. Often at fiestas we would talk; invariably the conversation would turn to some tale or other about Anselmo.

When Anselmo Valencia was born, his mother Leoway took one long look at him and declared, "Not this one." He was so tiny he fit inside a shoebox. It broke her heart to plan it, but she had no recourse—this child was so frail, only a life of suffering and sickness awaited him. So the young woman put the top on the size-twelve shoebox with her infant inside and handed it to her own mother to take away and leave. That way, even if Leoway changed her mind, it would be too late to take back her decision.

But Michala, the grandmother of the baby, saw something else, something in the baby shining faintly, as if the child's will had burned through the cloud of death that had occulted his first moments in the world. "No," said the grandmother, "No, this *is* the one," and she took the baby in the palms of both hands, turning him this way and that to see better. Then she went away from people. In the presence of the sun Michala raised the baby boy over her head as if he were a chalice or a sword.

"Father," she prayed, "I will do what I can for this one because he is the chosen one. I will do what I can for this one who is the hope of our people. I have seen him in dreaming. I know who he is." And she thanked the Creator for sending him to the people.

It was known to the dreaming women in Anselmo's childhood that Anselmo was the chosen one. Being a true Yaqui, of course, Anselmo did everything he could to deflect the power he was born with. He did not want to wear the mantle of such great responsibility.

So first he tried to die at birth, but even then his destiny commanded him, despite his frailness. In those times there was no Indian Health Service, certainly no easy access to pediatric medical facilities. The Yaqui have always let be: if a child was meant to live, it lived. The infirm either survive sickness or they don't. This is not a hard-hearted attitude so much as a tribal consciousness of the people's place in a vast universe through which they have traveled since the beginning of time. For generations since the great journey of the ancestors across the stars to Yaquiland, the people have survived by listening to life and bowing to the Creator's wishes for its expressions. It happens that a mother's love cannot save a child not meant to live. That's how it is.

Anselmo lived. For his first several years he was nearly blind. His eyes, even today when you look at them, appear cataracted, as the moon looks with its mantle of cloud and its halo. When he was nine Anselmo was playing in a cotton field in Eloy when the dust devils found him. People who tell the story say he was lifted by the spirits of the dust devils and thrown about like a rag doll, flipped by a leg and thrown, grabbed by the head and thrown. Over and over the dust devils tossed him around the cotton field.

When I asked Anselmo about it, he said that from the age of five he had been a drunkard. What he remembered was having the DTs in a field, being seized with violent fits. When he came to, he could see clearly for the first time in his life, and everything seemed different.

Anselmo got hooked on drinking in a very unusual way. When he was small, his grandmother Michala tied him to the leg of her sewing machine in the adobe house in South Tucson where he was born. Anselmo was full of mischief; being partially blind he often created even more trouble. Besides, his mother, Leoway, was away all day cleaning houses for the rich. The solution was to tie him to the sewing machine when no one could supervise him.

Michala's house was a sanctuary for Yaqui warriors wounded and fleeing the Mexican army in the 1920s, before the liberation from the slave camps in 1927. Leoway would use part of her cleaning money to buy guns and bullets for her people in the south. One day in 1926 an old Yaqui runner and warrior, don Refugio, came to recuperate from wounds. It was said that don Refugio could run invisibly from Torim to Tucson and back in

four days, to bring ammunition to the warriors in the mountains. Now he had come to the end. For months he lay in Michala's sewing room with a bad stomach wound. From time to time
his compadres brought whiskey to help kill don Refugio's pain.
Anselmo's job was to empty the tin can in which the old man
urinated and replenish a drinking cup with whiskey. Each time
he gave don Refugio a fresh cup of whiskey, he'd sneak a swallow himself and then listen as the old man told him stories and
secrets of the Baca Tete Mountains

When Rosario Moses left Leoway and Anselmo and his sister
Christina, they went with a kind man named Saturnino de Mayo
to live in Rio Yaqui with Saturnino's family. They made a place
in the jungle, outside Torim. Sometimes the children were left
with the grandparents of Saturnino, over near Navajoa, and it
was the old grandfather of Saturnino who did ant medicine with
Anselmo.

Anselmo made a circle in the dirt to play marbles. He made
the circle on the home of some red ants, and the ants bit him
badly. "Don't play there, the red ants will sting you," his grandmother told him. Anselmo just looked at her and went on playing marbles, all the while getting stung. Day after day, Anselmo
played marbles and would not budge. On the third day the old
man said, "The chief wants to play marbles here, so the ants are
going to have to be moving." Even as a child, Anselmo was
acknowledged to be the Elder Father, Achai. So the old man
took a tin can and a stick and connected them with a string. He
placed the end with the stick into the ant hole. He stood far away
and began to talk and sing into the can he held. For three days
Saturnino's grandfather spoke and sang to the ants, saying this
was the chief of the land, and the ants had to move because it
was the chief. On the third day the ants were persuaded; they
took their queen and went.

When they lived in Rio Yaqui with Saturnino de Mayo, Leoway had a garden. Every day they would get up at 4:00 A.M. to
water and work on the garden, so that the work of the day
would be done before the sun was high and hot. Back in those
days, when Anselmo was still little, there were great boas in Rio

Yaqui, and a huge one lived in the wooded jungle near their casita and garden. Leoway had chickens, and this boa would occasionally come down and take one. Anselmo observed his mother one day go out to the garden when she saw the huge boa, put her hands on his head, and look into that snake's smiling face, saying, "You don't take my chickens or I'll cut your head off." The snake minded her and, apparently chastened, was purged of its lust for chickens.

Snakes always dwelled with Anselmo when he was in Torim, and he petted the boa and knew that when his mother talked to the snake it was more than just a chicken-starved reptile—it was a being. It was then known in Torim that Leoway talked with the Great Serpent and that Anselmo was a friend of the Serpent.

The rattlesnake, being more capricious and dangerous than the boa, is, along with the coyote, one of Anselmo's animal familiars.

When he was young, Anselmo told me, and he lived in the village of Guadalupe outside Phoenix, he purposely conjured the Dark Flower World. He told me it was the first time he had with deliberation conjured anything. He was in his early teens when he began to conjure scorpions. He would lie under his great-uncle Nicky's porch, and the scorpions would come and sleep with him and never sting him, because he was conjuring them, becoming one with the forces of the Dark World. He conjured the Dark World for three years, until one night he heard the coyotes. Their call hurt the very marrow of his bones, and he knew that he had to come out of the Dark World or he would forever be a part of it. He stopped sleeping with the scorpions and came out into the light.

I asked Anselmo why people said he had gone into the Dark Flower World. He said because it was true.

To be a true magician you have to balance the dark and the light. There are many deer singers; most of them sing the glorious beauty of the Light Enchanted Flower World. Then there are some who go off and live by themselves in the mountains— and sometimes they are in the dark forever. When Anselmo conquered the Dark World he went into the Mouth of the Serpent. Ever since that time, Anselmo has been able to go between worlds with impunity, like the Death Lord.

Anselmo, in an uncharacteristic reversal, one day talked about Rosario Moses. "That man was given a choice in the Dark World. When you confront the Serpent, he will let you by only if your power is equal to his. Rosario Moses was a dark magician, and when the Serpent saw him, he let him by. When you get that far, you then have your deepest wishes granted. That man asked only for himself. He refused his duty to his people. All he could come up with in the Dark World was his selfishness, and, in the end, he died because of it."

You do not have to conquer the Light Enchanted Flower World, Anselmo said. We are all called to it and drawn there. Imagine a wild horse that lowers its head and lets the child touch and ride it. The horse does so because it cannot express itself without the innocence of the child. The child is the perfect vehicle for its expression.

"In the Seatica," Anselmo said, "you 'conquer' with innocence; but the Dark Flower World is about the power of the mind, it is mind-expanding, where the Light Flower World is emotional. In the Dark Enchanted Flower World, you must break fear barriers in the mind. In order to do that, you must have a very strong purpose. The Dark Enchanted Flower World is the realm of those who have a different kind of capacity and interest or ambition. The Dark World is the testing ground of the Yaqui magicians, warriors, and leaders.

"Yaquis are Yaqui, Heather. You have to be willing to give up your life in order to be a candidate to conquer the darkness, but the darkness almost always conquers those of us who try, even when we know better."

I couldn't stop looking at Anselmo and his friend Kitito. They were sitting on the brick ledge beneath the willow tree, and the sun was headed down. It caught both of them and they paused to look. They were in their rolled shirt sleeves and huaraches, passing a soda bottle back and forth. Then it hit me—I ran out into the backyard screeching, "It was you! It was you!" Kitito knew immediately what I was talking about, and covered his head as if I were beating him with a broom. Anselmo mimicked my swing from that day in the Rockies when I'd seen these very men in my house in the middle of winter. All three of us howled

and laughed and I hit Kitito on the arm. They were two clowns
when they got together!

It hadn't occurred to me that the strange men in Central City
had been Anselmo and Kitito. Obviously, they had not come in
person, but had sent their chilquins ahead—even before I knew
who Anselmo was. What I was just realizing had to do with an
event that took place on a snowy day in the winter of 1972. The
sinking Colorado sun glowed dully behind a metallic curtain of
clouds. The ridge out my window was slowly darkening, like a
knife blade grown black from being left in the sink. I noticed it
was cold in the house. Bobby wasn't home from school yet, so I
went outside to get an armful of firewood. On the way back to
the house my feet seemed to sink deeper into the snow than
they did on the way out to the wood pile. I reached the open
door of the house, stamped the snow off my shoes, kicked the
door shut behind me, and emptied the wood into the keeper by
the door. When I stood up and faced the room, I wasn't alone.

Two strange men were across the room, one warming his
hands at the fireplace, the other leaning against the kitchen doorway, his back on the doorjamb, his bare feet in the opposite
corner of the door. They both turned toward me, smiling politely. I thought they were migrant workers. They were speaking
and chuckling in a language I'd never heard before, maybe a
South American dialect of Spanish, which they ceased when we
saw one another. I froze with fear—I thought they might attack
me. Then I saw an incongruity—it was winter and the two men
were dressed in thin white cotton shirts, with the sleeves rolled
up, in blue jeans and sandals.

"What do you want?" I asked brusquely, groping behind me
for the broom I kept near the firewood. The one by the fireplace
said something to his friend and they both laughed. The man in
the doorway handed a small bottle to his companion, and the
man by the fire, who looked like a gypsy, with curly black hair
and a dark complexion, took the bottle and offered it to me.
There was a twinkle in his eye as he said something in the
language they spoke, and they both erupted into laughter at my
lack of amusement.

"Get out of here, both of you!" I screamed at them. In one
motion I ran from the door and landed a blow with the broom

right on the head of the man by the fireplace. I heard the handle of the broom crack against the stones.

I had shut my eyes with the exertion and when I opened them the two men were gone. I ran to the back door—but it was locked. I took a butcher knife from the drawer and entered the bedroom—they were gone. I went to the front door and looked out cautiously—no one, and the odd thing was there weren't even extra tracks in the snow, just my footprints going out and back, and Bobby's small footprints from that morning.

Anselmo had told me that he'd come to me even when I was a little girl. He'd often watched me in the shape of a bird. But that day in 1972 in Colorado, he could feel where I was and so he and his friend had their chilquins go ahead of them to see what was coming in the future.

"I told Pluma I was waiting for her," said Anselmo. "I wanted to see where she was, and what thanks did I get? She chases me and my best friend with her little witch's broom!" They made their eyes go big and laughed appreciatively at me, remembering. I, too, enjoyed their mirth.

The chilquin describes one's light body. If a magician develops his power—and many Yaqui children are born with this power—he does something called "making the chilquin go before." Your chilquin looks just like you and vibrates just like you, and an untrained observer could not tell your chilquin from your physical body. The only thing that makes the chilquin different from the physical body, as far as can be perceived with the five senses, is that the chilquin does not drink water, it does not eat food, but it can smoke cigarettes. Anselmo is noted for his chilquins, although I have seen him manifest only two chilquins at once: in addition to his physical body which was watching his son Roy dance, from my position under a ramada at a fiesta I saw Anselmo also smoking a cigarette with the chappeyekas while simultaneously leading the deer dance. Others have seen Anselmo in four places at once.

Yaquis have dreaming medicine and you seem to need it to use a chilquin. Parents do not encourage their kids to send a chilquin because they believe it will weaken their physical bodies. However, some children discover they have the power and do it for fun and pleasure. But the older people fear that those children will not live long. Not everybody seems to know they have a chilquin. But when somebody tells you they saw you someplace doing this or that, and your memory is that you were otherwise engaged elsewhere, then you realize you've sent a chilquin and were in two places at once. Some people learn they are sending a chilquin ahead by hearsay.

In my first months at Yaqui when Anselmo and I often traveled south to Rio Yaqui, I met a woman in Vicam Pueblo who had seen me in Torim two days earlier. "I knew you were coming," she told me. At first I was confused: two days earlier I had been in Tucson, not Torim. When I stopped thinking about it, though, I had the clear recollection of walking by the cane fence at Pilar's house, heading toward the old cuartel on the hill. I remembered that Pilar had offered me an orange from her basket, and I took it, but when I set it down on the table it was upon the altar in my bedroom in Pascua.

Most evenings after I came to Yaqui, if Anselmo was not busy with tribal affairs, we walked out past the temporary housing at the western side of the village and went to visit the place of the dead. Anselmo used these times both to restore himself after his hectic workday in the tribal office and to tell me stories and instruct me about the Yaqui ancestors.

In 1971, after preliminary congressional legislation cleared the way for tribal recognition, Anselmo held a meeting of celebration. At last a legal cemetery could be created on the land that would become Pascua Pueblo. In order for Pascua to be Yaqui, the dead had to be buried where the people were. At the meeting, Anselmo joked that now that the land for the cemetery had been set aside, all they needed was someone to be laid to rest there. Were there, he asked the gathering of his people, any volunteers? Everyone had laughed, but in the back of the room a hand shot up, and a young Yaqui in his thirties called, "I will!" People laughed again.

But within a week, the young man, Pancho Acuna, died in a freak industrial accident at his job. To this day, he is known as "the volunteer"; his grave is in the southwestern corner of the cementerio. After paying our respects at the Mount Calvario at the entrance of the cementerio, we walked among the rows of tightly laid graves. I asked Anselmo if he had taken the man's life so the people could have their place for the dead. "No," he said. "Something comes through me, Pluma. I don't do anything. It's the Creator."

Each grave was a story. As we sat down on a concrete bench beneath a mesquite tree near his mother's grave, looking at the simple white or unpainted crosses on the hummocks of dirt, some covered with plastic flowers, some with photos by the crosses, bright candles scattered about, I felt as if I were among rows of children who'd been tucked in for bed, and here was my husband telling me a bedtime story.

Sitting by his side in the twilight, by Leoway's grave, I saw the evening star. I had the strongest feeling that his mother was now a star. I asked him about it, and what the people say happens after we die.

"There is a special kind of time," Anselmo began. "Past, present, and future, all together. In that time our spirit is alive and aware. When we die, we go into that time and exist between lives of the body."

"Does that mean you believe in reincarnation?"

Anselmo explained that when the spirit departed from the body it spent one year of earthly time in eternity. After that year, the luto ceremony marked the return to earthly life of the departed spirit, and the dead person returned in a new body. We die neither in spirit or body, since we are returned again and again to the place of our creation on earth.

"In the eternal place," he continued, as the light seeped out of the western sky, "during our absence from earth and the life of the body, the spirit is rekindled by the fire that exists in the heart of eternity. It is from the perspective of that place between worlds that we can see all human time. That is how it is possible to see into the future, or commune with the ancestors. The dead are always among us. My people have never created any false barriers of the mind between themselves on earth and those who are no longer on earth. There is no permanent death for us.

"My mother is a star healer, Heather. She is here with us now. She did not have to return to this world. In her final life on earth the generosity of her spirit manifested itself in so many acts of kindness and healing that now she is free.

"But she lived here thousands of time. Yes. My mother is a star."

"Which star is Leoway, Anselmo?"

"For you? The Pole Star. From here she looks like Polaris. She is also the star within the center of your being. She is the star at the center of all the other stars in the mind of my people."

I asked Anselmo if he agreed that a life of service to the greater good of one's people could possibly free a person from having to return for successive lifetimes, which was something astrologers had told me more than once.

"That's true. I am very tired from being the father of my people. I am tired out from coming through the body since before the time of the great lizards."

"That explains why you look like a crocodile," I joked. "Sometimes."

"Now you know why," he said softly. He didn't seem to be in the mood for laughter, though he was not at all somber.

"Would you come back one more time with me? Maybe we would have our own children, like in my dream." I meant it in a lighthearted way. Maybe I was also testing him, hoping he'd say yes. But Anselmo said he could not come back again.

"You know, when you first came to me, I believed we would make a baby. Then I saw that your life force has another direction. The energy that would go into children for us must be redirected here and now in order to accomplish all the things that must be done to make the life of my people secure."

"Anselmo, when you die I want to die with you. You can't leave me here when you go." The suddenness of my sadness surprised me. I began to cry.

He put his hand on mine, a bold gesture for a Yaqui in public, even though night was falling. "You will be born into something better, Pluma. Don't waste your tears on sentimental thoughts. We have work to do here and now that will keep us together."

"The world would never be better without you in it," I said, wiping my eyes with my wrist, "not for your people and certainly not for me. You have to promise me I can be buried next to you when I die. Promise me, Anselmo."

"The world won't be without me when I kick the bucket. I'll be an even bigger deal than I am now," he smirked. "You can be

myself, as he belonged to himself, and out of total dedication to sacrificing one's self-interest, he and I could become free of that which enslaved us. The notion of "good" and "bad" does not extend to what non-Yaqui minds often mean by "good" and "evil." For the Yaqui, because the Creator's mind and purpose are infinitely creative, the works of the Creator are practical experiments. That which is dangerous is not dangerous because it is evil but because it is dangerous.

For Native American people, intelligence has a different function and description than it does for many European Americans. For the Yaqui, real intelligence is adaptability to the needs of the Creator. The people know that the mind of the Creator is endless. Everything is possible, and to say that there can be no such thing as, for example, space beings or mental telepathy is to place your intelligence above the Creator's.

"The Dark World is about power. It is unexplainable to those who haven't gone there. Its access is denied most people. The way into those mysteries is blocked by things like scorpions, the night eagle, snakes."

That was all he said. I rolled over and put my head on his chest, and we both fell asleep.

Anselmo Valencia burns with another kind of light. During the first luto I ever witnessed, I saw the diamond light come into Anselmo's eyes as he deer-sang.

A great deal of Anselmo's time was directed toward caring for the dead. Most weekends there was either a wake for those just passed, the velacion; or a fiesta for those reborn after being "dead" for a year, the luto. The luto ceremony celebrates the return to life of the person who passed away. The soul of the dead one is returned to earth where it enters into the act of conception of a man and a woman who wish to have a child. The relatives of the dead each have a black cord tied about their necks which they wear for twenty-four hours. After this symbolic period of grieving, the cord is cut and the dead one is released, as are the relatives, to life again. At luto the deer dances to celebrate the return to life.

Sometimes, after the newness of the luto weekends passed, we'd have to go from one village to another to officiate at the fiestas. On Friday do the velacion and bury the dead in one village. On Saturday in a second village the dead of a year before would live again . . . It was so simple: you live with the simplest fact—people live in the body and they die out of it to live again in it. That was the way of it, and that was the way of most weekends. At the ceremonies for the dead and the reborn, the older women would talk to me and tell me many things, small and eventful, about my husband because they knew how hard it was to take care of Anselmo—and how much work, both physical and spiritual, it meant for me.

The first velacion I went to was remarkable. One of the dreaming women, doña Lena, had died. Her wake was incredible—hundreds of people came to honor her. All night I watched the candles burn. I could see so *many* dark faces in the firelight, I couldn't believe what I was seeing in the candles. I asked Anselmo if it was imaginary or real, and he assured me it was quite real. In the candles I saw the story of doña Lena—how hard her childhood had been, the many family members she'd lost in wars, illnesses, untimely deaths. All night her story burned in the candles, and yet over everything I saw her joy, her medicine, her magic sing out in her spirit in the candle wax.

Lena was not the first dreaming woman to die as she had done. I thought she'd died because she was old. Later I would learn more about the agreements of the dreaming women in the center of whose circle was Anselmo Valencia. That night, sitting on a bench with some little boys who'd been dancing matachini, the freedom dance developed in the Mexican slave camps, I heard Pero tell one of his friends to look at Anselmo. I looked from the candles to where my husband was deer-singing. The kids were now looking at me to see if I saw what they did, and I did: Anselmo's eyes were possessed of a remarkable diamond light. I whispered to them that it was the Godlight.

Later I asked Anselmo what it meant. He said it was good. The power from doña Lena was truly extraordinary; that was what I had seen. And many comparably extraordinary things happened for the tribe in the months after the death of doña Lena: increased tribal funding for housing (more than any other Arizona tribe that year); an HMO program for the people; additional land for the expansion of the reservation; a program for self-help housing that created better-than-ordinary HUD houses; charcoal and adobe businesses; day care; a center for the elderly; Meals-on-Wheels; Yaqui bingo . . .

So the death of a key woman freed Anselmo and removed blockages beyond his control. I witnessed this phenomenon over and over. I was part of it myself.

When Anselmo returned to Arizona after the Second World War, no longer denying the mantle of power whose burden of self-sacrifice had driven him, as he liked to say, to a life of "the lowest of the low," Anselmo dreamed of building a new community for his people. He took a job with the Pima County Highway Department, married his first wife, had nine children. By the end of the 1950s, he believed the only hope for the Yaqui was to bring them as full participants into the twentieth century. He did not believe that the road to that future was in Old Pascua. After the temporary equalities granted Indians who served shoulder to shoulder with whites in the war, many Indians came back to their reservations only to return not to some new world which they had fought to save from Hitler, but to the same old life of devastating poverty. After the war, many turned to drink and drugs as a result of their disillusionment.

Throughout the 1950s, Anselmo was chief of Old Pascua village in Tucson. He studied with his uncle Juan Pistola and Anselmo's grandfather to learn his cultural obligations. In keeping with his duties as the spiritual leader, he collected herbs for medicine uses. Over the years he became intimately familiar with the desert terrain all around the Tucson basin and mountains, not to mention the Yaqui region.

Crossing the Santa Cruz River, Anselmo would take a dirt road out toward the old Valencia Ranch west of Tucson. In the late fifties Tucson was still more a big town than a city. Out that way he'd venture, toward Black Lizard Mountain. He was particularly drawn to an area on the north and west sides of the Lizard. One day he sat on two little hills that are like a woman's breasts, Tutuli Cawi, gathering herbs. Suddenly some dust devils came. Whirlwinds have always spoken to Anselmo Valencia. They are one of the forms through which the ancestors talk to him.

Come down, look around, the ancestors said. So he did, and he soon noticed movement in the fibers of the earth. Earth, like us, is a being, and she too vibrates, like her children. But just as people have soft, hard, and elastic elements in their form—an elbow functions differently from a stomach or fingernails—so too Mother Earth's being-fibers have a variety of densities. In some places on the body of the Mother the fibers move in such a way that they thin, and it is easier to go into the other world from such places.

Anselmo wanted to make a reservation where his people could have the luxury of time and space in which to bring themselves into the modern world. They had not had such a luxury for four hundred years, before the time of the Talking Tree. Despite the fact that many, even most, of his people did not want a reservation and recognition by the federal government, Anselmo knew it was the only chance they had for a land base to preserve their culture. Only land controlled by the Yaquis would provide the time needed to keep the culture intact.

Anselmo proceeded to research the land. The federal government owned it; it was in a part of Tucson that at the time was hardly inhabited, and there were no utilities close by, so he figured Anglos wouldn't be interested in it. It was precisely the inconspicuousness that favored his attaining the property, yet he'd walked it in monsoon season and observed that it drained and was not susceptible to floods. It did not have big-armed cactus, but it had its modesty—chaparral, lizards, ants—amply enriched by invisible qualities of access to the magic within the body of the Mother.

Still many of his people were not persuaded. The idea of the U.S. government conjured in people's minds psychological and spiritual enslavement to the white man. "But you already are slaves," Anselmo retorted. "So let the government take care of us. Look how many are already on welfare! The government is already chopping us up like stew meat.

"No, have some respect for yourselves. If we surrender to the government, we will survive and win the ability to say how it will be for us in the future. Otherwise, we get eaten alive by the culture of the Anglos. Look—the Mother wants us to protect this part of her so that no one can touch her and take her away. The law of the Anglos says the Mother can be owned, she can be bought and sold. Look how it makes them live apart from one another. If we don't protect the Mother, how will she provide for us? If we don't surrender to the government of the Anglos, we will end up lost in their way."

It was the circle of dreaming women who ultimately turned the tide for tribal recognition. "Yes, children," they told the people at meetings (as well as at their homes). "You will do what Anselmo is telling you. You will go whether you want to or not, and you will make the houses and cook the tortillas and make the village Anselmo is telling you about."

Once it was settled, Anselmo went hunting for support among the Anglos. He had many political friends and allies because he was not only a master of three languages; he also understood the Anglo mind. And Anselmo was charismatic, charming, sincere, mysterious, funny—he had many faces.

With the help of local politicians, especially Morris Udall, Anselmo secured land grant recognition in 1965, and thirteen years later, on September 18, 1978, President Jimmy Carter signed the Pascua Yaqui Tribe to full reservation status, officially recognized as a legal entity eligible for entitlement programs and a measure of sovereignty to address Yaqui affairs in a Yaqui tribal government format. After recognition, a tribal chairman was elected. Anselmo chose a slate for tribal council elections and for himself he created the role of executive director. Thus he consolidated his ancestral and contemporary roles, and for the first time drew a salary as any other leader of the day would. The Yaquis had finally become part of the modern world.

One night we were at a wake for the death of a young man who'd killed himself in South Tucson. It was the second time I'd been to a funeral of a male Yaqui. An old man, at least twenty years older than Anselmo, went down on his knees and put his head in Anselmo's lap. Yaquis are not demonstrative by nature, and least of all Anselmo, who sat there impassively. I was talking to doña Marcelena, when the man began choking out some words in Yaqui, asking, "Achai, will you forgive me now? Father, will you forgive me now?"

Later I asked Anselmo what had happened. Many years ago,

he said, a dance was held by this man to honor one of his beautiful daughters. At that time Anselmo was a worthless drunk. When he dared to dance with the beautiful daughter, this man came over and said, "Get the hell out of here, Anselmo Valencia. You devil, get away from my daughter." And Anselmo said, "Go to hell, old man," and the old man walked into his house, came back out with a gun, and emptied four bullets into Anselmo's chest at point-blank range. Anselmo took the gun away and shot the last two bullets into the air and threw the pistol. People say next—I heard this from three different women—that he disappeared right after he threw the gun and reappeared an hour later at the party, dancing as if nothing had happened.

Tell me your story, I said to Anselmo. His story was that he didn't have a story, he didn't know about any bullets. On the other hand, he had felt such a sudden burst of energy from the noise of the pistol and the force hitting him in the chest that it caused him to jump. The man's yard was surrounded by a tall fence and some even taller oleander bushes. From a standing position Anselmo catapulted himself over the tops of the bushes into the street outside, where he proceeded to run around the block several times until the excitement cooled out of him. Then he returned to the party. He said there was no explanation of why there were no bullets in his chest.

"I don't do anything. Things like this happen, and it has nothing to do with me, Heather. Achai is using me, that's all."

Over the next twenty years, each of the man's four sons took a bullet: one died in a gun fight, one as an innocent bystander during a robbery, and two killed themselves. So the old man was crying out for forgiveness, now that his last son was taken from earth. Anselmo, in all his dealings, was fair, evenhanded with enemies and friends alike. He was the father of his people, and in everything that happened he was an instrument of the Creator. The bullets that shot Anselmo came from Achai, not the sons or the old man, so there was, for Anselmo, nothing to forgive.

10❧ THE SERPENT AND THE HUMMINGBIRD

"ARE YOU AFRAID TO GO TO THE OUTHOUSE?" TEASE MY COMPANIONS of the dream place.

I am walking between two dark, robust women who are taking me across a small ravine. My relief is still far, and they are having a good laugh, but when I join in their merriment it hurts my bladder, which makes them laugh even harder. Beyond the cliff the ravine drops down and comes back up on the other side but at a lower altitude, so I can see roofs with corn spread on top, and around the houses goats and pigs and chickens. This despite the great darkness. Somewhere invisible to me yet is the hope of my body: the outhouse. It is such a simple thing, yet in the night it might as well be a matter of greatest faith, like the existence of the Creator.

The only light in the entire land is coming from the auras of the two women. "Are you afraid to go?" they tease me again. When we reach the outhouse they stand outside. Through the creaky door comes the indigo light from the two women. I realize I can make my way through the darkness because they are shining a way for me. And they are good company!

I know the darker, earthier woman: Macaria. We are great

friends and sisters. But the other is like Isis in blue—small, delicate, bird-like. This is Chonita, whom I'd met briefly the first night at Manuel's. She is somehow veiled, I see, where Macaria is outgoing, playful, bear-like. These two women are taking me deeper into the mysteries of the dreaming power and of the dreaming women.

"Who knows what lies beyond the outhouse, Elena? Want to see?"

Anselmo and I returned after the New Year, 1981, to visit the people in Rio Yaqui. Anselmo had political meetings to conduct in each of the pueblos. The weather, which had been exceptionally beautiful, was an added incentive. And, not least, the time was auspicious for an encounter that had far-reaching effects.

I had been so focused on Anselmo—bewildered, really, both by my happiness with him and by the unexpectedly difficult life of serving the Yaqui people—that I'd almost forgotten my connection with other women. In addition, Anselmo had been very stern about avoiding giving the appearance of *any* unhappiness through gossip with other women, and I did not want to be anything less than the perfect queen to Anselmo and the people. What a delight it was, then, to be in the company of Macaria and Chonita, these two sisters of dreaming! It was they who first hinted I should begin a group of women "like you" for the purpose of creating a dreaming circle. Under the ramada at Manuel's in Torim, as we prepared food together, the two of them planted seeds in me for my purpose and my service at Yaqui. They never said, "Elena, you must do thus and so." Rather, they would lead me into my own forum, always letting the choices be mine.

The first morning back in Torim, I sat between them at the breakfast meal. They asked if there were women *like me* in Tucson. Did women *like me* come to visit me? I understood from our interchange that they were telling me I was their sister not only because I was Anselmo's wife, but, they wanted me to know, we were sisters in dreaming. Were there women like me with whom to talk about my dreams? They never told me directly to start a dream circle on the reservation in Tucson, but their questions contained the blueprint, the form indicating what to do with power.

Ever since the elder women of the dream place visited me en masse in Kansas when I was pregnant with Bobby, blue has been the color announcing the presence of a dreaming woman, blue and the various shades of that part of the light ray. With hair pulled back and braided, Chonita was perhaps four foot ten, as pure as the blue veil under which I first encountered her in the dreams of my childhood and youth. Her hands were long and fine and delicate, and she was as old as Anselmo, her cousin. She was an aristocrat—she could have been a French princess. She had the purity and innocence of a child and the wisdom and strength of a grandmother, and her heart was kind. She had never known the happiness of making a baby; when the man she was madly in love with discovered Chonita was barren, he left her for a woman capable of giving him children. What Chonita was capable of was far greater, however, than biological reproduction. She had nothing when she moved in with her nephew Manuel Valencia—nothing of ordinary value. But she had the honor and protection of the community because everyone saw it shining from her: Chonita was the high priestess of the dream place, the seaneeya, and Chonita came to me and taught me, taught me more than any other, how to speak without words through the heart. As with all that is truly Yaqui, the dream and the material coil together.

Anselmo would leave me alone with Chonita in the homestead in Torim while he went to the farm. He said, "I want you to help Chonita prepare the food for when we return."

We went under the ramada at Manuel's. The vaca on the roof looked like a brown animal, so encrusted were the leaves and canes with soft dust. The ramada was held up by branches and sticks from the huchaco tree. I knew that the vaca was a cane, but I had no Yaqui word for it. Chonita pointed up into the leaves and said, "Cuchiim, cuchiim." I looked up and said, "Tutuli cuchiim," pretty cane, and she laughed and laughed. I looked up to see what was so funny. There in the cane was the handle of a knife. She couldn't reach it because she was so short.

So I reached up and got it down for her, and she said, "Ah, cuchiim, cuchiim!" The knife.

We prepared the dinner for the people who would be returning from the corn fields. "Seyem pul tenkuk"—What did you dream? You always have dreams, she said as we were working together on some guacavaci. "And you are in my dreams." She said. "Tell me the name that Chonukuk gave you."

"Onamwashnatena—high white lightning." Chonita laughed and nodded her head as she cut up corn ears, then looked up and stuck her tongue at me, in and out several times. Then she giggled like a naughty school girl. Because the white lightning is the tongue of the Great Serpent, Chonita said, it is a powerful name for a woman, one that a Yaqui woman wouldn't be given. If I had been named in Yaqui, she said, I might be called "Sewa oneeya," "Light Flower." I did not know till many years later, when I looked in a dictionary of proper names, that "Helen" signified "light-giver." Chonita, who had no awareness of my given name, Heather, nevertheless had come up with a Yaqui equivalent to denote "flower."

Chonita was not without mischief. Soon all the women made much fun of my Kickapoo name. Onamwashnatena sounded to Chonita like "onna matachini," which in Yaqui would be "the Salty Dancer." There was considerable hilarity over all these names for me. In the ramada, working with Chonita, all the names seemed right.

Chonita knows everything that is happening. She is the dream finder—in the dream, Chonita finds how it will be for her people. The people in Rio Yaqui would always know before I came that I was coming; Chonita would dream me, as well as what I was bringing and what sicknesses I had endured. Her health was very delicate; sometimes she burned sickness in her body because she was so open and sensitive. If there was pain in her people, she would burn their pain in her body. I myself have held her during fevers that would kill normal people. Around us the room would glow in the blue light of the dreaming women from time immemorial. The ancestors would be around us in the room. When I held Chonita and worked with my hands to draw away the fever, she communicated to me through her pain that she did not want me to burn karma in my body as she and

Anselmo had done. She knew I was sensitive enough to do it. But my purpose, she cautioned, was not in that direction.

So much of the instruction was by indication, suggestion, inference that I had no choice except to take an active role in learning. Nobody set out "teachings." Often, as with Chonita's warnings about health, there was no alternative specified as to what was better than danger. With Chonita, teaching was advice: don't imitate her, don't take on the ills of others and burn them in my body. But she never told me what I *should* do—only what was dangerous.

Chonita and the dreaming women of Torim taught me how powerful the collective dream realm is, how powerful the collective mind! That is the gift—and the curse—of the tribal peoples. There is nothing you can do that is not known. Your lovemaking is known, your lies, your truth, all are known. It is all known and understood—and accepted. Judgments in Yaqui are not harsh. When someone is smooth with the culture, it is felt in the dream realm, and is good. But when someone is not smooth with the culture, it feels like pain, a wound. Anselmo used to tell me that is how growth is produced—by pain. It is necessary; that is the only way humans can do it.

The moment is important. The Mother is important. In the dark silence, in mysterious ways, the dream fire flows. The men manifest the dream fire; the women conjure in the dark silence. When the Spaniards came, because they had no respect for women, things appeared to change. But that is just appearance. The women are not seen and heard; it appears the women have deferred to the men who form a protective circle around them. But the women are the source of real power. Although Anselmo is Achai, it is he who is in the protective circle of the dreaming women. They enable him to give form to the ancient, timeless acts of creating that have always been the women's realm of purpose.

I looked across the table at my husband. Our eyes glanced at each other a moment, and then we both continued talking to our companions sitting with us after our meal. The only man I ever wanted was a sorcerer, a magician. My magician had the face of the Death Lord and wore on his ring finger a star ruby that is the

same color as his aura. In the faces of the elder dreaming women
and the young women, Hilda and Macaria, I could feel Anselmo
Valencia. In the daylight it is hard to focus on the beacon of a
lighthouse. Among the dreaming women of Rio Yaqui, I was
beginning to sense how that beam of light that is Anselmo was
fed and charged.

It was less clear, then, how I was helped. But what I knew was
that the feeling of certainty came from those women.

All of Anselmo's clan are remarkable for their curly hair and
striking good looks. "Because we're such rats," he said to the
delight of those around us. Then he settled down and told me
about the tori rats his clan was named after. Even where there is
nothing else left on the land, Anselmo said, these little toris
make nests and proliferate. They have round, short fluffy tails,
big eyes, pointed noses, and bare feet and fur like a possum.
That is why the ruling clan in Yaqui is the Tori clan—everyone
depends on them, and all the people can survive on the tori rats.
I myself caught a tori.

As we were driving down the dusty road to the fields one day,
I saw what I was sure was a tori nest, an egg-shaped jumble of
sticks in a mesquite tree. "Stop!" I yelled when Anselmo confirmed that it was a tori nest. "Stop, I want to get a picture."

"You won't get a picture of a tori, Pluma. They are shy and it's
daytime. They like the night better."

"Stop the truck, Tori, I have to get a picture."

I ran up to the nest and called to the rats. "I am your new
sister," I said to them. "Come out and let's meet."

"Well, I'll be damned!" Anselmo muttered behind me. A tiny
tori had poked out his head to see me.

"Thank you, brother," I said. "Here is big Tori, and I am
Pluma." I snapped two photos, vainly waving Anselmo into the
picture, but as always he refused to let me photograph him. In
the old days—the people haven't eaten tori in forty years—this
little fellow wouldn't have gotten to stay in his little tori pueblo.
Inside the tori nest were apartments, Anselmo said. If there was
famine, the people would take a long stick and gently insert it,
twist, and the soft fur of the tori would snag on the stick. You
pulled it out and the tori came with it.

Anselmo remembered when he was young his favorite soup was pozole, with pinto beans, corn, meat, and salt. When he was little he would see the little tori feet clinging to one kernel of Yaqui corn—and he would eat them. I myself prayed that I would never have to eat a rat's feet.

Anselmo often warned me at first, "If you are the woman I think you are, you will eat whatever you are served and not be sick or complain." So far, in all the houses where we were honored and fed, I had eaten the lovely squash and beans, some meat and wonderful tortillas. I thought that I was in the clear, when, toward the end of our January visit, Anselmo took me to TiTi's house. She had the store and a real gas stove. "In your honor," she said, "I have made a special soup because you are Anselmo's bride." She presented me with a bowl of chicken soup with a huge, fleshy chicken foot sticking straight up out of the bowl, still attached to the leg which was impacted in the vegetables underneath. My stomach started to swim. Anselmo reached over and said, "That's too much meat for you," and took the chicken foot, leg and all, out of my bowl. I was so grateful I ate the rest of the soup gladly.

Nothing makes Tia Challa angrier than parrots flocking in her lemon trees. As we drove out of Torim, Tia Challa limped toward her lemon grove, waving her cane over her head. She wasn't in any mood to greet anyone—her cane slashed the air with force meant for parrot heads. Seeing Anselmo, however, she gave us a wave as she headed with determination toward the trees. The saucy birds went on munching her best lemons, squawking their sour music. The morning was blue and crisp, but Tia Challa's fury shook the scarf from her shoulders. Abruptly her cane touched base with the ground, and she stooped to retrieve the fallen shawl. By the time she reached the trees and smacked the lower branches with vicious swipes of her cane, the parrots had already left the trees, jumping in unison as if riding an unseen wave. They floated a moment like a scattering of mock lemon leaves tossed and taunting—then settled right back into the same branches.

We went around a curve and settled into the jumpy routine of driving the bumpy road. I rolled down the window. Anselmo rolled down his. We were both light and happy. January, the Janus-faced month, my first new year with Anselmo. I looked out the window at the landscape, which slowed down as Anselmo braked for the goat herd near Lencho, then flew by in a blur of laundry set out to dry on bushes above the irrigation trench. Two women looked up and waved, were gone. Who were they? Oh, your nieces. He's related to everyone. The smell of the Bahia behind us, does sunlight have a smell? . . .

Anselmo turned south on the blacktop highway, heading toward Obregón. He lit a cigarette and about a mile down the road gestured with his chin. "That's it," he said, indicating a small, rather ordinary-looking mountain on the east side of the highway. "Tosal Cawi."

So that was the sacred mountain. I might even have seen this when we drove in last week, I thought, but couldn't remember whether I'd seen it on the drive in or in dreaming. Its modesty surprised me, especially that it was right on the highway. But then, that is Yaqui, that also this mountain was here long before this road or this Mexico. January, Yaqui—nothing is just what it is.

As if he were listening to my thoughts, Anselmo replied, "Great treasures are always secret. They aren't for the eyes of everyone. Who among all these people driving by today would know Tosal Cawi is an opening to the other world?"

"Are we going to the Enchanted Flower World, Anselmo?" I asked. Recalling my experience in Magdelena, I had a premonition, or perhaps it was more like what a mother feels, having once gone through childbirth and subsequently having forgotten that pain in the thrall and flush of the new child, that each time you give birth there is that looming pain to go through . . .

"We are going up there," he said, turning onto a dirt track, leaving the highway behind us. "Today is a day for ceremonial magic. I want you to make a circle up on top, one we can enter together as a living prayer." We followed the wheel ruts up through alamo trees and cattails, gradually making our way toward the east side of the mountain, which was out of view of the highway. Tosal Cawi seemed hardly more than a volcanic afterthought, a small dit in the Morse code of landscape which skilled readers like Anselmo and his people understand. It was here, on Tosal Cawi the story went, that as a young man Anselmo Valencia entered the Dark Enchanted Flower World and conquered the Great Serpent.

"Is that true, Anselmo?" I asked after he parked by a tree. "Did you go into the Dark World and conquer the Great Serpent?" We sat there awhile without speaking.

"Rosario Moses had his chance with the Great Serpent, like I told you. I also have had mine. Only time will tell whose wishes will prevail."

He opened the door and got out. The forest had thinned considerably. Without a word between us I followed through the rocks and high grass onto a faint trail. I stooped down to look at the pretty white and pink flowers blooming everywhere in the grass on the way up. Near the top I started feeling nervous. Anselmo's voice was gentle. He kept walking but said over his shoulder, "So, Pluma, do you remember any of this from before? We have been here many times together."

I hadn't actually been up Tosal Cawi before, but it did look familiar. I sat on a rock for a moment to catch my breath. Anselmo paused to wait for me. "It is a very important place for you and me," he said softly. "It is very important for the people, too. When we get to the top, I will ask the blessing of the ancestors and open the door to the Dark World." He turned. I got up and followed and in a short climb we arrived at the summit. A strange bank of clouds had moved closer to the mountain. When we started it had been behind us; now it was to our right and slightly ahead of us.

The wind whipped around in little lariats, but I was pleasantly warmed by the sun, which was almost directly above. Anselmo suggested I take off my clothes while he prayed to the ancestors. I folded my pink skirt and blouse and used them as a cushion, tied the purple silk rebozo around my shoulders, and leaned against some rocks.

The summit of Tosal Cawi is like a shallow dish—there are small boulders that rim the little clearing where we were. When I sat down, all I could see was sky, the edge of the mountain itself, the strange cloud which had cycled still further counterclockwise around us. We were too high up to hear any cars or trucks. With a little wind in your ears, Tosal Cawi is very much as it looked to the first Yaqui people.

I closed my eyes. Off to one side of the mountain Anselmo was saying his prayers. I couldn't make out any words. The wind really began to sing in the rocks behind my head. It all seemed warm and silver, Tori's voice, the wind, the sun, the earth . . . They all started to go through me, as if my husband's voice were the leader of a strand of beads and I was being beaded. I heard the click-click and opened my eyes. I don't know if it was a raven, or rocks tapping together. I couldn't see Anselmo. When I shut my eyes again, a radiance was still there, building. I began to travel in it. I had the sensation of walking into something that was already moving around. At the same time I had the increasingly strange feeling of filling up physically with light. The thought occurred to me that I couldn't hold all the light. I became aware that Anselmo was crouching next to me. I knew that when I opened my eyes, we would not be in January 1981.

"Now pray," Anselmo said in my ear. I did not know what to ask. My heart was pounding so loudly I thought Anselmo had heard it. "Just do it as you always have. Pray to our Mother. Then we must make her an altar."

It was difficult to focus, because I seemed to keep expanding. I managed to pray for what was expected of me: the welfare of the people and their strength to transform in some new way. I prayed for Anselmo to have the strength he'd need to lead the Yaquis into a new era in which the survival of the people would be assured.

I got up and showed Anselmo where to place large stones in a circle around the little clearing. He carried many stones over, and together we set them into a ring. Then I inscribed a star within the circle, just as Aunt Charmaine had shown me, the outer ring being the entrance to the temple of Earth herself, the five-pointed star the figure for human beings in the circle of the Mother's influence. The star in the field of the Infinite; the human body open-armed in the reflecting pool of starlight; the unborn about to enter what existed before and will exist forever—

"Lie down in the center." Anselmo's voice startled me, but I reclined in the center of the star, placing my head to the north, my feet south, my arms extended east and west, facing the sky. The sun had become so intense it shocked me into closing my eyes. Again the sunlight gathered and focused, and for a while I felt as if I had become pure halo, I was so brimmed up with light. But then it oppressed me, like a painful weight within. I opened my eyes. I felt dizzy, as though my cells themselves had expanded to the breaking point. The ground at the corner of my vision was tipping or sliding. I couldn't grasp what I was seeing. I was only painfully aware that at any second my body was going to explode into tiny fragments and that if I didn't breathe and calm down I would die. I heard the cadence of Anselmo's prayer song and with great exertion I was able to shift my head and stop the ground from moving around. I didn't see the edge of the mountain; the ring of stones had changed into some sort of yellow and black pattern, as if I were inside a basket looking up close at the weave of the reeds.

Then the yellow and black strands started to move, very quickly, blurring around me. I rolled my head to the other side and a sticky, wet red tongue longer than a human body licked me all over. I am dying, I thought, and with the realization it suddenly was easy. The serpent opened its immense mouth—I stared straight into the black pit at the back of its throat—

I let go and my body released all its cells and disintegrated. Simultaneously I recalled the last instant when my body was whole and human and the serpent had come for it and begun to squeeze me. It was for a fraction of that instant an excruciating weight, and suddenly it was very pleasurable. The Great Serpent had shattered me and in the gap of time while I shattered, I was nothing; I was between daylight and starlight, between mountain and molten, between child and parents, this and that, now and then. I shattered, and thought, I wonder why dying is so hard. And then I knew that dying is the one thing a human being can never do—because we are eternal, starlight. The Great Serpent and I were the same, and I saw the memory of the woman I had been through the serpent's eyes, but the woman I saw was made of light, not flesh and bones. She exists to the serpent for less time than a flicker of its red tongue.

Anselmo's voice is at first muffled and far-off. At the same time it is in me like a searing needle piercing my heart. He is saying something in my ear, and I respond by breathing, breathing the way you do when you give birth, breathe the pain away, then breathe away the thought of pain. When I open my eyes I see the face of something like a boa constrictor with green eyes, except when I look closely, the eyes are dark, opaque, like Anselmo's. They are heartless eyes, which I cannot bear looking into, yet I know I must or I will no longer have a body.

"If you have fear or pain, this won't work for anyone," Anselmo whispers in my ear. His words in English are like a bucket of ice water. Suddenly the weight lifts and I am more in my body. Anselmo is kneeling beside me, as if he had never undressed. And instantaneously there is in me the knowledge that my husband and the Serpent are one, and I am floating on the great void from which everything is born. I do not know if this is a ritual we have created, or if my body can withstand any more, and then I stop thinking about it and feel a remarkable openness, a willingness, a love for the vastness of this creature that is life, as if for the first time I have comprehended how the form and formlessness of life ask my participation. I also know I could have refused, and I did not. Anselmo is watching me closely. "Now it will be changed, now the people have a chance. You came here, Pluma, to change things for us, and you have more courage than I imagined, you have great courage."

He stands up, leans over and covers me with my pink skirt. The sun is a bleached spot behind the bank of clouds.

When I first came to Yaqui, the whirlwinds came again and danced for me at the cultural arena, in the plaza, lifting confetti, leaves, candy wrappers, foil, even a parasol or two, and they pranced with all that human glitter in their wild heads and I saw the faces of the masked dancers that I would come to know, year after year, Easter after Easter. In this desert, after the lush bloom of spring and before the monsoon rains fall, the whirlwinds freely roam the land, talking and roaming.

Every medicine person I have ever known has been a living reminder that we cannot predict the form magic will take. We just have to be ready, in the moment. It is important that we appreciate the magic as it unfolds—Anselmo told me that, as did Aunt Charmaine and George Allen before him.

Long ago, looking over the Kansas plains, I saw the whirlwinds exactly as I had seen them in dreams of childhood. There, in 1970, before my medicine journey took on its more dramatic forms, I watched before me so many dust devils they appeared to be a herd of wild animals roving the Great Plains. I heard them talking, talking, talking, and those that came near me contained faces, as my dreams did, and the whirlwinds told me then that the dream is all around us, wherever we care to see.

On June 24, 1981, on the feast of San Juan, I was sitting under the ramada at the northern end of the Tucson Mountains, in Marana village, beyond the Rattlesnake Mountain. On San Juan's Day Anselmo had lost his son Giovanni many years earlier, and I, too, was grieving silently because being Anselmo's queen had isolated me so from other women to whom I was supposed to show nothing but joyousness.

The morning was hot. Small black bugs were everywhere. I was filled with the heat which seemed not only to be in the air but in the fluid pulse of the water drum, the rasp, the electric sound of the insects. Anselmo was deer-singing; I fell into a strange reverie in which many times and places that I had witnessed were again present. I heard the song about the ladybug. I heard the singers sing about the little javelina, the wild pig, rolling down the hill with his mother chasing after. Tears came easily to my eyes. There was a butterfly in the deer lodge. I saw it and my heart was filled with a sudden hunger to have a friend, one woman friend!

When the fibers of our beings are illumined, we can join in the heart of the Enchanted Flower World—something divine within us can reach out and take what we need from creation. In 1977 in Tucson, I had met an extraordinary artist, a woman named Dana Patterson, who wove in a medicine way with beadwork. Lately I had seen her many times in my dreams—the butterfly, the dust devils out in the Avra Valley marching to and fro like chappeyekas lit the fibers of my being with my need to meet Dana again, to find her. So I let my eyes follow the bright fibers into the spirit land and there I reached for her.

Three children were playing some distance from the deer lodge. Though the children, I realized, were not Dana's, I knew that somehow Dana was also looking for me. Into the aura around the three children the deer came; I looked and knew Dana and I would soon meet. During a break in the singing I went over to one of the little girls and asked her if she knew any of Dana Patterson's children. She said yes, she did know them. They went to grade school together. I asked the girl, who was the daughter of the chief of Marana Pueblo, if she'd get her mother for me. Soon the wife of the chief of Marana came over, and from her I learned Dana lived near Marana, out on Sandario Road. The woman gave me directions.

It is important that we appreciate the magic as if unfolds—Anselmo told me that, and Aunt Charmaine had told me that before Anselmo. Early the next week I drove our car from Yaqui up to Sandario Road, through the Saguaro National Monument, toward Dana's house. But I have never been much for maps, and the intersection between the real Sandario Road and the little lines snaking across a piece of yellow paper all got lost in the dance of the whirlwinds out in the valley below and away, and soon I was in some other time and place. The whirlwinds took me to the Papago sacred mountain, Baboquivari. There I was standing before the burned wreck of an old turquoise-colored car. The car itself had come to its rest in front of a sacred cave, used by mountain lions and coyotes for their winter rest, and used, I knew, by our ancestors who had been dancing and singing so powerfully recently. It occurred to me that I was not on the Sandario Road and that much time had passed. How did I get here and why was I not at Dana's house? Why was it so hard to find her?

Ahead on Sandario Road were a woman and three children, standing near a mailbox, waving. I stopped, got out and embraced her. Dana's eyes were wrinkled with gentle humor as she looked at me. "How can you who are such a medicine woman be so lost? We've been waiting for you!"

"I don't know if this can be said in English," Anselmo frequently warned. "The Anglo mind is not like ours."

Looking over what I have lived, before I came to Anselmo and his people, those simple sentences of his seem like the best door to go through, in or out. Looked at from the way of my upbringing, my life has been full of contradictions. But with my Indian mind, there is no contradiction. How can a medicine woman be so lost? When you follow trails of magic, you have to be careful where you go. Perhaps you have to be willing to get lost in the dream; my way has been my way. I like the thunder and the lightning, and I've been burned as well as blessed.

It didn't happen often, but occasionally Anselmo traveled without me to Rio Yaqui, for reasons of his own. Just after the Yaqui bingo business was started with the help of a wonderful Anglo whom I nicknamed "The Dragon," which is what everyone ended up calling him, too, Anselmo was away for a few days in Rio Yaqui. The Dragon and an Anglo dreaming woman named Cara were visiting me. We'd been talking, it was late, and we were all tired. I invited them to stay the night. We all shared, quite properly, the available space in my bedroom. I gave them the bed, took a blanket, and slept in front of my altar on the floor. The Dragon fell asleep in his business suit; Cara rolled on her side with her back to the Dragon, and I laid down my head and slept almost instantly.

Suddenly Chonita came into the room, the blue light glowing from her. Actually, she seemed to have emerged, like a madonna, from my altar. She said, "The Tori is fine, he's looking after the people, and they are also doing well. So don't worry if you haven't heard from him." When she stopped speaking, through the windows I saw dreaming women in the form of wolves and coyotes, their eyes lit with blue and aquamarine light. They peeked into the room to see who was lying in Anselmo's place, what was going on. "You see, Elena?" Chonita said. "See? We are always with you."

"Heather!" Cara said as loudly as she could without waking everyone else in the house. "Heather!" She was sitting up in bed, motioning me to look out the window. "There are coyotes out in the rose bushes, come see!"

"No, Cara, it's just the dreaming women," I said yawning. "Anselmo's all right, they just wondered who was in our bed. It's fine, go to sleep." I yawned and slept soundly all night.

*   *   *

When Macaria and Chonita in their sly way instructed me to start a dreaming circle of women like me in my house at Yaqui, I let Anselmo's daughter Andrea know it was time to form a circle of women. Over a few months various women would appear at my door. They would find me as I'd found Dana, who was of course part of my dreaming circle that eventually formed. Anglos and Mexicanas, blacks, Yaquis, Hopis, Arikaras, Navajos, Sioux—we found each other in a simple, medicine way. Andrea would put out the word, or through the most amazing grapevine women would find me. Red Jo, for instance, was a gifted masseuse who occasionally did work for the mother of one of Bobby's girlfriends. I met Red Jo in October of my first autumn on Yaqui. The dreaming women recognize and find each other in such apparently casual yet predestined ways. We are pointed out to one another.

There were many dreaming circles. In addition to the circle of women from all cultures and backgrounds that I began, I was part of an all-Yaqui circle of women who were approximately of my generation. That circle was composed of Macaria, Hilda, Chonita, and Prieta in Rio Yaqui; Chiyo and Sonja, Anselmo's younger nieces; Molly, Mercedes, and Maria, whom I dubbed the 3M sisters; Kooka, Maria Cantore, and her daughter Michele; and Anselmo's daughters Andrea and Margie. This was the core of the circle, though some women from Yaqui were also loosely affiliated with us at various times. This was the circle of contemporary women who could be relied upon to support Anselmo in all that he did.

There was also a circle of older women important to me, women of Leoway's generation, who were elder teachers to me. Many of the women of Leoway's generation I never got to meet in the flesh, but some I did. Leoway's circle included Tia Agustina, Tia Challa, Tia Teresea, doña Lena, Inez, and Nalda, among others, from both Rio Yaqui and Arizona.

All women, if they would lift up their eyes awhile and look, are interwoven from the beginning. But naturally at any one time in history, for those who feel the call of other dreaming women, it becomes apparent who should work together. In my Yaqui dreaming circle, as with the circle of elder dreaming women, what united us was our need to serve the Yaqui people and to support Anselmo Valencia, the chosen leader of the people.

The strength of a circle of women may at one age come from youthfulness and vigor. A young dreaming woman may not even know she is part of a circle. What she sees, as some of the young women in my circle did, like Chiyo and Sonja, who were helpers to me, is that you do a lot of errands, you do a lot of gathering of medicines for ceremonial uses. Because we are all there to help Anselmo and the people, the service to others is what a younger woman might focus on.

But as you mature you may realize you are also in the circle to learn; and when you are an elder, you are there to serve the younger dreaming women through your wisdom. Quite naturally you all become a circle of women who do many things, including teaching. The danger of describing it is the easy implication that a dreaming circle is something more formal than it really is. Often, after Tosal Cawi, I would forget and remember, forget and remember that real knowledge means surrendering control—even the magician's control—to serve the greater magic that is life. The knowledge comes after. Living, I followed life.

My first October in Yaqui, I was asked to come to the Flores house to sing for doña Francesca, who was dying. I went into her room in the adobe house in South Tucson. I was a complete stranger, yet she had met me in dreams and knew of me.

"I am going back to see the ancestors," she said as we held hands. Red Jo, whom I'd asked to come, began to massage her feet.

"Sing your songs for me now," doña Francesca said.

I sang. I don't even know what the words were, I didn't even know I had any songs for her. But the words, the sound, the feeling were there in my heart when she asked for songs. And she passed in the night.

There is a joke about Indian songs. At one Plains powwow or other, Rolling Thunder tells those assembled, "This is my Lakota brother. He is going to sing a song about a duck going south for the winter."

The Lakota steps forward and begins to sing. "Hay a nay a

nay a hay a—," until the song is finished. Rolling Thunder returns and addresses the people. "Now we are going to hear a song from my Seneca brother. He's going to sing about a warrior who goes on a vision quest."

The Seneca steps forward and sings, "Hay a nay a nay a hay a—"

The *words* aren't the meaning. They only point to the spirit which is carried by the song itself. I cannot tell the songs I sang. If it is spoken it becomes so different from what actually transpired between me and doña Francesca, which was personal, intimate, a gift from the ancestors who gave me the songs in the first place. All languages blend when you sing from the heart of your being. It isn't through intellect we understand one another. Without the heart and the mind of the heart, we are walking dead.

The Indian mind is different from the Anglo mind. For the Indian mind, there aren't inconsistencies in the workings of magical time and space, with how things can be in the spirit and the material places separately or simultaneously. It is the endlessness of the Creator's mind that makes everything possible. The Anglo mind has been encouraged to look for logical sequence, cause and effect, reasons, "order." For Indian people, this is a blindness, a limitation, a potentially fatal constriction of the flow of reality.

When a snake appears to a medicine person, he or she knows it has made an appearance because the spirit realm deemed it necessary. It's at both levels, spiritual and material, that the medicine person's mind operates by suspending all thinking processes. There is a watchfulness only. In watching the snake, the medicine man or woman disappears into the snake, into the moment, into the intent of the Creator. But, watching the medicine man or woman, someone immersed in the Anglo mind might easily but mistakenly assume that the medicine person was "doing" something to "cause" magic. Actually, a medicine person just gets out of the mode of "who" and has no thought of magic or outcome. When you have medicine, you have power because your presence in this world is suspended. Only the uninitiated would fail to comprehend that magic occurs not because of the presence of some powerful person, like a sorcerer, but because of his or her momentary absence.

I think it has been life's little joke on me that I've had such a strong sense of *what* I am, while I've so often found out from others *who* I am. Sometimes the difference between the two— *what* I am as spirit, as life, my eternal being; and *who*, in the narrowest, most personal, egocentric sense—blurred. Being with Anselmo, I easily assumed that my importance to the people was solely a function of being the wife of the spiritual leader of the people. I kept focusing on Anselmo, Anselmo, Anselmo. Part of me wanted to figure it out, the *who*.

Once Anselmo had to make an unexpected journey alone to Rio Yaqui. He asked that for his return I prepare a fiesta. For these feasts a cow had to be butchered and prepared in thin strips of steak; the intestines, known as mariguts, were sectioned and cooked in a certain way. It was beyond me, exasperating. Anselmo expected so much of me at all times, at all times to be at his level and understand even the details of the most ordinary of Yaqui realities such as food preparation. I asked don Luis to make the fires and called Andrea and Margie to help me do the food. Maria of the 3M sisters showed up. I still see her, bent over, cooking the mariguts, turning them, looking at me. I said, "You know, Maria, I get tired of doing these things for this man, and I sometimes wonder why I do."

She stood up straight with the spatula in her hand, looked at me, and said, "You do it for the same reason we all do, Heather. He's the center. He's the heart of things for this nation. What we do for our people we are doing also for the good of everyone else. We are lucky to be a part of this."

I said, "Yes, he does seem like the sun. He does seem like the god."

"But we are the power. We women. We are the real power."

I smiled: "Does *he* know that?"

"All Yaqui men know that. They are the thing you see. But we are behind it. We are the ones making the decisions."

"Me, too?"

"Of course, you, too! Look who you are!"

On Yaqui it became enough that others saw me. After a while *who* wasn't what mattered at all.

*   *   *

All the women in the dreaming circle stood up suddenly and held hands. There were thirteen of us in my living room, early in 1982, there on South Camino Vacum. It was evening, the room was dim. Something amazing was happening which we had all sensed and on account of which we were standing in awe. For out of everyone's mouth, eyes, and ears flowered a lambent amethyst light. I thought I was the only one seeing it, but Cindy said, "I can see everyone's aura," and little Brandy, Cindy's daughter, said, "I can, too," and I started to cry, I was so overwhelmed not only with my emotion, but something we collectively formed. I understood at that instant we were a unity, all these different women, and I knew they felt the same thing, which was grace; what was happening to all of us was grace.

And suddenly again, as if at once, several of the women looked at me and said, "Heather, I can see your lifetime, I can see her whole lifetime, I can see all her lifetimes!" Somebody said, "Heather, it's true, it's really you, you are like the queen of heaven with stars all around you, you're the queen!" Everyone was so happy for me and I didn't know myself what was happening or where it was coming from, and then I felt it, I felt it, I felt I was in the starry, starry void and wherever I was standing the void was behind me and I was surrounded by stars, stars. Dana was there and Cheri and all of a sudden there were more women in the room than we had started with, I hadn't seen them before, I knew they weren't there in their bodies, but they also had come to join us.

It was not long after this wonderful circle that Aunt Charmaine's husband, Julian, called the house to tell of Charmaine's death an hour earlier. Hearing the news I wept. It was Charmaine who had come to us, who had joyfully passed on what she was to all of us and given to me her own crown of power.

I hung up the phone and told everyone. Again I felt the connection with these women who were truly my sisters, who were me, and together we were something much greater than individual women. In the beautiful faces of these women, many of whom I barely knew, I saw myself whole for the first time, and Aunt Charmaine in the stars within my heart was expanding beyond her own body and years toward the simplicity of life in which we never die. "Heather," she seemed to say, "we are the same thing, the same one. Be awake, awake within the dream. We will always find each other, we cannot die, we just change form . . ." I had the greatest certainty that the dreaming women always were and always have been, and that they would keep finding each other, endlessly.

When I stood with the other dreaming women during Aunt Charmaine's passing, the stars seemed to beat in the veined night, returning to me, returning. And it can be so frightening when you go into the starlight. You're so afraid, because you can't touch anybody you know, you can't go anyplace you've ever been before, you're afraid and you don't want to stop touching, you don't want to let go. Yet when you do let go and surrender to the starlight, it's the ultimate surrender. Then we are what the god is, the all and the everything, we've come back to the heart of the shining void which is so magnificent. You love everything you've ever known with such complexity and completeness it's far more than our intellect can absorb. There in the starlight at my aunt Charmaine's death, I found her again, and my sisters, and myself.

Who we are will die. *What* we are is timeless, and we understand what we are at moments when we surrender our form. When we are open to the greatness of life, what we are cannot die. All my life I created dreams. So much of the time I was lost in them. It took me years—and teachers on both sides of the wall between worlds—to help me remember who had begun the dream.

My dream of Yaqui and the Dark Lord was a group dream and its power intensified a millionfold. Its nuances and all its intricate aspects were but one root in the network of the tree of creation. But I was lost in the dream long enough to experience completely that particular form of our collective human dream power. I stayed with Anselmo many years after Tosal Cawi. I didn't know at the time I was free to go, my tasks in Yaquiland over. I could not go, really, because I still didn't remember who had begun that dream. I still believed it was Anselmo and I wasn't able to walk through the door in time to my own freedom.

Chonita once told me that it is the responsibility of all of us to be happy, to bring our greatest joys and our biggest desires into the expression of formal experience. If you are a dreaming woman you are at the beginning of the web of creation. This web is extremely elastic, like a spider web. The old stories describe the web like this: When Cloud-Dreaming Woman's daughter Spider Woman created this earth, it was left to her daughters to carry on the endless dream weaving. But Spider Woman started things. She dreamed and spun out the things of this world. She did not know what she was dream weaving; only that she was dreaming . . . something. So she gave birth to the ugly right along with the beautiful, the sweet-natured and the misanthrope, the frog and the smooth-cheeked prince, atomic bombs and telephones along with every plant and chemical to cure or kill.

If you are a dreaming woman, however, you know you and your sisters are together making this world. Sometimes we know each other first, then the world we are making; other times we know the world first and find one another afterward. It is the same. We are making one unending weaving together. Among tribal people, ritual is the formal aspect that allows magic, and magic is much simpler than Anglo people have made it. Where the material and the dream realms meet, like land and sea, earth and air, time and space, something extra is left over for our use. We have to unite the private and the tribal mind all of us possess. We must release ourselves from the strangling fears of the unremembered and remember it fully. There *is* magic. It's what will join opposites together into new expressions of life.

The ceremonial rituals of Anselmo's people present the unending struggle between light and dark, between the universal and tribal and the specific and absolute. The deer doesn't dance for one man or woman, or even just the Yaqui people. The deer dances for everyone.

On Ash Wednesday, 1982, Dana dreamed she gave birth to a huge rattlesnake. In Yaqui, all creatures have a song. The rattlesnake, however, belongs to the Dark Enchanted Flower World, and his song is sung only in the Dark World because he is the familiar of the Death Lord and therefore under his, not human, protection.

In Dana's dream the snake revealed its medicine song. The dream awoke her, and she wove the dream into a band with a rainbow diamond pattern set on black. At first glance, each diamond is the same; only when you look closer can you see the superlative artistry of the weaver. The beads are tiny, and subtle shifts in color and pattern within pattern make each diamond unique.

Dana beaded for a month. Palm Sunday she brought the work to me. Seeing it, I at once called Anselmo. Anselmo loves the God eye. He wears little mirrors and eyes all over his regalia. He has hidden eyes throughout our house. At first sight of Dana's work, he was instantly impressed by the diamond eyes from which, we both saw, light emanated. Anselmo loved the band and wore it on his black hat, the following week, for the Running of the Gloria. After the first set of deer songs by the Church of Cristo Rey, the deer was escorted down to the deer lodge and installed, as has been done throughout time. All the participants took off their hats, regalia, and swords and placed them in a sacred mound before the deer lodge. The men clustered in a circle in the cultural kitchen next door for the beginning prayers and their meal together.

I had gone home to our house to prepare the regalia for a second deer dancer from Mexico who would dance in relief of the main deer dancer. I was assembling the leg rattles and gourds when Bobby came running into the room.

"Anselmo says to tell you not to cry. It is important not to cry, he said. If you do you'll weaken him."

"What? Just tell me what happened, Bobby."

"Someone stole Anselmo's new medicine hatband during prayers. Everyone was in the cocina and no one knows who did it."

I couldn't help being upset. The theft of the hatband during prayers was a breach of everything tribal and cultural, a violation of the sanctity of the spiritual work that occurs during a deer dance when through the people's intent the invisible medicine is created. The theft of the hatband was equivalent to stealing the elixir of eternal life.

"Come on, Mom. Anselmo wants you to give me his snake hatband and I'm supposed to take it to him right away."

I found Anselmo's hatband that had been made from a rattlesnake. The head of a small diamondback and its rattles were intact and had been fashioned into a powerful band. I took it myself to Anselmo, accompanied by both Dana and Bobby.

Anselmo took the rattlesnake band and put it on his hat. The rattlesnake is the only creature not allowed in the Light Enchanted Flower World, the Seatica. That Saturday, Anselmo wore his hat with the snake on it into the deer lodge, an act that terrified and astounded many who witnessed it. Dana and I sat together behind Anselmo as he sang the song of the rattlesnake in the Light Enchanted Flower World. With his song, Anselmo invited the serpent from the Dark World into the Light Enchanted Flower World.

Dana was eager to know what Anselmo was singing. I leaned near her and told her: "The 'Song of the Rattlesnake.' " Anselmo was calling the snake in because the snake knew all the dark and hidden places where a man might conceal things.

Then something extraordinary happened. Alcario Red Tail was half Yaqui and half Papago. Every year at Easter Alcario walked over seventy-five miles, all the way from Vaya Chin on the Papago reservation where his father lived to his sister's house at Pascua. Suddenly Alcario came into the lodge, just as Anselmo finished the third stanza of the rattlesnake song. As the song ended, Alcario handed Anselmo Dana's magnificent hatband, which his father had stolen. The old man had been called by the force of the old form of life to resist change.

From then on Anselmo wore the snakeband into the deer lodge as a signal that the people must live blending the Dark and the Light into one world. For nothing, even in the world of the Yaqui, is possible without form, and the form, Anselmo was showing his people, had to change to allow new possibilities for life to happen. Things from now on would be more unstable, unpredictable—and more powerful. That day I witnessed Anselmo fulfill his purpose with the simple and eloquent introduction of unprecedented forms of magic: an ancient song, a new hatband.

Sunday night after the social dance, we strolled to Granny's grave and sat down. "Tori," I said, "what happened with the snake?"

"There is a story about Grandfather Rattler. Grandfather is the master of the Dark Enchanted Flower World, but the Humming-bird is the mistress of the Light Flower World, and Grandfather isn't welcome there because he just loves hummingbird eggs. The hummingbird doesn't want her eggs to be stolen. Then there'll be no new birds.

"But if Grandfather should happen to get one of those hum-mingbird eggs and he should happen to swallow it, then a feath-ered serpent would be born, something that has never before existed. Who knows what such a birth might unleash? The world as we know it is so sensitive to change—something as tiny as a hummingbird egg could, under extraordinary circumstances, change the course of history.

"Yet nothing is really different. The dreaming women have dreamed this new world already, and now it is time to make it happen. My people have to grow up, Pluma. That is why you have come. You know that already."

I wasn't sure I did know it. "How would I see myself without you, Tori? How would any of us see ourselves without the cul-ture. Or without Granny?"

I leaned down and patted Leoway's grave and thanked her for bringing me to Anselmo, and I thanked God for the people.

"You're welcome," Anselmo said. I slapped his hand, then took it and kissed it.

We made love in the darkness.

Standing in front of our new dressing mirror in my new home in my new clothes, the two of us were looking at the two of us. In the darkness of last night we made love in bodies that became transparent with love and so much light that opening my eyes once I saw a blue light had filled our room like the storm glow that fills an electric bottle. Later I became more familiar with the blue light and recognized it as the harbinger of my dream life with the elder Yaqui women. But then, in those days, it was all about love. Despite so much I had lived already with Anselmo, I didn't know the dream catches you, even though it is an ex-pression of reality and gives form to what we perceive. Each dream has its shortcomings and its traps.

If I dreamed after we had made love, today it seemed this was the dream itself, these two happy people in the mirror, the lithe dark man with the curly black hair, his artisan hands on the woman's shoulders, her blond hair falling partly on the red gauze dress, partly on his coppery arms; he in forest green shirt and denim pants, she with the hibiscus in her hair—a portrait posed for some hall of glories that would never have an Egypt, no Machú Picchú dedicated to love. Maybe then, I can't remember, I already had a sense that this couple in the cherry-wood dressing mirror wasn't us at all but two people who came for us at night and slipped our bodies on like silk pajamas. There they were fading gently before us like stars at dawn until the demands of light and activity hid them from us, until the months and years wore them away like those soft figurines of volcanic pumice stone. Sometimes, even now, I see the lovers floating farther down the stream, those lover selves, worn out from service until they had nothing but habit for each other, floating back into the Rio Yaqui, into the Sea of Cortez, past Torim, past the day before anyone had even seen a conquistador or a Cortez, past the Talking Tree, past the formations of giants in the bay, past the bay and the field of waves harvested by earth, the man and the woman nested together and their features smoothed so slowly away they never noticed they had become nobody, floating from the sea to the ocean of air, passed on to the energy fields of pollen and tasseled rays of light shaking and stirring in the great river of ash where everything destroyed assembles and rises and flashes an instant like this thought illumining the two lovers in the mirror.

"Look in the mirror, Pluma. Every morning when you rise, remember the woman looking back at you is a queen, she's the best on earth! Look at her, Pluma—you must remind her every day, you must tell her what I am telling you: 'She is the best woman on earth.' "

He had slid his arms around me and was holding me. I was so happy I cannot remember it. That happiness absolutely burst the envelope of the human veil which restrains this thing we are.

He said, "Mirrors have medicine. Those in the mirror give the mirrors life. They feed and prosper on what they see. This mirror will always look for you, Pluma. It will work for you. This is your mirror, to be filled with our medicine together. It will witness us in joy and sadness. And it will empower you."

Some mornings in those first years on Yaqui, Anselmo would stand in front of the mirror with his hands on his hips, feet apart, his head cocked to the side, smiling so broadly all his teeth showed bright white. He'd look in the mirror and bend forward slightly, arching an eyebrow, and with mock vanity admire what he saw. Then he'd say, "Well, how do you like your little, wrinkled old man?" He'd turn to me wherever I was standing in the bedroom and shake his head. "How can a beautiful young woman like you look at this wrinkled old man and call him 'beautiful'?"

"Tori," I would reply, "it's you who commands the mirror. Doesn't the mirror tell you you are the best there is?"

"The reflection of you in my bed tells me I'm the best there is!" he said with a grin.

After enough time went by in Yaqui, I couldn't keep track of what year it was. But I remember Easter morning, 1982. The deer lodge was hot. I looked out as Anselmo led a prayer. A group of little boys had stirred up dust in front of the sacred area and was circled into a tight huddle over something on the ground. Then five-year-old Mikey was walking toward Anselmo's son Roy, his small hands outstretched as if he were carrying water. It was a small sparrow, its pale yellow beak open and its eyes shut. It looked dead to me. "Why does he die?" Mikey asked. "Can you make him alive?" Roy handed the bird to me where I sat behind Anselmo. For this bird to die at the end of the ceremonies seemed to me a bad omen. I showed the bird to Anselmo, who immediately started the "Song of the Sparrow." After the verse was sung once it was sung again, and the bird got up as if it had only been sleeping. The sparrow stood up in my hand and spread out his wings and trilled. Through my hand and up my arm the vibration of his song ran like a current. The deer singers went on singing, and then the bird hopped onto Anselmo's shoulder. They went on singing, and the bird fluttered its wings and chirped some more and flew off into the blue sky. And still they went on singing as if it was the first day in history, or the last.